THE

BLDG
BLOG

BOOK

Architectural Visions of Early Fancy in the Gay Morning of Youth and Dreams in the Evening of Life by Joseph Gandy (1820), courtesy of the Trustees of Sir John Soane's Museum.

soane.org

→ bldgblog.blogspot.com

THE
BLDG
BLOG
BOOK

GEOFF MANAUGH

CHRONICLE BOOKS
San Francisco

Library of Congress Cataloging-in-Publication Data available.

ISBN: 978-0-8118-6644-6

Manufactured in China.

Designed by MacFadden & Thorpe.

10 9 8 7 6 5 4 3 2

Chronicle Books LLC
680 Second Street
San Francisco, California 94107

www.chroniclebooks.com

TABLE OF CONTENTS

An "urban district above the water," proposed for an island site in Seoul, South Korea, by Minsuk Cho and Jeffrey Inaba.

massstudies.com
inabaprojects.com

1

ARCHITECTURAL CONJECTURE, URBAN SPECULATION

Dollywood (2005) and Grid (La Brea and Olympic) (2005) from the ongoing series Utopian Debris by Bas Princen. In a 2008 interview with Marc Pimlott, published in Oase #76, Princen explains that he is interested in "the ruin of the modern": "I would almost say that these things"–referring to the landscapes he photographs–"are only filled with beauty when they are portrayed, and looked upon by a viewer from a comfortable distance. To see the beauty you need distance; you need to exclude the actual context; you need to give it an aura of it being an unreal place."

basprincen.nl

I STARTED BLDGBLOG in the summer of 2004, inspired more or less by four things: I was writing a novel about surveillance, terrorism, independent film, and the London Underground; I was auditing a course about Archigram, the 1960s British pop-architectural supergroup that once dreamt of bolt-on instant cities, "mobile villages," and inflatable utopias; I was reading a lot of J. G. Ballard (*Super-Cannes, Concrete Island, The Drowned World, Crash*); and I was feeling generally hemmed in by the city in which I then lived. While my initial impulse might have been to complain—noting every little thing about the world that bothered me—I decided, in fact, to do the opposite: I made a conscious decision to write only about the things that interested me.

I've often joked that BLDGBLOG is organized around one thing only: the *pleasure principle*. It's not theoretically rigorous or disciplinarily loyal or beholden to one particular style of design—even one historical era—but that's the point. To discuss the buildings of Christopher Wren, for instance, in the context of Restoration politics, the very beginnings of the British Empire, the importance of Christianity, the birth of the private patron, and so on, might be academically appropriate and occasionally interesting, but to discuss the architecture of Christopher Wren in the context of overgrown ruins in the Cambodian rain forest, or 21st-century psychogeography—or the early writings of Rem Koolhaas—suddenly sounds like quite an exciting conversation. Or discuss Christopher Wren in the context of video games—or spy thrillers, or the undersea fate awaiting London in 3,000 years—and see what happens. Suddenly people with no interest in architecture, and certainly no interest in Christopher Wren, can join the conversation.

In other words, forget academic rigor. Never take the appropriate next step. Talk about Chinese urban design, the European space program, and landscape in the films of Alfred Hitchcock in the span of three sentences—because it's fun, and the juxtapositions might take you somewhere. Most importantly, *follow your lines of interest.*

With BLDGBLOG, the fundamental motivation has always been to write about things—ideas, buildings, books, landscapes, cities—that excite me, that make me want to keep writing, keep thinking, to go out right away and talk to friends. After all, why not remind myself—and others—of all the interesting things that actually exist in the world? Even if those things *don't* exist; even if they're just speculations and plans. Why not concentrate *only on them*? After all, I genuinely believe that writing is a way to pull oneself out of the grime and scabs—to excavate oneself—but, of course, the opposite can also be true. Through writing you can bury yourself, lose yourself, push yourself not away from but much deeper into darkness; flipping through your own journals, or scanning your own blog at night, you see only reminders of the things you hate, signs of the things that frustrate you.

So why not *do the opposite*? It's a psychological experiment in which you're scientist, lab, and patient all in one. Before going to sleep, you pick up the notebook beside your bed and see that it's full of only the things that invigorate you. To be clear, there might be something there that you don't like—but it can be exciting to think about nonetheless. I don't "like" secret overseas detention camps run by the U. S. government, for instance, and I don't "like" climate change—but, as facts, they are both fascinating, and they can even be discussed in the context of architecture. They can even be discussed in the context of Christopher Wren.

BLDGBLOG was born out of these circumstances, then, and from almost literally day one it was full of archaeology, astronomy, and underground cities; Gothic cathedrals and Celtic burial mounds; Mars, green roofs, and translucent concrete. Somewhere between science fiction and architectural theory, J. G. Ballard rubbed shoulders with H. G. Wells, W. G. Sebald, and H. P. Lovecraft; there were London floods, earthquakes, William Blake, and James Bond. Ruins, climate change, and the apocalypse. Cape Canaveral. Hadrian's Wall. Homer. Anything that could, in however distant a way, be related back to architecture, in its broadest and most interesting conception.

Why architecture? Because we're surrounded by the built environment at almost literally every moment of the day; it is the frame through which our experiences are filtered. And if this is the world that we've built for ourselves—or that someone's built for us, whether we wanted them to or not—then we should ask ourselves whether it's working out as planned. Rethinking architecture—rethinking landscapes, cities, and the way we've designed our everyday lives—is a shortcut to rethinking the whole world, and a great deal of this boils down to expanding our definition of architecture. Where architecture can be found, what it can be, and who created it. If academia is to be believed, then architecture is something in the drawings of Vitruvius or Le Corbusier; if today's architecture critics are to be believed, architecture is just parametrics and Zaha Hadid. Either way, it's claustrophobic.

Architecture surrounds us at all times, everywhere; we live within shaped environments. From airports and shopping malls to blockbuster action films, from *Bioshock* and prison camps to the canopies of giant sequoias, there are structures and spatial frameworks everywhere. Mars rovers are architectural; they are structured explorations of landscape and space. Haunted house novels are architectural. Mt. Everest base camps, Tokyo storm drains, abandoned biowarfare ranges in the former Soviet Union, and the inaudible songs of Libyan sand dunes: These are all wide open to architectural discussion.

In fact, one of the best parts of creating BLDGBLOG has been in setting myself constraints: Forcing myself to relate things back to architecture has made it all feel more like a game. It's too easy to write about anything at all, anywhere in the world—or off of it, as the case may be—to have quick opinions about this, that, and the other thing. Isn't that what blogging is supposed to be? The challenge, though, is connecting all of this to the built environment, to landscapes, cities, and naturally shaped space. It's *Six Degrees of Separation* in architectural form: Relate aerial turbulence in the Himalayas to the Woolworth Building in New York City in no more than six steps. Link dinosaur fossils unearthed in Arizona to the Berlin subway system—via heretical theology and the novels of Cormac McCarthy. The stories and images that you find along the way constitute something a bit like BLDGBLOG. After all, architecture will always involve telling stories—it is as much fiction as it is engineering and materials science.

When I was still a teenager, I flew out to visit my brother, who lived two time zones away. We had a few hours to kill at the end of my trip, so we drove downtown to walk around; eventually we ended up in the state capitol. As we walked inside, I looked up to see that the building—a neoclassical space of well-financed government control—extended several more

THE ARCHITECTURE OF SPAM
The *Spam Architecture* series by Alex Dragulescu, currently a researcher at MIT's Media Lab, was "generated by a computer program that accepts as input, junk e-mail. Various patterns, keywords and rhythms found in the text are translated into three-dimensional modeling gestures." It is spam in architectural form. If you applied this to large-scale architectural design, you could actually live inside junk e-mails, computer viruses, and unsolicited ads for Viagra. You could also turn digital photographs of your last birthday party into elaborate architectural structures; export your Ph.D. thesis as a five-level inhabitable object; transform every bank statement you've ever received into a small Cubist city. Your whole DVD collection could be informationally re-presented as a series of large angular buildings. Or you could reverse the process, and input *SketchUp* diagrams of Notre Dame cathedral—generating an inbox-clogging river of spam. E-mail the Great Wall of China around the world in an afternoon. Turn the collected works of Mies van der Rohe into junk e-mail and send it anonymously to the director of the National Building Museum—who then deletes it without knowing what it was.

sq.ro

↑ previous page
KoKoKu by Fashion Architecture Taste.
fashionarchitecturetaste.com

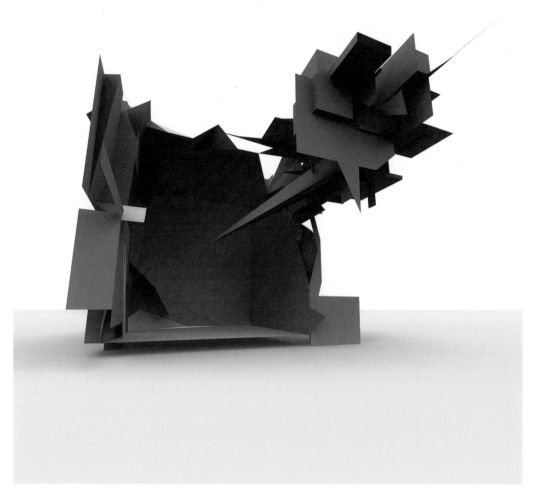

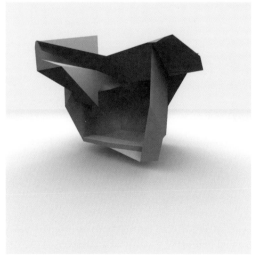

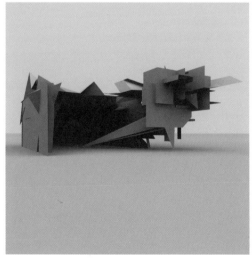

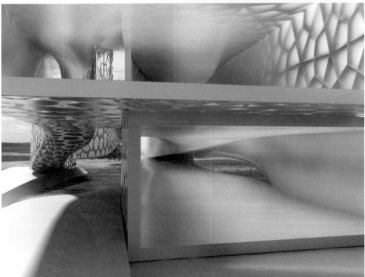

JELLYFISH HOUSE

The Jellyfish House by San Francisco–based architects Lisa Iwamoto and Craig Scott is "modeled on the idea that, like the sea creature, it coexists with its environment." The house has thus been designed with "a mutable layered skin, or 'deep surface,' that mediates internal and external environments." The external environment in this particular case is rather interesting, as the Jellyfish House has been proposed for construction on an artificial island in the San Francisco Bay that once served as a military base. There, the house would be part of a much larger landscape proposal involving soil remediation, replenished wetlands, and a complex "water filtration system" that operates within the walls of the house itself. "Phase change materials" and even a UV–sterilized "water jacket" complete the technical specs of the project.

iwamotoscott.com

ARCHITECTURE PARLANTE

Architecture parlante is "architecture that speaks." Perhaps the
most famous example of this is
18th-century architect Claude-
Nicolas Ledoux's unrealized
scheme for the salt-mining town
of Arc-et-Senans. Ledoux's plans
included buildings that were
shaped, often absurdly, after
their function: The barrel maker's
house was shaped like a barrel,
and so on. This was christened
architecture parlante because
the architecture revealed its own
function: it "spoke" its purpose
for all to see. An impressively
ridiculous modern-day example
comes to us from South Korea. In
2007, the Internet briefly flared up
around the sight of Sim Jae-Duk's
new toilet-shaped home; Sim
had made his career "beautifying
public restrooms," according to
the Associated Press, and so one
could argue that this was a classic
case of *architecture parlante*. It
was a toilet-beautifier's house
in the shape of a toilet. On the
other hand, *architecture parlante*
can be more subtle than this. For
instance, the FBI headquarters
in Washington, DC, gets heavier
and wider at the top, expanding
outward through cantilevers;
it looms over you and shadows
you from above as you pass by.
It does what the FBI does—if
you'll excuse this rather libertar-
ian interpretation—it just does
so in architectural form. It is
architecture parlante.

levels above us. Standing there on terraced marble walkways
that criss-crossed the domed interior were other tourists looking down into the space where my brother and I stood. Higher
above them were offices and closed doors and hallways—yet
there was no visible means of ascent. I was aware that I could
be watched from above, in other words, and that it was possible
to go much higher—to become one of the watchers—but I didn't
see how it could be done. The architecture embodied a political
message: *There are people higher than you, and they can watch
you, follow you—and, theoretically, you can join them, become one
of them. Unfortunately you don't know how.* This might have been
my first real experience of architecture's *interpretability*—the
fact that it can *say something*, or embody a message. Buildings
can physically represent certain story lines as strongly, and far
more viscerally, than a written text. Architecture encodes messages; call it my own belated discovery of *architecture parlante*.

One of the first things I thought of, in fact, standing there
with my brother, was *The Trial* by Franz Kafka, an unacknowl-
edged architectural masterpiece in which all the buildings
are confused, self-connected, and inconsistent with themselves. Architectural space, in Kafka's novels, is always somehow impossible, made up of surprising overlaps between law,
religion, and civil society. I'd even say that *The Trial* is actually a book about topology, with Kafka more of an architectural
guide, his work a handbook to the outermost limits of political spatialization. Josef K., the book's main character, wanders
through courtyards that open onto further courtyards. Stairways lead to more stairways, and attic spaces open onto hidden
law offices—which stand beside government courtrooms that
double as apartments for the building's evening cleaning crew.
"There are law court offices in practically every attic," Josef K.
is told, and never before has the confusion between the limits of
state power and the spatialization of personal privacy been so
well explored. Kafka's architecture is like a text through which
the state explains itself—or deliberately *does not*—to its people.

Telling stories through architecture is nothing new or even
necessarily interesting. It's actually become something of a
formula for science fiction and fantasy: whole books are often
little more than extremely detailed descriptions of space. They
are "cityscapes." There are no real characters to speak of, and
there is no real plot; there are just loads of overwrought balconies, amazing castles, and a few underground mazes or two.
The architecture itself *is* the story. It is the literature of urban
speculation.

But that's not what I mean. What I mean is that architecture, as a discipline, can itself be used to tell stories. In fact,
some of the most interesting student work today comes complete with elaborate plots and story lines, supplied for no other

ARCHITECTURAL INFECTIONS: AN INTERVIEW WITH JEFF VANDERMEER

In light of my frequently stated belief that some of today's most original, historically unencumbered, and imaginative architectural ideas can be found in video games, films, and science fiction novels, I decided to talk to novelist Jeff VanderMeer back in 2006 about his own inventive and novelistic use of built space. From his fungal city of Ambergris to the medicalized underworld of *Veniss Underground*, VanderMeer's vision is architectural in the most exciting sense.

Jeff VanderMeer: I get my inspiration from real life as much as possible, and *then* from history books and *then* from other writers. I find Italo Calvino's *Invisible Cities*, for example, stultifyingly boring. Although I like the idea of a setting also being a character, it has to *be* a character—it can't be the only thing in the book.

There have been definite examples where I feel like the city in question, in a piece of fiction, is not connected to anything real—and it's almost like what happens in bad characterization. In bad characterization, you can't really imagine anything happening to the character outside the pages of the book. There are cities in fantastical fiction that work the same way, where the writer has obviously put a lot of care into creating the city but it's somehow *inert*. It's simply there as a place for the author to set a story. I think the best cityscapes are kind of like characters. They're slightly illogical. There's much more to them than is described in the book. There's all this stuff

that you don't know—and can't possibly know. For example, there is a layering effect in many great cities. You don't just see one style or period of architecture. You might also see planning in one section of a city and utter chaos in another. The lesson behind seeing a modern skyscraper next to a 17th-century cathedral is one that many fabulists do not internalize and, as a result, their settings are too homogenous.

Of course, that kind of layering will work for some readers—and other readers will want continuity. Even if they live in a place like that—a baroque, layered, very busy, confused place. Even if, say, they're holding the novel as they walk down the street in London. One thing I find interesting is what people choose to believe and not believe. In the early history of Ambergris, from my novel *City of Saints*, the more fantastical stuff is actually taken from Byzantine history and other periods. A lot of stuff that's true to life, people, in e-mails, will say how cool it is that I made that up.

There's not really a method beyond that; it's just what strikes me. Like going to the York Minster, in England: that blew me away and inspired the cadaver cathedral in *Veniss Underground*. Standing inside that building, which was so absolutely amazing, like nothing I had ever seen before—because I had never had a chance to go inside an old cathedral—how alien it looked and how ethereal and yet so solid—I literally just stood there looking at it, looking at the inside, looking at the ceiling, for more than an hour. Being in there, and having been stalled on *Veniss*, that structure—that piece of architecture—saved my novel.

I suddenly understood how to transform something from the real world into something imaginary.

BLDGBLOG: Speaking of *City of Saints*, I was particularly struck by the idea in that book that "much of the 'gold' covering the buildings was actually a living organism similar to lichen" that's been "trained to create decorative patterns." What does this imply about the possibilities for a living architectural ornament, or even an *architectural infection*: diseases and infestations that act to enhance a man-made space?

VanderMeer: Scientists have already created buildings that are self-cleaning using certain types of bacteria, I believe—so this is as much a "science fictional" idea as a fantastical one, that's for sure. I'm all about extrapolating fungal technologies. It creates an extra frisson of satisfaction in the reader, for one thing.

In my novel *Shriek* there's a whole passage devoted to this. At one point, the narrator comes to realize that there's an entire other city under the skin of what she can see—because her brother has constructed these glasses that kind of allow you to see with a sense that human beings don't actually have. And what she sees is that every single building is just coated with fungus, invisible to the naked eye, and with living things forming separate symbols and signs. It's on every wall that she looks at. It's like a fungal architecture imposed on top of the city. There actually is all this micro-bacterial activity—things we can't see—so it's not too different from reality.

jeffvandermeer.com

Photographs by Øyvind Hagen for StatoilHydro, courtesy of StatoilHydro.

statoilhydro.com

reason than to explain why a particular building should exist or require designing. These stories very often exceed today's mass-market fiction in imaginative strength—to such a degree that I might suggest, only half-jokingly, that the reason fiction sells so badly in the United States today is because all of the people with real ideas have moved on to study architecture or urban design. American fiction has been left languishing in the hands of people at summer writing workshops in Iowa, obsessed with the morality of suburban fatherhood.

Of course, some fiction does articulate larger, very often political, points—and some of that writing even uses architecture as a vehicle to explore these ideas. Architecture, as in the works of Kafka, becomes something that is in and of itself symbolic. For instance, the premise of Rupert Thomson's 2006 novel *Divided Kingdom* is that the whole of Britain has been broken up into four sectors, and that the population itself has been forcibly "rearranged" according to emotional temperament. Walls and fences begin to appear; soon people complain of "border sickness" as they are further hemmed in by a series of Internal Security Acts. London itself is "divided so as to create four new capitals," and all bridges over the Thames have been "fortified, along with watch-towers at either end and a steel dragnet underneath." Apparently learning from Robert Venturi and Denise Scott-Brown, there is even a "tourist settlement called the Border Experience" constructed near one of the crossings, complete "with theme hotels, fast-food restaurants, and souvenir shops," and, in one sector, like something from the early visions of Archigram, all the motorways "had been converted into venues for music festivals or sporting events." It is interesting to note here that Thomson cites *S,M,L,XL* by Rem Koolhaas as a literary influence.

Parts of *Divided Kingdom* read like descriptions of Dubai in the first decade of the 21st-century—or what Mike Davis once described, in the *New Left Review*, as Dubai's "monstrous caricature of futurism." For instance, Thomson's narrator is at one point led down into a basement warehouse, where, standing beside a lifeguard on a boardwalk in the dark, he and his colleagues are shown something called the Underground Ocean:

The lifeguard's voice floated dreamily above us. Any second now, he said, the scene would be illuminated, but first he wanted us to try and picture what it was that we were about to see. I peered out into the dark, my eyes gradually adjusting. A pale strip curved away to my right—the beach, I thought—and at the edge furthest from me I could just make out a shimmer, the faintest of oscillations. Could that be where the water met the sand? Beyond that, the blackness resisted me, no matter how carefully I looked.

Packard Jennings and Steve Lambert, 2007
A Project of the San Francisco Arts Commission's Art on Market Street Program. |
www.sfartscommission.org/pubart/projects

SAN FRANCISCO AS IT SHOULD BE

For this series of posters, originally displayed inside bus shelters along Market Street in San Francisco, artists Steve Lambert and Packard Jennings teamed up to reimagine public transport in the Bay Area. In these alternative versions of the city, office workers ride zip lines across the water to Oakland, the BART system has been redesigned as a mobile underground library, the entire peninsula has been turned into a nature preserve, and Candlestick has become a place to grow fresh vegetables. In my favorite detail, a cross-city roller coaster has been installed to replace the aging cable cars.

visitsteve.com
centennialsociety.com

"Lights," the lifeguard said.

I wasn't the only delegate to let out a gasp. My first impression was that night had turned to day—but instantly, as if hours had passed in a split-second. At the same time, the space in which I had been standing had expanded to such a degree that I no longer appeared to be indoors. I felt unsteady, slightly sick. Eyes narrowed against the glare, I saw a perfect blue sky arching overhead. Before me stretched an ocean, just as blue. It was calm the way lakes are sometimes calm, not a single crease or wrinkle. Creamy puffs of cloud hung suspended in the distance. Despite the existence of a horizon, I couldn't seem to establish a sense of perspective. After a while my eyes simply refused to engage with the view, and I had to look away.

"Now for the waves," the lifeguard said.

My point in citing all of this is to suggest that fictional proposals and architectural plans work extraordinarily well together in the imaginative rethinking of the world. Architecture is, in many ways, a very specific type of science fiction; it is its own genre of speculative thought.

To choose just a few random examples of what I mean from within the world of architecture, in the spring of 2007 Jeffrey Inaba and Paul Nakazawa at the Southern California Institute of Architecture (SCI-Arc) asked their students to explore an elaborate political scenario involving the economic future of water and the changing nature of international sovereignty—all so that students could design the infrastructure for a new kind of import economy. The inspiration for that studio reminds me of an earlier project by Agents of Change, an East London–based architecture firm that, back in 2002, asked themselves what might happen if multinational agribusiness giant Monsanto were to buy the entire London borough of Hackney. Their resulting vision was of a city transformed into a sea of roof gardens and crop fields—an Agricultural Action Zone (AAZ). The economically depressed borough would present "new growing opportunities," the architects write, thus "liberating the ground's agricultural potential." Meanwhile, Grace La at the University of Wisconsin–Milwaukee, working with Dutch architecture firm MVRDV, had her students envision a future city around the availability of airborne real estate in an era of flying cars; called *Skycar City*, the resulting projects rethink urban space from the relatively mundane perspective of private transport.

Any one of these ideas could become the primary element in a short story collection, science fiction novel, or Hollywood

→ next page
Four images by Daniel Dociu show the range of imagined landscapes and architectural spaces available to an artist working in game design today. Images are *Guild Wars* content and materials, copyright ArenaNet Inc. and/or NCsoft Corporation.

tinfoilgames.com

↓ next spread
A fake newspaper spread by Agents of Change.

theaoc.co.uk

GAME/SPACE: AN INTERVIEW WITH DANIEL DOCIU

In an interview with game designer Daniel Dociu, posted on BLDGBLOG in April 2008, Dociu remarks that the "beauty" of designing architecture for video games is that "you don't have to be stylistically pure, or even coherent. You can afford a certain eclecticism to your work. I can blend elements from the Potala Palace in Tibet with, say, La Sagrada Familia, Antoni Gaudí's cathedral. I really take a lot of liberties with whatever I can use, wherever I can find it."

BLDGBLOG: Of course, if you were an architecture student and you started to design buildings that looked like Gothic cathedrals crossed with the Bauhaus, people outside of architecture school might love it, but inside your studio—

Daniel Dociu: You'd be crucified!

BLDGBLOG: It'd be considered unimaginative—even kitsch.

Dociu: Absolutely. That's probably why I chose to work in game design. There's so much creative freedom. I mean, you do compromise and you do tailor your ideas and the scope of your design to the needs of the product—but, still, there's a lot of room to push.

Bankrupt Hackney turn to Monsanto for city farm community

Geoff Shearcroft
Political correspondent

The London Borough of Hackney have sold Hackney City Farm to biotech agricultural firm Monsanto and declared the surrounding area an Agricultural Action Zone (AAZ) in a deal that promises a significant package of benefits for local people.

In a move characterised as "bonkers" by City Farm co-ordinator Caroline Smithington, Monsanto have bought a 99 year lease on the City farm site in exchange for an undisclosed fee and a commitment to invest in the newly created AAZ.

Hendrik A. Verfaillie, President and CEO of Monsanto, flew in from St. Louis, US, last week to finalise the deal. Speaking yesterday at a press conference in a hastily erected structure in Haggerston Park, he confirmed that Monsanto would be working closely with the local people to improve the area.

"We are a caring company with a vision of the future, a vision of abundant food and a healthy environment. Here in Haggerston there is great poverty and a far from healthy environment. In constant dialogue with the local people here we want to build our shared vision."

The deal brought a wave of protests from environmental groups. Monsanto first rose to the attention of the UK consumer in 1998 as the leading company resonsible for genetically modified crops.

"We at Monsanto acknowledge we are seen in a pretty dim light here in Europe at the moment," acknowledged Verfaillie. "We failed to listen to our customers worries. We realized that we needed to hear directly from people about what they thought, what their concerns were and what they thought we ought to do."

Nick Parney, spokesman for Friends of the Earth, was the first to respond to the deal. Speaking at the Urban Agriculture conference in Shanghai he condemned Monsanto, the government and Hackney council for creating what he called a "giant city laboratory, with the young, the elderly, the infirm and the unemployed sacrificed as lab rats to pay for their irresponsible masters' bankruptcy."

Although the full details of the deal have yet to be published, local councillors have hinted at a 'growth' package of up to £25m. Covering over 30ha, the AAZ includes the City farm, Haggerston Park, two schools, public and private housing and a stretch of the Grand Union Canal.

Following last year's announcement that it was bankrupt with over £40m debts, Hackney Council has come under considerable pressure from the government to sort out its finances. In December the council announced it was halving the City Farm budget, a reduction of £50,000.

The Monsanto deal would appear to resolve the farm's future as well as bringing a massive shot of investment into Haggerston.

Christopher Coleman, Labour councillor for Haggerston and Moorfields, described the deal as an exciting pilot scheme that offered the possibility of a "dynamic model of high density, sustainable city living. Continuing the government's 'Business in the Community' initative, Monsanto's involvement in our borough offers a host of opportunities; more jobs, more facilities, easily accessible fresh food and a greener, healthier environment for all."

Local residents were split in their reactions. Maggie Glean, 27, a single mother who relies upon the farm's creche seemed unconcerned about Monsanto's products. "Hackney council has run itself into the ground with our taxes and is unfit to be running our community facilities. If Monsanto are prepared to step in then good luck to them."

Despite Hackney's shortcomings Smithington is still appalled at the new owners of the farm she runs. "A large multi-national corporation like Monsanto clearly has its own agenda that is totally opposed to the local, community spirit of this farm.

This farm provides an essential social and educational role within the local area, a role Monsanto are very unlikely to fill. They seem to have promised the earth to the council but their recent history would suggest their promises are not to be trusted."

Colin Might, 67, who has lived in Haggerston all his life, struggled to see why the American agricultural corporation were interested in Haggerston. "I don't see why they want to come sticking their noses into our farm. And I don't want none of those killer tomatoes round here."

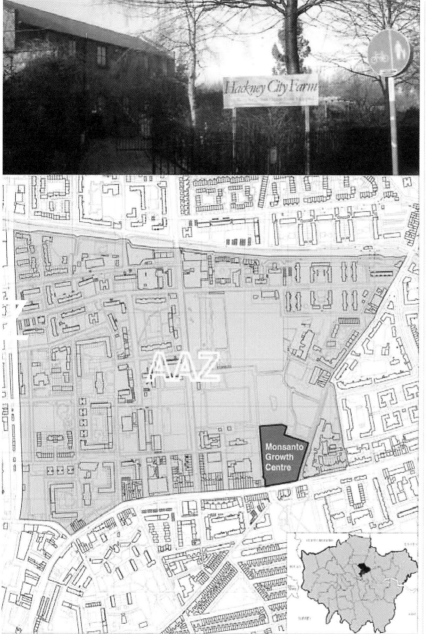

Monsanto City Farm situated in Hackney's newly created Agricultural Action Zone, East London Maps: Geoff Shearcroft and Hackney Council

UK researcher warns of a growth in the housing market

Horace Trent-Campbell
Research correspondent

Richard Croft, 24, a researcher at London's Royal College of estate Agents, has published a report that could revolutionise the houses we build. Or rather grow.

Croft suggests that today's starter homes will be replaced by a 'House on a Mouse', the volume house builder's answer to the human ear grown on the back of a mouse.

In his report, 'Work in Progress - the new biology of architecture', Croft explores the architectural implications of the latest developments in biotechnology.

MIT-developed smart gels, elastic metals and even living cellulose will make up the buildings of the future in Croft's biological brave new world.

On a more practical level, the report argues that our buildings and cities must increasingly be based upon biological logic as opposed to mechanical if they are to create the complex, sustainable environments that scientists, planners and politicians are agreeing we need to survive the 21st century.

If houses of the future mimic living plants then not only will our homes grow to accommodate our families and friends over time but bills will be a thing of the past as organic solar

screenplay—and any one of these ideas could be expanded far
beyond the genre of an architecture proposal to form a kind
of future prediction or scenario plan. Architecture, in each of
these examples—and there are hundreds, if not thousands, of
such examples from schools, design firms, and blogs all over the
world—is literature, poetry, and mythology all in one. Architecture becomes nothing less than a way to reimagine how humans
might inhabit the earth. It is large scale. It is planetary. It spi-
rals all the way down to the magnetic structure of atoms and
borders on being *everything*.

None of which should be news to anyone—but we've been
too hypnotized by Dubai to ask real questions. During the process of taking that Archigram class five years ago, for instance,
I realized that the entire Archigramian project, if one can say
there was such a thing, had been misunderstood. This seemed
true even in the confines of that classroom. Archigram, we students were meant to think, had been interested in using hi-tech
cladding systems, modular ductwork, and electronic hinges on
mobile windows—or whatever—and that was it. That was the
end of it. Instead of looking at Archigram's call for social and
spatial liberation—and at how architects could *enable* such a
liberation on a truly global scale through literally more flexible design—we were simply meant to think that Archigram
had wanted faster escalators. Archigram had asked everyone to
rethink everything—and, if we didn't like the world, to change
it—but you would have thought, studying Archigram in school
today, that they had been interested in nothing more than Space
Age kitchenware and appropriately footnoted citations. At that
point, the most stultifying shopping mall designs from 1970s
Japan had to be studied as if they were direct outgrowths of
Archigram's most manic speculations. We were shown photos
of pedestrian arcades in Tokyo and vast, climate-controlled
department stores full of discount home stereo equipment, and
we were asked to believe, slumped there in a basement lecture
hall, that this had something to do with the same architects
who had once proposed building sovereign robotic mega-
structures, Walking Cities, drive-in housing, and offshore
micro-utopias on stilts.

Of course, those Japanese malls *did* have something to do
with Archigram—but, then, a lot of things have something
to do with Archigram. But instead of looking at future lunar
bases, Antarctic ice labs, flat-pack Olympic stadiums, Department of Energy nuclear waste entombment sites in the mountains of Nevada, or even floating superhighways in Dubai, we
got stranded in a distant suburb of Osaka, looking at boutique
clothing shops, wondering where all the big ideas had gone.
So much for "zoom," then—Archigram's name for architectural innovation. So much for wanting "to put the zap back into

Palmtree Island (1971) by Zamp Kelp/Haus-Rucker-Co.

ortner-ortner.de

EQUIPMENT FOR LIVING: AN INTERVIEW WITH PETER COOK

In May 1961, young London architects Peter Cook, Warren Chalk, Dennis Crompton, David Greene, Ron Herron, and Mike Webb produced the first issue of *Archigram*, a decidedly low-tech "architectural telegram" that would go on to become one of the most well-known architecture publications of the 20th century. Archigram—both the publication and the group—brought together ideas and illustrations from comic books, space travel, mass manufacturing, automobile design, the works of Buckminster Fuller, and the military (among countless other sources) with their own polemical writings, to imagine a future world of "throw-away architecture," temporary installations, Walking Cities, and utopian seaside piers. The city, in Archigram's view, would be an ongoing festival, urbanism itself a social event of near-constant renewal and change.

In *Archigram 4*, Peter Cook wrote of the group's "preoccupation" with finding "ways out from the stagnation of the architectural scene, where the continuing malaise is not just with the mediocrity of the object, but, more seriously, with the self-satisfaction of the profession." Four decades later, this stagnation and self-satisfaction have hardly gone away.

Cook, born in 1936 and knighted in 2007 for his "services to architecture," remains a lively—and very funny—thinker of architecture. Over the course of even a short conversation, Cook will freely invent new applications and possibilities for design. Still a practicing architect, Cook spoke with BLDGBLOG about where he finds the experimental, the avant-garde, and the unexpected in today's urban environment.

BLDGBLOG: Architecture schools and publications today seem almost desperate for a new avant-garde—even for a "new Archigram"—but they seem only to be looking within the field of architecture to find it. For the sake of argument, let's say that BP, with its offshore oil rigs, or the U.S. military, with its rapidly deployed instant cities, or private space tourism firms are the new Archigram. They, too, are experimenting with spatial technologies and structures. Is it possible that the "new Archigram" won't involve architects at all—but will be, say, rogue engineers from the construction wing of an international oil-services firm?

Peter Cook: Actually, I don't think it's that. I think it's to be found in people who are working, in a sense, with the environment. Which doesn't necessarily mean the *built* environment; it means things that are *experienced*. I think a lot of people in the communications industry, and a lot of things to do with the music world, and the showbiz world, and the people who invent gizmos are the new Archigram. I think people who make tents, and people who

make luggage, people who make trolleys, people who make packing materials, and lightweight containers, and forklift trucks, and protective headgear…. You know, if you took something in between Smart cars, artificial grass, rock operas, and producing wine out of sardines [*laughs*], then that would be the new Archigram. It's not likely to be found in the background of architecture–although architecture is still an amazing springboard territory in many ways. It's easy to speculate and dabble and invent. It's sociology at one end, and how people make jam at the other.

For instance, we have our studio here in London by a market that, at lunchtime, sprouts mobile vehicles all selling hot food. It's an instant village of eating. It's a phenomenon. People buy this stuff and they sit on a public lawn nearby–and that becomes a beach, as much as if it had sand, and the vehicles become restaurants, as much as if they had kitchens. But it all then trundles off on

wheels. It just sort of moseys into the city, which is amazing. I think what is available for people to do with their time now is extraordinary. You can literally spend part of your lunchtime in the opera: Instead of dressing up for the opera and going in the evening, you can weave bits of the operatic experience into breaks in the day's work.

Things have sort of merged in a way, and I think, as architects, we're still fascinated by that–or some of us are. The only thing is that you get a whole lot of architects now who want to be more solid brick than ever before. It's as if the prospect of everything being architecture–you know, the famous Hans Hollein phrase, *Alles ist Architektur*–well, that has now been realized. I think a lot of architects are scared by that. They don't *want* everything to be architecture.

BLDGBLOG: The role of the architect, then, is less one of creating new spaces than of creating the

conditions for future events. Architects *assemble events*?

Cook: In terms of putting together all of these bits and pieces, yes. I think there's tremendous territory there for constantly re-evaluating what we mean in a city by a master plan, or a circus, or a plan of action. For example, we've just bid for a competition called the Brooklyn Art Master Plan, and it's all to do with taking advantage of the artists who are moving into Brooklyn–trying to organize this territory and draw it to public attention. Whether you do it with searchlights, banners,

Images by Peter Cook and Peter Cook/Archigram.

Left: Archigram's Instant City goes glam.

Right: The Hedgerow project rethinks rurality, bringing a power supply–and architecture–deep into the woods.

crabstudio.co.uk
archigram.net

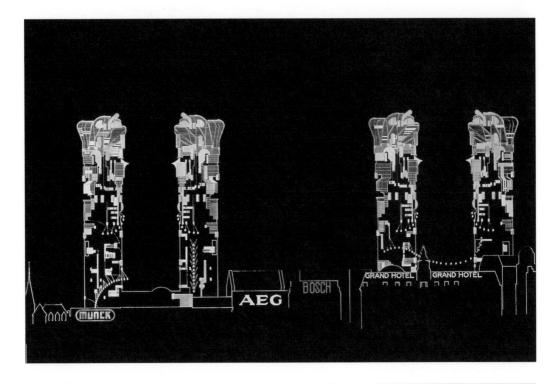

or web references, I'm not quite sure. But it's an interesting thing, because it's not a master plan in the sense of somebody laying down a boulevard. It's a *strategic* thing. I'm sure there should be far more of these, and not just for art conditions—like if you had a kind of weekend master plan for this part of London. We only tend to do that if somebody says, *oh, it's a festival—we'd better make sure that people are not bored on a Friday afternoon.* Whereas, actually, the whole city is a sort of ongoing festival. I'm interested in that.

These things can be creative parasites, too. We've been talking about parasites in architecture for years now—where somebody comes along and plants something on your building, or on your roof—but people are still nervous of them. For instance, I'm designing a project in Madrid right now where I want to deliberately lift the building off the ground and say, *look, anybody can come and put kiosks underneath it*—and, actually, anybody can come and

do things on the roof, as well. But the city is very nervous about that—certainly of doing things on the roof—so they want us to *design the kiosks*, which is not intellectually what it was about. I wanted a free-for-all sort of situation, where the solid bit of building is really kind of a dog into which fleas can embed themselves—but the city wants those fleas to be designed to fit aesthetically with the dog, as it were. [*laughs*]

I think we can do far more than we're being allowed to do in terms of artifacts and what you do with artifacts. Sometimes the determination to make something actually work—and certainly the determination to try to make it *economic*—gets in the way of imagination. I find myself constantly battling between two halves of myself: one that says, *wow, it could really do that,* and another one that says, *oh, you've got to make it understandable, or economic, or circumspect in some way.*

BLDGBLOG: We're speaking during what has broadly been referred to as *the building boom.* Dubai, Shanghai, Manhattan, Beijing, Moscow—all of these places have been undergoing record levels of construction. But it's very conspicuously not referred to as *the architecture boom.* Does the difference between a *building* boom—sheer construction—and an *architecture* boom interest you at all?

Cook: Well, I've been to Dubai once, a few months ago. I found it singularly uninteresting, actually. It was incredibly bland—even formalistically.

In a way, though, the design scene today is more accommodating that it's ever been. It relishes new forms and shapes and so on—but most of what it relishes are way behind what people are really imagining. Buildings in Dubai tend to be one-liners. They might be *interesting* one-liners, but I think the really interesting stuff is always the hybrid, the parasite—the piece that's partly

enclosed, and partly electronic, and partly collapsed. Partly here today and gone tomorrow—or whatever it might be. Those things are much more difficult for the Dubai psychologists to deal with, because they're not *easy*, and they don't necessarily look like anything else.

BLDGBLOG: At the same time, though, Dubai has helped to popularize architecture. New skyscraper designs now pop up on the front page of the BBC.

Cook: Architecture has captured the interest of the press and the public to some extent. I think that was sort of inevitable, after many decades of just looking like a box. For good or ill, architecture has a popular appeal these days, even if it doesn't do that much more—it just changes the face of the enclosure. But I have a bias for things that look like something sometimes—and then reconfigure, or do something that you didn't expect them to do. Instead of

having to wear a different mind-set—if the thing is mobile, or changeable, or made of a flimsy material—you can carry the same mindset.

My wife and I had a chunk of money some years ago, so we bought a nice car, rather than a crappy car. My wife does all the driving—and the thing that sold it to her was the sound system. She said, *wow, I've never heard a sound system like this*. So she bought the car—and I think that's perfectly reasonable. If you want to have the best concert experience, then you go and sit in the street in your car—you can probably get it better than in your living room. Once you have things like that, it's great. It's only half a step more till, say, the car is more comfortable than the chairs you have at home. So why sit in the living room at all? You would go sit in the car—and maybe go back to the living room to have a smelly meal or something.

I'm exaggerating a bit here—but it's only a tiny exaggeration.

Images by Peter Cook.

Left: Lantern Towers in Oslo.

Right: Arcadia Riverside, London.

Bottom: Housing in Vallecas, Spain, designed by Peter Cook/CRABstudio.

crabstudio.co.uk

architecture," as the group's most outspoken member, Peter Cook, later explained to *Dwell* magazine. So much for Archigram itself, whose ideas got lost somewhere between the Mall of America and the Millennium Dome.

There was more to it, in other words. Architecture is not just better elevators. If you allow yourself to look beyond mere buildings to things like military detention camps, *Halo 3*, and even the street-by-street routes of urban marathons, then you'll see that the spirit of Archigram—assuming there really was such a thing (and, if so, that we should still be talking about it)—never went anywhere. Or, rather, it went *everywhere*. In fact, putting all questions of politics and morality temporarily aside, it's not out of the question to suggest that the U.S. military has succeeded in a surreal but almost total implementation of Archigram's architectural project, however inadvertent— whether you're talking about plug-in housing, flexible electrical supplies, or airlifting instant cities into the middle of nowhere. It's not even outside the realm of believability to say that the mobile modularity and nomadic new towns called for by Archigram are even now being shipped under military escort off to distant theaters of war, occupation, and natural disaster. In other words, the "new Archigram" that critics seem to be looking for so desperately *already exists*, but it's been overlooked by the same academics who look dully and predictably to the collected works of Norman Foster, Richard Rogers, and the Japanese Metabolists.

It's too often assumed that if you want to talk about architecture, then you need to talk about the work of *architects*. Frank Gehry is architecture, in other words; William Burroughs, inflatable children's toys, and *The Odyssey* somehow are not. The obvious problem here is that, to find more exciting examples of architecture from the present day—and to explore architectural culture more fully—you need to look beyond mere *buildings*. As Mike Webb of Archigram once wrote: "When you are looking for a solution to what you have been told is an architectural problem—remember, the solution may not be a building."

Architecture is not limited to buildings!

Being an architectural critic means *writing about architecture*—even writing about Mies van der Rohe, sure—but it also means writing about architecture in its every manifestation: Whether it's built or not, designed by an architect or not, featured in a video game or not, found outside a novel or not, ruined or not—even whether it's on planet Earth. If architectural critics can get people to realize that the everyday spatial world of earthquake safety plans and prison break films—and suburban Home Depot parking lots and bad funhouse rides—is worthy of architectural analysis, and that architecture is everywhere and involves everything, then perhaps we'll learn to stop taking

SPATIAL DEBAUCHERY: AN INTERVIEW WITH SAM JACOB

Along with Sean Griffiths and Charles Holland, Sam Jacob is director of the East London architecture firm FAT–Fashion, Architecture, Taste. FAT's buildings feel a bit like punch lines to complicated jokes you're not quite sure you heard correctly—and they are notoriously graphic, in the sense that colored brickwork and exaggerated, patterned facades form an ironic, possibly unintentional, hi-tech nod to 19th-century British Arts and Crafts. Sam is also the author of *Strangeharvest*, easily one of the best architecture blogs on the web today. I talked to him about the role of the non-architectural in today's architectural thought.

Sam Jacob: I think, if you say that these things that aren't quite architecture actually *are* architecture, then you start to think: Well, how come architects aren't involved in designing them? How come they don't call up an architect when they need to build a massive gas pipeline all the way from Wales to central England? There are so many architectural moments that could happen within a project like that. Well, it's partly because architects, on the whole, don't want to get involved in that kind of stuff—but it's also because it's not perceived as something that you would need an architect *for*. I suppose you could say: if all of that stuff *is* architectural, then, as an architect, you should get involved in it, and you should argue why it's relevant for an architect to be involved. That would mean, from a business point of view, expanding your possible client base so that you could work for all kinds of strange organizations. I suppose that's not unusual, either—the Eameses were working for the U.S. military and Basil Spence worked in the Second World War designing decoy oil refineries so that the Germans would bomb these bits of cardboard rather than the real things.

But I'm also interested in expanding the idea of architecture in terms of thinking about what the term means in a more general way. So, for instance, working with someone from an advertising background, or working with an artist, or a writer—that gives you an ability to look beyond the confines of what is normally considered *architectural*. With those sorts of projects you're not building a building, you're kind of making a scenario—which, if you think about it in the right way, at the right time of night, after the right amount of wine, is architecture. These are often temporary projects which hijack a moment that already exists, and turn it into a moment where something else could happen. Because, fortunately, architecture is not just about building stuff. You can have a pretty good career as someone involved in architecture, even as an architect, without ever building anything. If, as an architect, you sit there waiting for stuff to happen—it's inevitable that you're going to reproduce the status quo. I think that, in whatever way, architects can make stuff happen, whether it's to do with ideas or to do with buildings.

Once you start to recognize these things as significant moments in the life of a city, or in someone's

The Blue House in Tower Hamlets, London, and *Sint Lucas Art Academy*, in Boxtel, Holland, both by Fashion Architecture Taste.

fashionarchitecturetaste.com
strangeharvest.com

experience of the city, then they offer up architectural scenarios.

BLDGBLOG: I'm also curious if there are any nonarchitectural books—like novels—that might have influenced your thoughts on design.

Jacob: There's this great novel called *Against Nature* by Joris-Karl Huysmans. It's about a dissolute Parisian who decides that he's had enough of his life of debauchery, and he wants to separate himself from the rest of the world. So he moves out to the suburbs of Paris somewhere and he buys this house. The first thing he has to do is to do it up—but he ends up torturing himself about exactly what shade of orange to use, and how it looks in the daytime, and how it looks by candlelight. He even builds a kind of ship's cabin as part of the house. It gets more and more ridiculous. He buys a big Turkish rug that he thinks is great—but then he thinks, *oh, hold on a minute: it's too static*. So he buys a giant tortoise to crawl around on the rug—but then he goes, *oh, that's a bit too dark*. And so he has the shell of the tortoise encrusted with gems.

Each chapter goes through a different sphere of his life, exploring things that he might be able to appreciate. Music, for example: He starts going through all the different kinds of music in the world, and eventually the only thing he can bring himself to listen to is Gregorian chant. He does the same with literature; he does the same with art; and he does the same with food. He ends up having to use this amazing contraption that steams his food and turns it into liquid—because he's tried eating all kinds of things, but it's all made him feel bloated and lethargic.

As a look at the relationship between *architecture* and *lifestyle*, I think it's great; as a satire of how design is appreciated, it's really on the mark. It's like *MTV Cribs*, only more extreme.

In fact, the author wrote another book about a French bureaucrat—a lawyer for the government—who has to retire, or something like that. But he hates his life so much, now that he doesn't have his job, that he builds a replica of his old office in his house; then he hires someone to give him problems to work on, with textbooks and things. It's ridiculous—but written in a very straight way.

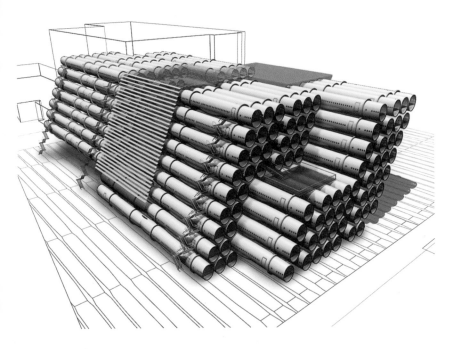

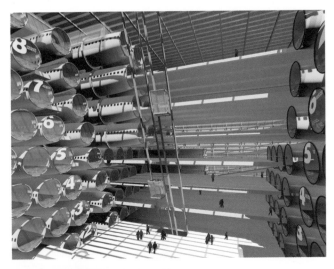

LOT-EK's design for the New Jalisco Library in Guadalajara, Mexico, uses the discarded fuselages of old Boeing 727/737 airplanes as the structure of the building.

lot-ek.com

those spaces for granted. If the world is framed by architecture, then the world can be rebuilt.

What I wanted to do with this book, then, was to pull out certain threads from the blog that seemed worthy of a more extended discussion. There are countless themes on the blog that don't necessarily lend themselves to exploration in a book format—like photos of exploding volcanoes or brief rhetorical questions about suburban waste management. I had no interest in producing a catalog of weird buildings, for instance, or turning this into some kind of encyclopedic tombstone for the blog. This is in no way an exhaustive survey of all things BLDG-BLOG. In some ways it's actually a rather narrow attempt to take on just a few major themes—the underground, climate change, architectural acoustics, and future landscapes—and to explore them in a way that would be at odds with the normal attention span of a blog reader (myself included). I wanted to use the book *as a book*, in other words, to see if I could develop certain ideas and references more fully, to the point that they'd become coherent chapters. After all, a BLDGBLOG book could easily have had chapters about Mars, urban surveillance, simulation, and micro-sovereignty; I could have written chapters about gardens, science fiction, and the architecture of occupation in Iraq. Instead I chose the underground, weather, sound, and landscape futures, and I dug in a little further.

Interspersed throughout the book, though, are clusters of smaller, interstitial entries; these are short, bloglike minichapters, and there are nearly 80 pages of them. Skim them, read them out of order, revisit them if you wish—they're the brief and simple ideas that I liked too much to leave out.

Finally, I want to reiterate that BLDGBLOG is fundamentally about following, and not being ashamed by, your own enthusiasms, whether or not they are rigorous and appropriate for the academic mores of the day, or even interesting for your family and friends. This is extraordinarily important—as is not celebrating something simply because it's "good" or loved by others. If you don't like something, you don't like something. I'm reminded here of the old reggae cliché: *who feels it, knows it.* Adolf Loos might be, academically speaking, "good" architecture, but if his buildings leave you cold—if you're not feeling it—then find something else to talk about. Chances are, you're not the only one who wanted to change the conversation. ⊗

CORB v2.0

...MAN ARE NOMADIC IN NATURE.
...N AVERAGE AUSTRALIANS WILL
...VE IN 14 DIFFERENT HOMES
...RING THEIR LIFETIME. THIS
...OMADIC TENDENCY IT USUALLY
...ESIRED, NOT IMPOSED. OUR
...OMAD LIFESTYLE IS TYPICALLY
... CHOICE, CITING BOREDOM,
...ATUS ENVY, CONTINUOUS
...ANGE IN FAMILY DYNAMIC,
...ROWTH OF PERSONAL WEALTH,
...ANGE OF WORKPLACE ETC..

POSTMODERN HOUSING
(IN MORE WAYS THAN ONE)

THESE CONTAINER STACKERS
COULD MOVE THROUGHOUT A
HOUSING COMPLEX RANDOMLY
CHANGING THE HIERARCHY AND
ARRANGEMENT OF THE
APARTMENT LAYOUT. THEY ARE
WASTED HERE ON THE DOCK.

Architect Andrew Maynard's Corb v2.0 uses container-stacking cranes to perpetually rearrange a new suburb. "Changing your view or neighbors with the seasons or on a whim is not a problem at Corb," the architect writes. "Changes in family dynamics or space requirements are easily dealt with."

maynardarchitects.com

Inflationary Spaces of the Aero-Gothic Future

In the summer of 2005, Swiss architecture firm Instant designed *ON_AIR*, an inflatable addition to KW, an art gallery in Berlin's Mitte district. This inflatable space with transparent walls served as a new entryway both to the building's inner galleries and to the small courtyard garden located just beyond; it even came complete with its own staircase and balcony. The project was an internal prosthesis for the building, in other words, a new interior that could be deflated and moved elsewhere.

To function properly, and to support the weight of museum visitors, Instant used "tensairity," an inflatable variant on structural tensegrity, itself a concept first developed in 1968 by sculptor Kenneth Snelson with the input of Buckminster Fuller. Instant worked in collaboration with Airlight, another Swiss firm, whose website boasts that their pneumatic structures are so strong that "it is already possible to build temporary bridges even suitable for heavy transports"; indeed the design for KW was apparently so strong that it could hold a small truck.

When I initially glanced at the project, however, I misunderstood it to be an entire museum addition, of perhaps indefinite longevity—a permanent, inflatable art museum. Alas, it was just a temporary installation, and is now long gone. While thus deluded, though, I found myself imagining what might happen if you could design inflatable additions to other types of buildings, like suburban houses: your in-laws come to town, or your weird and apparently unemployed uncle who doesn't really talk to anyone stops by, and there's no room for them inside the house. No worries: the smiling patron of this particular household pops open some hinges on the back French doors, and *voilà*: The house's central air-conditioning doubles as an air pump, and you all watch in pleased awe as a twin house, identical in form to the one you're now standing in, takes bloated shape in the lawn behind you. Even your uncle mutters that he's impressed.

Whole suburbs of inflatable houses!

It's easy to imagine a new chapter for Italo Calvino's *Invisible Cities*, in which our untrustworthy narrator is taken out into the gardens of the king—whose courtiers proceed to inflate an entire palace, over a half-dozen acres, full of flamingos and orchids, unrolling in the summer heat. A thousand rooms. Towers and halls. Somewhere in the midst of all that is the chamber you'll be staying in…

Then I remembered Tobias Hill's 2004 novel *The Cryptographer,* in which an ultra-rich Bill Gates–like figure purchases an entire borough of London, walling it off and transforming it into a private homestead (an agonizingly brilliant setup for a book, though the story itself falls flat)—and I thought: You could *inflate* an entire borough that has never otherwise existed, sprawling across the marshy floodplains of east London. Call it Hackney 2, or Stoke Airington. It's one seamless piece of fiber-reinforced PVC foil. It looks like a huge plastic bag lying across the landscape—until the fans kick in. Two days later there's a whole new city, complete with streets and traffic lights *built into* the plastic. The lamps have shades; all the buildings' windows have shutters. It's a *Gesamtkunstwerk* so total it would make Mies van der Rohe panic. To pay the initial investors back, you hire it out as a film set and produce award-winning mobile phone commercials there. Or strangely extravagant pornos, using transparent sets, described as "artistically stunning" (though sales remain low).

Perhaps there should be a film in which a dozen strange men show up in New York City carrying identical briefcases. Like a scene from *The Thomas Crown Affair* or the plot of an early Tom Clancy novel, they're being tracked by undercover agents who have been following them street by street. But they get away. Just like that. All twelve of them manage to evade their pursuers for long enough, dashing down alleyways, that no one sees when they drop off their briefcases at predetermined points. They set them down on the sidewalk, near trash cans, in front of coffee shops, and they walk away. Then, one by one, their briefcases start to whir with tiny ventilators, and the hinges unlock, and the lids spring open, and we see carefully folded, layered sheets of plastic—which begin to inflate, flopping out through the streets, into Central Park, across

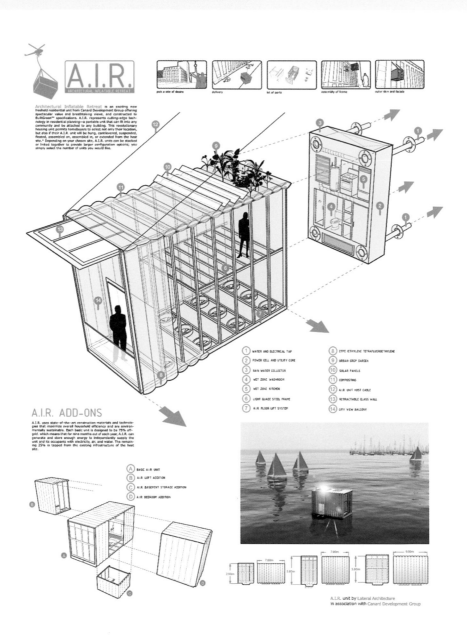

A.I.R.

ARCHITECTURAL INFLATABLE RETREAT

Architectural Inflatable Retreat is an exciting new freehold residential unit from Canard Development Group offering spectacular value and breathtaking views, and constructed to BuiltGreen™ specifications. A.I.R. represents cutting-edge technology in residential planning—a portable unit that can fit into any community and be attached to any building. This revolutionary housing unit permits homebuyers to select not only their location, but also if their A.I.R. unit will be hung, cantilevered, suspended, floated, assembled on, assembled in, or extended from the host site.* Depending on your chosen site, A.I.R. units can be stacked or linked together to provide larger configuration options; you simply select the number of units you would like.

pick a site of desire   delivery   kit of parts   assembly of frame   outer skin and facade

1	WATER AND ELECTRICAL TAP	8	ETFE (ETHYLENE TETRAFLUOROETHYLENE)
2	POWER CELL AND UTILITY CORE	9	URBAN CROP GARDEN
3	RAIN WATER COLLECTOR	10	SOLAR PANELS
4	WET ZONE WASHROOM	11	COMPOSTING
5	WET ZONE KITCHEN	12	A.I.R UNIT HOST CABLE
6	LIGHT GUAGE STEEL FRAME	13	RETRACTABLE GLASS WALL
7	A.I.R FLOOR LIFT SYSTEM	14	CITY VIEW BALCONY

A.I.R. ADD-ONS

A.I.R. uses state-of-the-art construction materials and technologies that maximize overall household efficiency and are environmentally sustainable. Each basic unit is designed to be 75% off-grid, which means that for nine months out of each year, A.I.R. can generate and store enough energy to independently supply the unit and its occupants with electricity, air, and water. The remaining 25% is tapped from the existing infrastructure of the host site.

A BASIC A.I.R UNIT
B A.I.R LOFT ADDITION
C A.I.R BASEMENT STORAGE ADDITION
D A.I.R BEDROOM ADDITION

A.I.R. unit by Lateral Architecture
In association with Canard Development Group

The A.I.R. module by Toronto's Lateral Architecture is an "architectural inflatable retreat" that can be bolted onto existing structures. "Depending on your chosen site," they explain, "A.I.R. units can be stacked or linked together to provide larger configuration options; you simply select the number of units you would like."

lateralarch.com

In 2006, Rem Koolhaas and Cecil Balmond collaborated to produce an inflatable pavilion for the Serpentine Gallery in London. Photograph by Nicola Twilley.

serpentinegallery.org

the waterfront, filling up like lungs to form high-rises and tenement buildings and, soon, skyscrapers. A counter-Manhattan, made from structured air, invading the city it replaces. The whole thing is bulletproof. Stab-proof. Bomb-proof. It's like Cloverfield's inflatable cousin in architectural form.

Back to Instant and their inflatable design for KW. What if it had been more ambitious— and perhaps more interactive? What if you could show up at KW with your own air pumps and—after clearing the building of people— inflate a *whole new interior*, perfectly matched to the architectural plan, subdividing galleries, adding stairs and lofted office space? You come back a day later and twist a valve, blocking air from entering one room—and so another room unfolds somewhere deeper in the structure, perhaps so far away that you'll never even find it. This, in turn, causes a corridor to inflate, leading onward to another room—where you have a choice: You can either open a valve and inflate the rest of the ground plan, or you can leave the valve closed and cause a four-story tower of inflated rooms to lift itself up above the courtyard....

You have dreams at night that some kind of subsidiary structure has been tucked away in the walls all around you, and that, if only you could find the right place to attach some air pumps—if only you could find the right valves—you could proceed to inflate perhaps a whole new city, something so titanic it would dwarf the very planet you now stand on. It's a *Choose-Your-Own-Valve Adventure*, unfolding a vast inflationary architecture across the universe like a Beatles song, stepping down corridors between planets.

This leads me to wonder if there's perhaps some Hindu myth, or an obscure *Upanishad*, in which a multi-lunged god of air parades his wizardry of inflated worlds past stunned worshippers—or a Christian heresy, from medieval France, in which the breath of God, a holy spirit animating base flesh, became interpreted as *God, Inflationist, Lord of Balloons*. The primordial inhalation blew out to form palaces of life, hovering in mid-air. Had the heresy survived, a new breed of cathedrals would now dot the European landscape, supported by inflatable buttresses, inaugurating the Aero-Gothic... Aero-Romanesque... Aero-Baroque...

Architecture as a Form of Deliberate Paranoia

As a teenager in suburban Philadelphia, I hung out now and then with a Canadian guy who owned a drum machine. He'd been programming huge amounts of really great music into it for at least six months, he said, but, being naive to the thieving ways of the world, he came home one day to find that his drum machine had been stolen. This act of musical larceny propelled him into a state of unremitting paranoia so intense, and so interesting, that I still think about it nearly 15 years later.

From that moment on, every time he went out to hear music—mostly at raves in New York City—he claimed that, at some point in the night, he had heard *one of his own songs*. Flagrantly stolen from his own drum machine, and then inscribed to vinyl—to be spun, live, for the dancing masses—his music popped up at least once every few hours. Wide-eyed, emotional, convincing: there he was, explaining that this song was really his.

I mention all this because I wonder what the architectural equivalent would be.

Perhaps a student somewhere, who's spent literally hundreds and hundreds of hours sketching strange buildings—detailing elevators that lead to more elevators, and hotel rooms that connect to secret swimming pools in which hundreds of people sit, talking—finds that his sketchbook has been stolen.

Fifteen years later, this person goes on vacation with some friends—but the hotel they're staying in looks familiar. Too familiar.

It's his building.

"I designed this thing!" he screams, rattling door handles and staring through rotating glass doors at the swimming pool outside. He's visibly sweating, and a large vein is pulsing in the center of his forehead. Everyone takes a step back. "This is *my* hotel!" he shouts, kicking an ice bucket down the hall. The man gets so loud that his friends start to panic, going so far as to punch him in the face, hoping it will knock him out. It doesn't. This enrages him further. *Should I call 911?* his girlfriend wonders.

Within 20 minutes the police show up. Our friend is arrested and strapped facedown to a table at the station, where they inject him with horse tranquilizers. He wakes up in the nearby hospital, where he is held for three days.

But the thing is: He was right. He *really did* design that hotel. It really had been copied from his stolen sketchbook. That swimming pool *really was* his idea. Even worse: so was the building across the street—a building he's about to see when they discharge him from the hospital. And those buildings downtown? He designed them, too. He designed this whole city: he sketched *the whole thing* in that book that was stolen from him so long ago.

Except he's the only one who knows it. Not a single one of his friends believes him. People make fun of him, call him "Charles Manson," and point out the window at different buildings as if to antagonize him. "Did you design that, too?" they taunt.

To escape the madness, the man moves to a new city, packing his bags and buying a dog—only to realize that this city, too, looks strangely familiar…

(Coming soon: *Sketchbook*, starring Christian Bale.)

A Game is the City Abstracted: An Interview with Kevin Slavin

With Frank Lantz, Kevin Slavin co-founded Area/Code, an immersive games-development and entertainment firm based in New York City. In their own words, Area/Code "takes advantage of today's environment of pervasive technologies and overlapping media to create new kinds of entertainment." These new kinds of entertainment are "urban environments transformed into spaces for public play"—"game events driven by real-world data."

In Lantz's *Big Games* manifesto, outlining the firm's basic design philosophy, he writes:

> Big Games encourage a playful use of public space. They have their roots in the neighborhood games of childhood; in the campus-wide games and stunts of college; in the nerd-culture of live-action role playing and Civil War re-enactments; in the art-culture of Happenings and Situationism; in urban skateparks, paintball fields, and anywhere people gather together to play in large numbers and large spaces.

> Big Games are games, not academic exercises, not tech demos. They must be easy to understand but deep enough to encourage thoughtful play. They must have challenges and rewards. They must run the gamut from purely abstract formal systems to richly rendered narrative experiences. They must connect people to people whether they are strangers, rivals or old friends.

> Big Games are human-powered software for cities, life-size collaborative hallucinations, and serious fun.

In May 2007, Slavin spoke at *Postopolis!*—an event co-organized by BLDGBLOG at New York's Storefront for Art and Architecture—and we continued that conversation by phone to discuss how mobile games can change one's experience of urban space.

BLDGBLOG: What do specific cities, or specific neighborhoods within cities, contribute to certain games?

Kevin Slavin: When we did *Crossroads* down in the West Village, it was due to the confluence of a couple of different things there. First, it's a grid—but not a perfect grid. We didn't want it to be perfect geometry, but we also needed the conceit of a grid for the game. It's also near the river, so the buildings are low enough that GPS satellite transmissions don't bounce, and we could get visibility to three satellites at once. It was interesting that the topography of the game was determined partly by history, partly by urban planning, and partly by access to optical satellite links. It was a game that we couldn't have played in Midtown.

BLDGBLOG: Could the same game then migrate through the city based on whether new construction has obstructed satellite signals?

Slavin: Totally. The thing about designing games for the real world is that you don't have the benefit of a board game, where you're in control of the environment. If you and I are playing chess, I can't just move the pieces however I want because you'll see it—and, if it's a video game, I can't just move pieces however I want because the code will prohibit that. But the real world changes all the time and it's really, really hard—as any urban planner will tell you—to design something for an environment that is not systematized. There are all kinds of tricks—like placing the game close to the river to optimize your chances of getting an optical satellite link—but we've also found that some cities will simply reject a game, almost like it's a virus, while other cities will just metabolize it. There were cities in which the problem was homeless people, and there were other cities where it was the police.

Every city has a different response to these kinds of interventions.

BLDGBLOG: Has setting games in particular cities actually led to a deeper understanding of the way each city works—or the way its residents think, for that matter?

Slavin: When we were doing *ConQwest*, we were working with high-school kids in cities like Salt Lake City, Phoenix, and Boise. It was a commercial project so everything was licensed and fine—nothing went wrong, in that sense. But when we were dreaming it up, our idea was that the game would let the kids experience the city in a way they'd never experienced it before. What I discovered on the ground, though, is that, when the kids showed up, they were seeing the city in a way they had never seen it before: *in person.* Which is to say that cities like Salt Lake, Phoenix, and Boise just didn't play a role in these kids' lives. The idea that they would go downtown to do something was absolutely strange to them.

We were in these cities that weren't really cities—they were cities without a civic life. And whereas we felt like we were providing a new perspective, what we were really doing was providing any use for downtown at all for high schoolers. Because really, what else would they be doing there? You know, they don't work for an insurance company! It was a totally foreign place for them. We discovered it when we were handing out maps: They were really studying the maps, and it was clear that they had never been on these streets before.

That was really vivid evidence of how far away people are from the everyday life of the cities that they live in.

BLDGBLOG: Architect Sam Jacob once wrote on his blog about the spatial origins of the soccer pitch. Apparently, soccer was once played throughout the village, with the church, say, as one goal and the jail as another. "It was a game played once a year for a whole day," he writes, "where the entire village and the surrounding countryside became the pitch. The street, the buildings, the trees, the fences… every last bit of landscape." In other words, the *entire urban field* was the space of the game. But this was eventually abstracted and standardized into the landscape that we call the soccer pitch—and a regulated game space could then be exported around the world.

Slavin: That's beautiful. That makes me think of a project we're doing in London now. We got a call from someone representing the Home Office there because teenage violence is so out of control in the UK: It's all these 16-year-old kids binge drinking and the numbers are really scary in terms of how many people get seriously hurt. The guy representing the Home Office said something that was actually so insightful—he said, "I don't know how to qualify what I'm about to say—and I hope this is how you think about these things—but what we're looking for is an activity we can give them to make their time more *valuable.*"

And I thought that is really interesting. It's a funny thing that games can do, especially because, in fact, they're making the time *useless.* They produce useless activities that you consider to be valuable.

While we were working on that, though, Frank recalled the history of basketball. Basketball was invented by a minister who had been given the task of trying to give a bunch of rowdy kids some way to get through the New England winter. It was a sport that they could play indoors, and nobody had really thought about something like that before. Basketball was basically invented to get kids to run around and have a way to fight that was regulated and productive—precisely through being unproductive.

BLDGBLOG: That brings us to the political aspect of games: that they can also be a distraction. Why form a union or resist your government when you can go play basketball?

Slavin: Right. Because you know what else would make kids' time more valuable? Jobs. How about that? [*laughs*] But we don't make jobs, we make games!

areacodeinc.com

The Undiscovered Bedrooms of Manhattan

A friend of mine once told me about the "typi-cal dream of a New Yorker," as he described it, wherein a homeowner pushes aside some coats and sweaters in the upstairs closet only to reveal a door, and, behind that, another room, and, beyond that, perhaps a whole new wing secretly attached to the back of the house… Manhattanites, in particular, are looking for more space.

So I was thinking that you could go around Manhattan with a microphone, asking people who have had that dream to describe it—or you could ask people who have never had that dream simply to ad lib about what it might be like to discover another room tucked away inside a closet somewhere. What additions to their space do New Yorkers secretly long for?

Of course, you'd probably need to record about 5,000 people to get even a dozen or so good stories—but then you could edit it all down and listen to the unbelievable variations: people who find secret attics, or secret base-ments, secret closets inside closets, even secret children's bedrooms, secret bathrooms, hidden roof gardens, or a brand new four-car garage plus screened-in porch out back. One guy finds a sauna, and a cheese cave, and then a bicycle-repair shop… *What does it all mean?* And if you once dreamed about finding a secret UPS load-ing dock attached to your back door… what would your therapist have to say about that?

You get all the stories together and you make a radio piece out of it. A month or two later, it's broadcast during rush hour, on a Friday night. Soon commuters are pulling over to the side of the road and staring, shocked, at the radio—because you've given no introduction, and no one out there has any idea what this is. *Some guy found* a boathouse *attached to his apartment in Manhattan* . . . ? one driver wonders, con-fused as hell. And the stories keep coming.

There's a skyscraper with a whole hidden floor . . . ? someone thinks, momentarily amazed—before driving into the car in front of her. A woman on the Upper East Side found *what*? Or: All along he had a *basketball court* behind the bedroom wall?

The New Jersey turnpike gets backed up for miles. The Brooklyn Bridge is at a stand-still. *Where are all these secret rooms—and why don't* I *have one*…? Radio listeners at home are knocking on walls, taking measurements, drafting letters to the Rent Control Board.

But as the credits are read, and the radio sta-tion cuts to commercial, everyone realizes that those were all just stories. Just dreams. There *are* no secret rooms—they think.

So they pull back onto the highways—and you go down in radio history. Within two weeks you've signed a six-figure deal with Henry Holt to turn it into a book, and Paul Aus-ter volunteers to write the foreword. You call it *The Undiscovered Bedrooms of Manhattan*. It's mistakenly shelved under *Erotica*.

Ancient Lights

The phrase "ancient lights" is shorthand for a "right to light," guaranteed under British law, whereby windows that have had 20 years' worth of "uninterrupted" daylight cannot be blocked by the construction of new buildings. The Prescription Act of 1832, together with the Rights of Light Act of 1959, offers legal protection for homeowners who have had windowed access to daylight for at least 20 years; no neighboring structures can be built that might infringe upon that access without permission from the window's owner. As established in the case of *Kelk v. Pearson* (1871), the holder of a right to light is entitled to "sufficient light according to the ordinary notions of mankind"—but what these "ordinary notions of mankind" might be, we do not know.

Fast-forward to the present day, and England's Royal Institution of Charted Surveyors (RICS) inspiringly suggests that you should never "settle for living in the shadows." The RICS believes, rather, that "many people are allowing adjacent buildings to block their natural light, unaware that they have a legal right to it. Light blocking can be classified as a 'nuisance' alongside noise and air pollution and culprits range from large new commercial developments to a neighbor's building extension or a new garden shed. Even a tall hedge can be a problem." The tone of the RICS abruptly shifts at this point, however, as it explains that you can—and, in fact, must—prevent your neighbors from acquiring ancient light rights. There is a "need for vigilance to prevent neighbors acquiring a right to light," they warn; after all, such an acquisition "may hamper future development and investment possibilities" on your own property. "It is possible to prevent a building acquiring a right to light," we're told, "but despite the procedure being simple, it is rarely used."

The "procedure" here is to build a kind of *ghost architecture*. In other words, following consultation from the RICS, you would draw "a notional screen of unlimited height" around your home, together with other "imaginary legal partitions," thus defining the light rights of your property. You'd then ring your neighbor's doorbell, hand him an envelope, and explain what you've been doing. He'll nod quietly, cease construction on his new guest bedroom—and throw a brick through your window the next day. You retaliate. Soon, all your neighbors have joined in, choosing sides, letting the air out of your car's tires, and stealing your morning paper. Within two weeks, the quality of life on your street has plummeted; there are threats, loud noises, lewd graffiti, and an unexplained smell....

Meanwhile, throughout greater London, the phrase "ancient lights" can be seen painted near windows, staking claim on the light in the sky.

A Spatial History of Mirrors

In his 1994 book *Crystallography*, poet Christian Bök describes "a medieval treatise on the use of mirrors." This treatise, according to Bök, suggests that when two mirrors reflect one other, the endless abyss of mirrors-in-mirrors created between them might form a kind of spectral architecture. Further, the medieval treatise says that "any living person who has no soul can actually step into either one of the mirrors as if it were an open door and thus walk down the illusory corridor that appears to recede forever into the depths of the glass by virtue of one mirror reflecting itself in the other. The walls of such a corridor are said to be made from invulnerable panes of crystal, beyond which lies a nullified dimension of such complexity that to view it is surely to go insane. (…) [A]fter an eternity of walking down such a corridor, a person eventually exits from the looking-glass opposite to the one first entered."

The treatise's author then "speculates that a soulless man might carry another pair of mirrors into such a corridor, thereby producing a hallway at right angles to the first one, and of course this procedure might be performed again and again in any of the corridors until an endless labyrinth of glass has been erected inside the first pair of mirrors, each mirror opening onto an extensive grid of crisscrossing hallways, some of which never intersect, despite their lengths being both infinite and perpendicular." The author warns, however, that one could become "hopelessly lost while exploring such a maze"—for instance, "if the initial pair of mirrors are disturbed so that they no longer reflect each other, thus suddenly obliterating the fragile foundation upon which the entire maze rests." Whole crystal cities of mirrored halls would *simply disappear*—along with anyone still exploring inside them.

Aboard the International Space Station, an astronaut, crazed with loneliness, sets up two mirrors…and promptly escapes into a hinged labyrinth of crystallized earth-orbiters, his radio crackling unanswered in the control panel left behind. British public school children sing hymns to the Disappearing Astronaut.

At the End of the Tunnel

Certain architectural hallucinations have been associated with near-death experiences (NDEs); these include the classic "bright light" at the end of a long tunnel. While one could forge an entire career studying the neurophysiology of the near-death experience, what I think deserves more exploration is the *actual tunnel*—the architectural space within which NDEs seem to occur. Is there a particular type of structure that people see when it comes to nearly dying? If so, are those structures simply optical phenomena or neurochemical epiphenomena—or are there cultural and historical influences at work? If you're an architect, are your NDEs particularly detailed? And what if you see a bright tunnel, inverted, ending in a space of pure darkness…?

What about the architecture? Does everyone see the same hallway—or do some people see large rooms, or skylights, or even underground car parks, or caves, or maybe some huge mechanical garage door that slowly creeps open like the beginning of a suburban horror movie? Is there an *architecture of death*? Can it be measured, and studied, and taught to others? Could it be *built elsewhere*? After all, if death does have a structure, if death has a *spatial format*, you could say—then clearly the end of life could also be architecturally reconstructed, based on eyewitness accounts, here on earth, in the present moment, with us. We could visit it, in groups, and emotionally prepare.

So what would happen if an architect (who works mostly on public parks) teamed up with an anthropologist (who studies narrations of the near-death experience) and a neurophysiologist (who understands the basic cortical mechanisms) to design a themed environment specifically meant for triggering NDEs? It'd be a kind of post-Buddhist thanatological fun ride, complete with people passing out, then waking up, blinking and vibrant, determined to change their lives—hugging strangers and starting things over. *Hallways of Rebirth*, it might be called—and the first person to make it to the end of that hallway without passing out wins $10,000. It's harder than it sounds.

Mies van der Rogaine

I was thinking one day about performance art pieces involving architecture, and I thought that there should be a man who travels around the world, visiting cities and jungles and deserts and islands, all so that he can take Flomax inside famous architectural structures. It would be the new art of pharmaco-architourism.

In fact, I was speaking to a friend once about "gonzo" architectural journalism, and how most people seem to think that would just mean getting high before interviewing Rem Koolhaas, or taking hallucinogens and flying off to Dubai—but who's to say that architecture would be any less interesting if you experienced it all jacked up on prescription diuretics? High on Cialis? Reexamining every church in Rome while you swagger through the city in a libidinal haze…surely some interesting journalism would result. You could call yourself "The Cialisian" and get a monthly column in *Vanity Fair*. For Christmas, you receive a specially tailored set of loose trousers.

Next year you lather your head with a spot of Rogaine foam inside every building Mies van der Rohe ever designed—and, by the end of the piece, your hair is so long you're actually refused entrance to Berlin's National Gallery. You write a book about it, which becomes an instant, if controversial, bestseller. You title it *Mies van der Rogaine*.

Or perhaps you take heroic quantities of Prilosec in buildings built before A.D. 1500, and pitch the resulting articles to *Abitare*. Pop some Adderall and plow through the High Gothic monuments of Europe, publishing your research in the *New York Times*. Next year it's Lipitor, or Effexor, or a whole rucksack full of Advair inhalers, as you write about anything built by Le Corbusier. And then, of course, there's Clozaril, for your forthcoming book on Gaudí….

The Structure

An indestructible foam, resistant even to nuclear explosions, is developed by the Department of Energy to contain radioactive spills: When a nuclear power plant melts down you simply spray it with this foam—and *voilà*. It locks into place, sealing the site away from humans—away from all living tissue—for ten thousand years.

One day, though, a massive shipment of foam is being taken out of Los Angeles by train when the pressurized cars containing it rupture. There is an explosion; the foam sprays everywhere, coating buildings, raining down onto cars and pedestrians; and it hardens within mere seconds.

Resistant to saws, fire, blunt force, and bombs, the site becomes known as The Structure. It is a huge, white web of hardened foam—and it will outlast human civilization. Families take tours of it; Greenpeace makes posters of it as a cautionary tale; architecture studios map its complicated arches, inspiring buildings as far away as Mumbai. It is the 8th Wonder of the World, some people say as they drive by, snapping photographs.

The Wonders of the World: An Interview with Mary Beard

Mary Beard is a professor of classics at Cambridge University and the general editor of *The Wonders of the World*, "a small series of books that will focus on some of the world's most famous sites or monuments." Published in the United States by Harvard University Press and by Profile Books in the United Kingdom, the series has thus far covered topics ranging from Mediterranean archaeology and the birth of Egyptology to the history of British railways and memorials to World War I.

BLDGBLOG: I can think of a dozen or so places that would make fantastic books—the catacombs of Paris, the Maginot Line, Hoover Dam, Cape Canaveral, and so on—maybe even the International Space Station—but perhaps those don't really fit the editorial mission of the series. Would any of these sites qualify as Wonders of the World?

Mary Beard: We want to range from the absolutely bog-standard, normative greatest hits that would be anybody's idea of a Wonder of the World, while, at the same time, we want to increase the range of those Wonders. There's a trade-off there, between not wanting to be boringly predictable, and, on the other hand, not wanting to be maverickly odd.

One of the things I want to do is to take some of the greatest hits, like St. Peter's and Stonehenge, and show people how interesting and complicated and different they are—different from what those people might have imagined. But I also want to take things that people might never have thought of putting in the category of a Wonder.

BLDGBLOG: Like Simon Bradley's *St. Pancras*?

Beard: I think St. Pancras in England is an absolutely extraordinary building, and, behind it, the rail sheds are incredible—in the engineering and in the architecture. Similarly, with something like Gavin Stamp's *The Memorial to the Missing of the Somme*: What happens if you take something that people would say, "Oh, a war memorial"—and you say, No—think of it in a different way. Think about this as a Wonder of the World. And then you think about that monument differently.

I'm also interested in natural wonders: The Grand Canyon is only made a natural wonder by cultural reappropriation. Without that, it's just a canyon. So why not the Grand Canyon? Similarly, too, the Alps were any old mountains—till they became *Mountains*. And the Lake District was just boggy hills till the blasted poets got at them.

But I don't know how far you can go down that line of being subversive. In some ways, we're always teetering on the margins of where we might go next. One of the things that I've often said is: "I wonder what happens if you do Auschwitz?" Can you do sites of *horror*? Can you turn *wonder* around in that way? It would be hard to know how to do that in the series in a way that isn't mawkish or that, in some way, makes the monument tawdry. It's hard to know.

BLDGBLOG: That's interesting, actually, because there's been a lot of attention lately to so-called *dark tourism*—where people visit sites like Auschwitz and the Cambodian Killing Fields. So there is a connection between *wonder* and *horror*.

Beard: There was a book—which was not in the series—by William St. Clair, about Cape Coast Castle, a British slave-trading castle on the west coast of Africa. That turned out to be extremely interesting. It expanded from being a Wonder partly because St. Clair found an enormously rich set of unexploited documentation. But we did talk quite a lot about whether the slave trade could produce *wonder*—if the slave trade could produce a Wonder of the World—and what that would mean.

I think the boundaries of the *Wonders of the World* series are interesting—but, in the end, if all you did was invest in the margins, without re-looking—and I think it is a radical re-looking—at some of the things which seem more familiar, it would be a bit of a waste.

BLDGBLOG: In other words, doing a book about something like Cape Canaveral would be a little too avant-garde.

Beard: I *would* go with a monument of space technology, actually, because I think you'd read it differently within the series. It's just that I wouldn't have too many volumes on Cape Canaveral and other things like that. It's a question of productive balance. In the long term, I hope that the books will rub off on one another: you'll read Westminster Abbey differently because you've read it after you've read about Cape Canaveral—and vice versa.

It seems to me that all these books really do, in a sense, is say: *Look, these buildings matter.* They're not just bricks and mortar. They've been fought about. People want to own them—to make them theirs—because they know that they're important. Quite *how* that happens, I think, is always an important story. Do we think culture is moveable and global and shared? Or do we think that culture is national—it belongs to the soil on which it was created? Should culture be owned by the people whose ancestors created it?

I saw a statement quite recently—I don't know if he was correctly quoted—by the Greek minister of culture, saying that, in his ideal world, everything produced in Greece would remain in Greece. At that point you think: Right, this is not about the restitution of things that have been illegally bought or smuggled; this is about a particular version of *archaeological nationalism*. At that point, I start to feel very uneasy—and I would hope that this series of books might help people to see that a narrowly vulgar archaeological nationalism is a very problematic idea.

I was in the Metropolitan Museum of Art relatively recently, and I was walking through those rooms that have been reconstructed from British country houses, and I thought: Do I feel pleased that these rooms are here? Or do I feel like what *have you got your hands on these for*? Which do I feel? Obviously, to some extent, I feel both—but, on balance, I feel more pleased than cross. The idea that bits of my culture can be found globally—that I can go into a museum in New York and see something from Gloucestershire—actually pleases me as much as it makes me anxious. I did also go to the Mellon Center for British Art, in New Haven, a few weeks ago—a marvelous collection of British art—and it made me say: Here I am, a very well-educated, culturally middle-class Brit, and this collection of British art in New Haven, displayed in a way that I'd never seen British art displayed before, has made me think differently about my own culture, in a way that would have been impossible had these been in the UK.

So, leaving aside the fraught issues of criminality or theft, which is one thing, the idea is whether we can think of these things as bits of shared cultural property. I mean, what happens when a building becomes a Wonder of the World? One of the interesting consequences, I think, is a series of tough questions. In what sense do we own these things? In what sense can these things really be *shared*? Do we feel pleased that there's a bit of the Parthenon in the Louvre—or do we think it should go back to Athens?

BLDGBLOG: I think a lot of this comes down to the specific historical relationship between the countries involved. The United States having British artifacts in a museum means one thing, whereas, say—

Mary Beard: Having the Benin bronzes means quite another.

BLDGBLOG: Exactly. It has a different set of political implications. But that's also why it can be hard sometimes to distinguish between archaeology as a *science*, and archaeology as a *political pursuit*. Archaeology becomes politics, or even empire, pursued by other means.

Mary Beard: Yes, I think there's always a trade-off. Different sides will tell you different stories and give you different interpretations of the same series of events. It's always murky.

2

THE UNDER GROUND

The William B. Rankine Hydroelectric Tailrace tunnel at Niagara Falls, Ontario, photographed by Michael Cook. "Imagine a tunnel more than ten stories underground, a hundred years old, bricklined, wet, and completely inaccessible save by descending through a narrow slit in its ceiling thirty feet above the floor," Cook writes. "Now imagine that this tunnel flows into Niagara Falls, emerging behind the pummeling curtain of water that nearly everyone in North America journeys to see at some point in their lives. This tunnel exists."

vanishingpoint.ca

I ONCE READ ABOUT a British farmer who was driving a tractor one day across the back hills of his property. The land had been in his family for generations; he knew every hill, ditch, thicket, and water hole, practically every plant. But, that day, cresting a small rise on his way home for dinner, his tractor's front wheel got stuck. *That's strange*, he thought. *There are no holes around here.* So he tried backing up, going forward, rocking the tractor, accelerating—but it wouldn't move. It took at least 20 minutes to get the tractor free, at which point the man hopped down to take a look at what had trapped him. It was a hole, all right—but a very interesting one, because the wheel of his tractor had actually dislodged a stone in the domed ceiling of an ancient burial chamber. He wasn't standing on a hill at all, in other words, but on top of a man-made landform on which centuries of grass and wildflowers had grown. Peering into the darkness, he could even make out what appeared to be a tunnel leading off across his property—where there was another small hill, with a remarkably similar shape to the old barrow he was standing on. And another, he saw, and another—at which point all those hills suddenly looked quite different. The farmer stood up, gazing out across his family's land, stunned.

Whether it's a question of archaeology, urban infrastructure, natural caverns, or the plot of an old Jules Verne story, there are whole built worlds and landscapes in the darkness beneath our feet. These spaces—vast, sprawling, and pieced together over centuries—are accessible and worth exploring. In fact, the toroidal world of self-intersecting drains and sewers built beneath developed cities all over the world—such as London's old brick sewers, designed in the 1860s by Joseph Bazalgette—together with medieval catacombs and modern storm water complexes, gives shape to the dominant mantra of modern architecture, that *form follows function*, with an intensity, and a necessity, that surface structures seldom achieve.

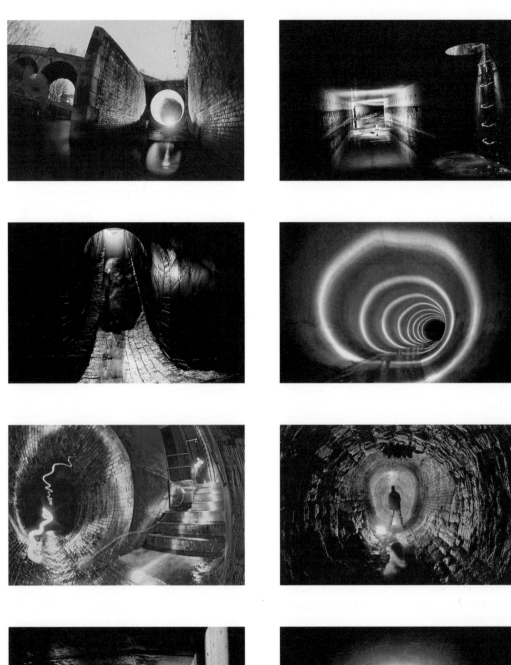

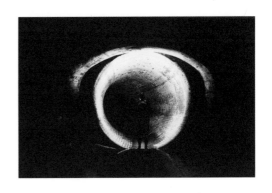

URBAN KNOT THEORY

↑ previous spread
Sixteen photographs by Siologen of International Urban Glow. This is architecture as dreamed of by Adolf Loos: shaved of ornament, exquisitely smooth, and nothing if not functional. While architecture schools were busy teaching their students to design like Mies van der Rohe, civil engineers were perfecting the modern movement beneath their feet.

siologen.net/pbase

Rumor has it that a university outside Manchester, England, teaches its courses in mathematics and knot theory not inside comfortable, well-lit classrooms—the university has none—but down in the sewers, drains, valves, and storm tunnels built long ago beneath the city. Those subterranean vaults of old Victorian brickwork are measured, sketched, and catalogued every year by new students who spend whole weeks at a time mapping the curvature of spillway walls and graphing intersections of unexplored side-channels. The results are then compared to diagrams of Euclidean geometry. Manchester's storm overflow sewers, then, are topological models, deliberately designed to teach knot theory in built form.

Other rumors claim that a former student of that program went on to become chief engineer for the city of Brisbane, Australia, where he now leads the construction of new pieces of underground civic infrastructure; every sewer and spillway built beneath Brisbane is designed by him alone. As a result, whenever you flush a toilet there, a bewildering and exhaustively contorted world of concrete knots and brick culverts comes to life, engineered to faultless precision, washing everyone's waste out to sea. Manifolds, loops, and prime number sequences: the entire history of Western mathematics can be derived from the sewers of Brisbane, monuments to geometry in the form of urban plumbing.

Four photographs by Siologen of International Urban Glow.

siologen.net/pbase

Two photographers in particular—publishing their work under the names Siologen and Dsankt—have been busy documenting these topologically complex systems built beneath cities throughout the United Kingdom, Australia, Europe, and beyond.

Siologen ranks tunnels according to their "connectivity, variation, and age," he explained to me in an e-mail, and he travels around the world to explore new systems. Some drains, he claims, resemble car parts, huge engines attached to the underside of the city, resonating with the echoes of unseen pumps. Sidedraught Induction, Siologen writes, referring to a system of drains in Manchester, "reminds me of a Stromberg carburetor."

The drains are named—"the person who finds them, names them," Siologen says—ranging from The Motherload to the ROTOR Bunker, to Maze, Zardox, Supercharger, and The Works. Post a name, with photographs, onto enough urban exploration websites, and the label soon sticks. The world's sewers become a known geography.

↓ next spread
The River Fleet in London, photographed by Samuel Seed/Dsankt. "Congealed sewage on the floor and bleached toilet paper trailing from the wedge," Dsankt writes. "This is London."

sleepycity.net

Dsankt, meanwhile, actually boats into the underworld, boarding small skiffs in the rivers of outer Brisbane and following tides up intake valves, ducking beneath dangling scraps of sewage. His visits to the subcity are thus very carefully

timed: Should the waters rise faster than expected, both he and his boat will be crushed—shipwrecked in a world of abstract concrete rooms, slowly but lethally flooding.

Regional geographies impose their own variations. For instance, Australian drains actually *sound different* than drains in the United Kingdom. In Sydney, there are "weird acoustics due to the jagged facets of rock in the walls," Siologen explained, whereas London's tunnels "sound wet"—and smell like shit. "Mostly, it's the sound of rushing water you hear, with the clank of cars running over loose manhole lids and, of course, the splashing of people walking through."

I'm reminded here of Gene Harrogate, a character from Cormac McCarthy's 1979 novel *Suttree*. Obsessed with robbing the banks of Knoxville, Tennessee, from below, Harrogate begins "to tunnel toward the vaults underground where the city's wealth was kept." He travels through "dripping caverns, stone bowels whereon was founded the city itself," stepping into a "region of ruptured ducting and old clay drains." Harrogate has found that the city is more like a sponge than a solid mass of paved streets and architecture. There are sinkholes; the surface is porous. When Harrogate sees that an entire truck has fallen through the streets of the city and down into the caves below, he engages in an amazing, if brief and difficultly punctuated, exchange with the novel's eponymous anti-hero, Cornelius Suttree:

> I reckon once a feller got in under there he could go anywheres he took a notion right in under the ground there couldnt he? (...) That goddamned truck like to of fell plumb out of sight.
>
> I saw it.
>
> What if a whole goddamned building was to just up and sink?
>
> What about two or three buildings?
>
> What about a whole block? Harrogate was waving his bottle about. Goddamn, he said. What if the whole fuckin city was to cave in?
>
> That's the spirit, said Suttree.

I decided then to talk to Michael Cook, an urban explorer based in Toronto who is that city's "master sewer-spelunker," according to Cory Doctorow of *Boing Boing*. Cook runs the well-known urban exploration website *Vanishing Point*, but as that

SUBTERRANEAN SAXOPHONY
Unreliable sources suggest that the earliest Victorian sewer engineers had all been trained as musical instrument makers; it was something of a hobby of theirs, a second job. As a result, many storm drains beneath London bear the shape of saxophones, tubas, and flutes. Distant changes in air pressure—such as a rainstorm over the Cotswolds—can cause the whole system to shudder; a subliminal whistle can thus be heard on the edges of the wind, a soundtrack for the city so beautiful it's often hypnotic. If you wait long enough in certain alleys in Soho, you'll hear it, droning beneath the rustle of crisp bags and rubbish. In fact, it's rumored that the dying words of composer John Cage were: "Make sure they play my London piece.... You have to hear my London piece..." He was referring, many now believe, to a piece written for the subterranean saxophony of London's sewers.

A cable splay beneath the streets of London, photographed by Samuel Seed/Dsankt.

sleepycity.net

site makes clear, Cook's interests extend well beyond taking photographs of subterranean spaces; they include the ecological consequences of city drainage systems, the nature of public underground space, and the implications of industrial decay for future archaeology. As he writes on *Vanishing Point*:

> The built environment of the city has always been incomplete, by omission and necessity, and will remain so. Despite the visions of futurists, the work of our planners and cement-layers thankfully remains a fractured and discontinuous whole, an urban field riven with internal margins, pock-marked by decay, underlaid with secret waterways. Stepping outside our prearranged traffic patterns and established destinations, we find a city laced with liminality, with borderlands cutting across its heart and reaching into its sky. We find a thousand vanishing points, each unique, each alive, each pregnant with riches and wonders and time.

BLDGBLOG: To start with, what do you actually bring with you on these trips? Do you have some kind of underground exploration kit, full of Band-Aids and extra batteries?

Michael Cook: I have a pair of boots or waders, depending on the circumstances. I'll also bring one or more headlamps, and a spot lamp, and various other lighting gear—plus a camera and a tripod. That basically sums it up.

I also have a manhole key—that's just a loop of aircraft cable tied onto a bolt at one end and run through a piece of aluminum pipe that serves as a crude handle. Most of the manhole lids around here have between two and twenty square holes in them about an inch wide, and they're reasonably light. Assuming the lid hasn't been welded or bolted into the collar of the manhole, it's relatively quick and painless to use this tool to pull the lid out.

BLDGBLOG: A lot of these drains look like surreal, concrete versions of all the streams and rivers that used to flow through the city. The drains are like a man-made replacement, or prosthetic landscape, installed inside the old one. Does the relationship between these tunnels and the natural waterways that they've replaced interest you at all?

Cook: Oh, definitely—ever since I got into this through exploring creeks. At their root, most drains are just an abstract version of the watershed that existed before the city. It's sort of this alternate dimension that you pass into, when you step from the aboveground creek, through the inlet, into the drain—especially once you walk out of the reach of daylight.

Photographer Michael Cook emerging from the Depths of Salvation drain beneath the nighttime streets of suburban Toronto.

vanishingpoint.ca

A mist-funneled tunnel photographed by Michael Cook.

vanishingpoint.ca

↓ next spread
All photos by Michael Cook.

Top left: Tailrace outlet, William B.
Rankine Generating Station, Niagara
Falls, Ontario.

Top right: Cook writes that this is "deep
inside the century-old wheelpit that is
the beginning of the Rankine Generating Station," Niagara Falls, Ontario.

Bottom left: Garrison Creek Relief
Sewer, Toronto. "Lit on the left are
three (of four) ducts that serve as
an overflow from a combined sewer,"
Cook explains. "We spent six hours
inside this part of the system, which
runs from roughly Dundas Street to the
Western Beaches Storage Tunnel at
the lake shore. The tunnel is a concrete
arch with a rounded brick floor, and
some sections are well over three
meters in height."

Bottom right: Inside Toronto's Sisters
of Mercy Drain, where "we walked,
and walked, and walked," Cook writes.
"Here the pipe was plain and featureless, winding its way north beneath
Parkside and Roncesvalles."

vanishingpoint.ca

Even sanitary sewers often follow the paths of existing or
former watersheds, because the grade of the land is already
ideal for water flow—fast enough, but not so fast that it erodes
the pipe prematurely—and because the floodplains are often
unsuitable for other uses.

BLDGBLOG: I'm curious if you've ever been injured or gotten
sick down there.

Cook: I can't say that I've ever gotten sick from it. Sometimes,
the day after, you can feel almost hungover—but I don't know
what that is. It could be dust, or it could be from the amount
of moisture you breathe in. But it passes. It might even be an
allergy I have.

In Minneapolis/St. Paul, they actually have a name for the
sickness they sometimes come down with after a particularly
intense sewer exploration: Rinker's Revenge. It's named after
the engineer who designed the systems there. And a colleague
caught giardia recently, which he believes he acquired exploring a section of combined sewer in Montreal.

So, obviously, there are disease risks in doing this, though
they're not as extensive as one might want to imagine.

BLDGBLOG: How connected is all this stuff? Is it like a vast,
underground labyrinth or just a bunch of minor tunnels that
only look connected because of the way that they've been
photographed?

Cook: Most of the drainage systems I've been in are pretty
linear. You have a main trunk conduit, and sometimes you'll
get significant side pipes that are worth exploring. But as far
as actual maze-quality features go, it's pretty rare to find systems like that—at least in Ontario and most places in Canada.
It requires a very specific geography and a sort of time line
of development for the drains. You might end up with a lot of
side overflows and other things, which makes the system more
complicated, if the drain has several different places where it
overflows into a surface body of water—or if there's a structure
that allows one pipe to flow into another at excess capacity. That
sort of thing allows for more complicated systems—but most of
the time it doesn't happen.

You can still spend hours in some of these drains, though,
because of how long they are. And sometimes that makes for a
fairly uninteresting experience: drains can be pretty featureless
for most of their length.

BLDGBLOG: What do they sound like?

Cook: I'd say that each drain is acoustically unique. Each has its own resonance points—and even different sections of the drain will resonate differently, based on where the next curve is, or the next room. It all shifts. I often explore that aspect a bit—probably to the annoyance of some of my colleagues. I'll make noises, or hum. Even sing.

As far as environmental noises, the biggest thing is that, if there's a rail line nearby, or a public transit line, you often get that noise coming back through the drain to wherever you are. It's very frightening when you first hear it, till you figure out what it is—this rushing noise. It's not a wall of water. [*laughs*] But the most common recurring noise is the sound of cars driving over manhole covers—which gives you an idea of which covers you don't want to exit through. It also helps you keep track of the distance, and where you are—that sort of thing.

BLDGBLOG: Within Toronto itself, are you still finding new drains, or is the city pretty much exhausted by now?

Cook: We are still finding new tunnels beneath Toronto, and we're on the trail of others that we know about but just haven't discovered access to yet. When Siologen came over here he found a whole bunch of new drain systems—systems nobody else knew about. He had the time and the inclination to go and scout out a whole lot of stuff that I'd never gotten around to doing—basically by riding all the buses. That, and looking at a lot of little creek systems, and searching around for manholes—all of that.

But there are people who happen to read in the paper about some new tunnel project, or whatever, and so they pass that on to people who do this sort of thing. I guess some people have even found stuff after it's been featured in skateboarding magazines. Some of the largest pipe in the world is used as spillways for hydroelectric projects—big dams and that sort of thing—and usually the first people who find out about this stuff are skateboarders. Usually they try to keep the locations pretty quiet—just as we do.

BLDGBLOG: I'm also curious if there's some huge, mythic system out there that you've heard about but haven't visited, or even just an urban legend about some tunnels that might not even be real—secret government bunkers in London, for instance.

Cook: I guess the most fabled tunnel system in North America is the one that supposedly runs beneath old Victoria, British Columbia. It's supposedly connected with Satanic activity or Masonic activity in the city, and there's been a lot of strange stuff written about that. But no one's found the great big Satanic

Inside the Ontario Generating Station at Niagara Falls, photographed by Michael Cook. "Beyond the penstocks," he writes, "we could see the physical end of the distributor, as well as surge pipes reaching up towards their spillway structures and the tantalizing though inconclusive evidence that a connection may exist between the two distributors. The penstock openings were too wide to safely skirt around however, as falling into them would have meant nearly certain critical injury or death."

vanishingpoint.ca

The William B. Rankine Hydroelectric Tailrace tunnel at Niagara Falls, Ontario, photographed by Michael Cook.

vanishingpoint.ca

system where they make all the sacrifices. You know, these legends are really…there's always some sort of fact behind them. How they come about and what sort of meaning they have for the community is what's really interesting. So while I can poke fun at them, I actually appreciate their value—and, certainly, these sort of things are rumored in a lot of cities, not just Victoria. They're in the back consciousness of a lot of cities in North America.

BLDGBLOG: What aspects of urban exploration do you think deserve more attention?

Cook: Even among explorers, we don't pay enough attention to *process*. I think every piece of infrastructure—every building—is on a trajectory, and you're experiencing it at just one moment in its very extended life. We see things, but we don't often ask how they came about or where they're going to go from here—whether there will be structural deterioration, or if living things will colonize the structure. We tend to ignore these things, or to see them in temporal isolation. We also don't give enough time or consideration to how this infrastructure fits into the broader urban fabric, within the history of a city, and where that city's going, and whose lives have been affected by it and whatever may happen to it in the future. I think these are all stories that really need to start being told.

Which is something I'm starting on. It's just not something that necessarily comes naturally. It requires a lot of work, and a lot of thought while you're on-site—which maybe you're not really inclined to do, because you're too busy paying attention to the immediate, sublime nature of the experience.

I think the real question is: Are these photos of asylum hallways and drainage tunnels ultimately going to be useful to anyone else at some point in the future? And the answer is: probably not. Probably we're photographing the wrong things for that.

BLDGBLOG: It's like bad archaeology.

Cook: Yeah, basically. It's like we're just digging things up and not paying attention to where they were placed, or what they were next to, or who might have put them there. Ultimately, we need some sort of framework, and to put more effort into additional information besides just taking a photo. That doesn't necessarily mean publishing all that information so that everyone can see it—but just telling stories in other ways, and creating narratives about the places and the things that we're seeing. Otherwise, these are just postcard shots. We're taking postcard shots of the sublime.

LONDON TOPOLOGICAL

The under-London world of interlinked drains, sewers, Tube tunnels, and bunkers, accumulated organically over hundreds of years, curving around beneath the city in rhizomic tangles of unmappable, self-intersecting whorls, seems to hold an unfading sway over the urban imagination. Paris may have its catacombs, New York its subways, and Vienna its sewers with their cameo appearance in Orson Welles's classic film *The Third Man*, but the semiclandestine postwar underworld of London all but calls out for conspiratorial speculation. The very fact that London is known to host a World War II–era complex of supposedly disused government bunkers, connecting state offices together like some sort of apocalyptic weaving diagram, means that there will always be a role for its tunnels in films, novels, games, and TV. Not only that, but the city is under constant threat from flooding—and so this underground world has a strange air of survivalist urgency: London sits atop a buried hydrological fortress that keeps the city's streets free from encroaching waters.

As proof of the ongoing vitality of underground London's imaginative appeal, one need look no further than Neil Gaiman's popular novel *Neverwhere*, the literally Underground horror film *Creep* ("Your journey terminates here," its posters read), or even the opening scenes of 2002's *Reign of Fire*, starring Christian Bale, in which a construction project on the Tube uncovers an ancient dragon, which goes on to breed and take over the world—and, yes, the film is as bad as it sounds.

London, for all intents and purposes, is built more on rebuttressed volumes of air than it is on solid ground. There are an awful lot of tunnels down there.

"The heart of modern London," Antony Clayton writes in his 2000 book, *Subterranean City: Beneath the Streets of London*, "contains a vast clandestine underworld of tunnels, telephone exchanges, nuclear bunkers and control centers...[s]ome of which are well documented, but the existence of others can be surmised only from careful scrutiny of government reports and accounts and occasional accidental disclosures reported in the news media." This unofficially real underground world pops up in some very unlikely places: According to Clayton, for example, there is an electricity substation beneath Leicester Square that "is entered by a disguised trap door to the left of the Half Price Ticket Booth, a structure that also doubles as a ventilation shaft." Incredibly, this links up with "a new 1¼ mile tunnel that connects it with another substation at Duke Street near Grosvenor Square." And that's not the only disguised ventilation shaft: there are also "dummy houses" at 23–24 Leinster Gardens. Complete with windowsills, lintels, and molding,

LIGHTS OF ALIGNMENT

Neolithic archaeological sites, like the cairns and barrows of Bryn Celli Ddu (Wales), Newgrange (Ireland), and Maes Howe (Scotland), are famous for, among other things, the fact that their entryways align with the rising sun on the morning of the summer solstice. But what other solar alignments exist that we have yet to discover? Might some alignment, however accidental, be found between the solsticial sun and the sewers of central Paris? Three hundred years from now, every sewer system in the city begins to shine, light escaping from manhole covers, the surface of the urban earth faintly glowing.

these buildings aren't buildings at all: they are more like vents for the underworld, disguised as faux-Georgian flats. They are facades—with nothing behind them.

There's a scene in Umberto Eco's novel *Foucault's Pendulum* where the narrator is told: "People walk by [this certain house in Paris] and they don't know the truth." What's the truth? "That the house is a fake. It's a facade, an enclosure with no room, no interior. It is really a chimney, a ventilation flue that serves to release the vapors of the regional Métro. And once you know this you feel you are standing at the mouth of the underworld…"

There is also a utility subway "with access through a door in the base of Boudicca's statue near Westminster Bridge." You open that door in the base of the statue and, like something out of an Alfred Hitchcock film, you discover a tunnel that "runs all the way to Blackfriars and then to the Bank of England."

Here, then, is where the dizzying self-intersection begins, systems hitting systems, as layers of the city collide. For instance, there is an abandoned Tube station at King William Street, but "the only access… is made via the basement of the recently built Regis House" next door—and the entrance is just "a manhole in the basement." It's like a version of London, rebuilt to entertain quantum physicists. At one point, for instance, King William Street's old tunnels "run directly above the existing Bank Northern Line platforms—if you look up you can see directly into these tunnels through several ventilation grilles in the roof." Clayton further explains that, when being given a tour of that now abandoned station, "the locked entrance to the disused platform was hidden behind some grey panels… making it look like a storage cabinet."

Everything leads to everything else; there are doorways everywhere. When Nick McCamley, author of the 2000 book, *Secret Underground Cities*, stumbled upon just such a "secret underground city" with a friend in Wiltshire, the BBC explains that they found it simply by climbing through the rubber flaps at the end of a long conveyor belt:

> Running along the back of the building was a conveyer belt. The belt disappeared through a hole in the end wall covered by a rubber flap.

> Curious, the boys lifted the rubber flap and climbed through. Before they knew it, they were whistling down a sharp 45-degree incline:

"We couldn't stop ourselves," says Nick. "We slid off down and finished up about 100 feet underground."

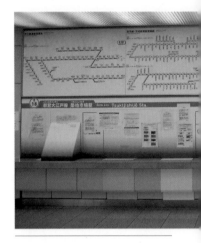

TOKYO SECRET CITY
According to a 2003 article in the *Japan Times*, researcher Shun Akiba might have discovered "hundreds of kilometers of Tokyo tunnels whose purpose is unknown and whose very existence is denied."

Shun, who believes he is now the victim of a conspiracy, claims to have stumbled upon "an old map in a secondhand bookstore. Comparing it to a contemporary map, he found significant variations. 'Close to the Diet in Nagata-cho, current maps show two subways crossing. In the old map, they are parallel,'" he says. This unexpected parallelism of Tokyo's subway tunnels—a geometrician's secret fantasy—inspired Shun to seek out old municipal construction records. Yet no one wanted to help; in fact, he was treated as if he were drunk or crazy. This mysterious lack of interest actually invigorated him. Shun immediately "set out to prove that the two subway tunnels could not cross: 'Engineering cannot lie,'" he believed.

But engineers can. To make a long story short, Shun discovered "seven riddles" about this secret sub-Tokyo of tunnels; the parallel subways were only number one:

> The second reveals a secret underground complex between Kokkai-gijidomae and the prime minister's residence. A prewar

map (riddle No. 3) shows the Diet in a huge empty space surrounded by paddy fields: "What was the military covering up?" New maps (No. 4) are full of inconsistencies: "People are still trying to hide things." The postwar General Headquarters (No. 5) was a most mysterious place. Eidan's records of the construction of the Hibiya Line (No. 6) are hazy to say the least. As for the "new" O-Edo Line (No. 7), "that existed already." Which begs the question, where did all the money go allocated for the tunneling?

Shun even "claims to have uncovered a secret code that links a complex network of tunnels unknown to the general public. 'Every city with a historic subterranean transport system has secrets,' he says. 'In London, for example, some lines are near the surface and others very deep, for no obvious reason.'" There are even subway tunnels neither "shown on maps" nor "indicated in subway construction records." Underground car parks, unofficial basements, locked doors near public toilets—and all "within missile range of North Korea." So what's going on beneath Tokyo?

A map of the Tokyo subway system, photographed by Nicola Twilley.

Deep underground and not knowing how they were going to get back out, the boys were running out of matches.

Fumbling around in the dark, Nick felt a box on the wall with switches.

"So I turned a few switches and this corridor lit up ahead of us," says Nick.

A corridor that went on for about half a mile.

That was just the start of it.

"All the corridors had rubber conveyer belts," says Nick. "We found you could push buttons by the side of them and they would start up and we could ride them."

The amazing labyrinth of air-conditioned tunnels and chambers went on for miles. Passageways branched off at right angles into further passageways and on and on.

I, too, could go on and on. Stretching like veins and capillaries throughout the compressed waterproof clay of underground London are flood-control complexes, buried archives, and lost rivers sealed inside concrete viaducts. There are also the Camden catacombs. As *Subterranea Britannica* writes, these catacombs were "built in the 19th century as stables for horses," and "their route can be traced from the distinctive cast-iron grilles set at regular intervals into the road surface; originally the only source of light for the horses below."

My favorite story of underground London by far, however, is also the best known. I'm referring, of course, to British investigative journalist Duncan Campbell's December 1980 piece for the *New Statesman*, now something of a classic in urban exploration circles. What exactly did Campbell do?

"Entering, without permission, from an access shaft situated on a traffic island in Bethnal Green Road," Antony Clayton explains, he "descended one hundred feet to meet a tunnel, designated L, stretching into the distance and strung with cables and lights." Campbell had, in fact, discovered a government bunker complex stretching all the way to Whitehall. On and on he went, for hours, riding a folding bicycle through this concrete looking-glass world of alphabetic cyphers and location codes, like structures from the school of the subterranean military abstract: "From Tunnel G, Tunnel M leads to Fleet Street and P travels under Leicester Square to the then Post Office Tower, with Tunnel S crossing beneath the river to Waterloo." Here, giving evidence of Clayton's "accidental disclosures reported in the news media," we read that "when the IMAX cinema inside the roundabout outside Waterloo station was being constructed the contractor's requests to deep-pile the foundations were refused, probably owing to the continued presence of [Tunnel S]." But when your real estate is Swiss-cheesed and under-torqued by an unreal world of remnant topologies, the lesson, I suppose, is that you have to read between the lines.

In London, a simple building permissions refusal might be a sign of something else entirely. As Clayton writes:

> It was reported that in the planning stage of the Jubilee Line Extension official resistance had been encountered, when several projected routes through Westminster were rejected without an explanation, although no potential subterranean obstructions were indicated on the planners' maps. According to one source, "…the rumor is that there is a vast bunker down there, which the government has kept secret, which is the granddaddy of them all."

Which leaves at least me wondering what it might be like to wander through London with a ground-penetrating radar device, scanning for anomalous voids and bunkers as they spiral off to the very limits of perceptibility. A vast chain of basements, like a natural cavern, is discovered beneath a house in Westminster—the rooms honeycombing down to where the strongest radar cannot penetrate. You spend a whole summer mapping London's basements from above. After all, Clayton adds: "No doubt many more bunkers, tunnels, and secret underground structures will be 'discovered' beneath London in the future." This brings to mind the village of Wroxeter, in the west of England. Wroxeter made the news in the mid-1990s when a series of ancient Roman foundations was discovered beneath its streets; this discovery wasn't made through excavation, however, but through the use of ground-penetrating radar. It was non-invasive archaeology, so to speak: history as a vague mass of radar-reflective shapes underground. So could you hack someone's handheld radar to make them think there are ancient cities when there is, in fact, mere soil—or mere soil when the earth is hollow with mysterious voids?

Continuing to read between the lines, meanwhile, Clayton describes how, in 1993, after "close scrutiny of the annual Defense Works Services budget the existence of the so-called Pindar Project was revealed, a plan for a nuclear bomb-proof bunker, that had cost £66 million to excavate." All of these places have quasi-mythological names: Pindar, Cobra, Trawlerman, ICARUS, Kingsway, Paddock. Clayton refers to a 1999 article in the *Observer* that describes Cobra as "an air-pressurized network of low-ceilinged corridors" in which

STATION Z

In the event of complete governmental obliteration during WWII, England had a backup plan: Station Z, "an alternative center of government," *Subterranea Britannica* explains, located "in the western counties," made up of "bombproof underground citadels." Like some new race of Celtic demigods, the British government would evacuate into the earth, hiding out within a series of strange mounds, sending its deranged final broadcasts from the underworld across a landscape of rain-filled craters.

Station Z itself "consisted of a three story above ground surface block with an inner court yard. Below this was a basement roofed over by 3.5 feet of reinforced concrete and below it a sub-basement protected by another 6 feet of concrete (probably in two layers); with comparable protection at the sides, the sub-basement was considered to be entirely bombproof." Now that Station Z is militarily useless—as well as unnecessary: today's backup British government appears to be the White House—the international photography firm Kodak has purchased the site. The above-ground buildings, however, were demolished in 1996, leaving only these monolithic hollows in the darkness below:

> Access to the bunker was maintained via one of the emergency exits but the bunker was allowed to flood. Until recently, the sub-basement was flooded to a depth of several feet but the water has now been pumped out with only a little standing water remaining. The pumps are still in place to ensure that the flooding does not reoccur and new ventilation trunking has been installed to ensure a supply of fresh air throughout the bunker.

Kodak has "no planned use" for the flood-prone basements, it says.

THE REVERSE WORLD
In a September 1997 article for *Outside* magazine, author Erin Arvedlund took readers on a spelunking tour through underground Moscow with a local explorer named Vadim Mikhailov. Mikhailov began to venture down into what he calls "the reverse world"—the world of Moscow's sewers, bunkers, and tunnels—at a very young age. "Stuck in a sprawling gray city," Arvedlund writes, "too poor to travel, where else was there for a restless young adventurer to go but down?" She writes of "subterranean bunkers, supply depots, and enormous vaults" constructed for the czars, and "a vast underground network of brick-lined canals" built at the behest of Catherine the Great. There is even Ivan the Terrible's infamous torture chamber. When the Soviet Union eventually came along, she points out, Muscovites "burrowed even further": They built "secret tunnels and subway tracks, KGB listening posts, and fallout shelters for the political elite, hundreds of meters below the surface." Because "someone somewhere is surely listening," this has produced "an ambivalent relationship" with the underground world; "the very ground on which one walks," we read, "is not to be trusted."

The roofed-over Ballardian darkness of Lower Robert Street, London, photographed by Geoff Manaugh.

top-secret government strategy meetings take place; however, they are but one tiny part of "the warren of underground corridors that run from Downing Street along the whole of Whitehall and through central Westminster." Even the act of constructing these places is clandestine: "Workers on the [Whitehall basements] project had to sign the Official Secrets Act and any maps and plans used had to be handed in at the end of each day."

For all of that, though, I haven't mentioned the so-called CTRL Project (the Channel Tunnel Rail Link); or *Quatermass and the Pit*, a 1967 Hammer Horror film in which deep tunnel Tube construction teams unearth a UFO; or the future possibilities such material all but demands. Such as *BLDGBLOG: The Game*, produced by LucasArts, set in the cross-linked passages of subterranean London—where it's you, a torch, a dozen weapons, and hordes of bird flu–infected zombies coughing their way down the dripping passages…looking for *you*.

HELLO. WELCOME TO MY SQUASH CAVE.

But why just visit the underground when you can live there full-time? The urban surface of London is no longer interesting enough for the ultra-rich; they're now building downward, into the earth. As Helen Davies of the *Times* reported on August 19, 2007: "A Roman bath, a cinema for two dozen friends, even a subterranean tennis court—the super-rich are transforming their London homes, even if it means digging dozens of feet underground."

Some of London's most financially advantaged residents, we learn, including oil tycoons and Indian steel magnates, have begun "seeking permission to excavate under the garden . . . making space for a three-storey garage with car stacker, a swimming pool, a gym, and a private home cinema." There are "walk-in showers with waterproof television screens and glass walls that turn opaque with the press of a button, and cost £1,000 per square meter." There are even "high-end builders," for whom business is booming; they "frequently dig down as far as 50 ft to create new floors, basements and swimming pools, while the original house is propped up on giant steel pillars."

This urge toward subterranean architectural eccentricity is transforming the very earth beneath London. We learn, for instance, that "billionaire Russian oligarchs, private-equity traders and hedge-fund managers are engaged in a multi-million-pound game of one-upmanship as they vie with each other to dig ever bigger, wider, and deeper extensions." *Digging* also helps London's super-rich to avoid strict planning and conservation laws, as the houses they've been extending into the earth are usually listed structures and thus can't be visibly altered. Many of these houses thus now "have more space below ground than above it," we read.

Apparently, there is even quite a market for "adjustable-height swimming pool[s]" built underground:

At the flick of a button—because everything is remote-controlled—the bottom can be raised or lowered by a giant hydraulic jack, forming a deep swimming pool for the heavyweight millionaire or a toddler-friendly paddling pool for his offspring.

Which isn't even the most extravagant example of home hydro-logical engineering:

One home in north London even has a bespoke chute covered in a special slippery paint, which enables the owner, who loves swimming first thing in the morning, but hates the fuss of dressing, to step out of bed and slide straight into the water a couple of stories below.

Further, "a secretive hedge-fund tycoon" has submitted a 168-page planning application—perhaps the de facto literary masterpiece of an upper class that has set about entombing itself below sea level—within which he requests permission to build "a 16 ft-deep swimming pool with high board," among many other things, all of which will be deep underground.

BUNKER MALADIES: AN INTERVIEW WITH TOM VANDERBILT

In Tom Vanderbilt's 2002 book *Survival City: Adventures Among the Ruins of Atomic America*, he describes something called "con-cretitis," as well as other "bunker maladies" associated with Cold War-era underground U.S. military installations. While the idea of a "sick building syndrome" is nothing new, it is almost always mentioned in reference to things like mold, off-gassing flame retardants, and formaldehyde. I decided to ask Vanderbilt if he thought there might be a kind of *psychological* sick building syndrome as well—and, if so, which would come first: the buildings (concrete bunkers, high rises, etc.) or the psychological state? Are such building types, and the materials they're made from, actually projections of psychological states—paranoia, neurosis, etc.—or do those buildings, in fact, generate new psychopathologies?

Tom Vanderbilt: Your question reminds me of my visit to "Sorry, Out of Gas," an exhibition at the Canadian Centre for Architecture, which looked at how architecture responded to the sudden energy deprivations of the 1973 OPEC oil embargo. The range of ways people responded to a possible future of dwindling petroleum resources, part of a larger sort of neo-Malthusian doom about the pressures of life on "spaceship Earth," is striking. Some turned to long-neglected passive and active solar technologies and architectural designs, like the Trombe wall; some dusted off old windmills not seen since before the days of rural electrification.

The most interesting response, in my mind, was the move underground, into "earth sheltered" houses. One project featured in the exhibition was the work of Jay Swayze, a one-time fallout shelter contractor turned underground house designer. His Las Vegas house for Jerry Henderson, the onetime head of Avon cosmetics, is poignant. First, the house looks like a normal suburban house, with a grill on an Astroturf lawn, but it's enclosed in a kind of cavern. There are scenes from Henderson's life painted on the walls, like some inwardly seeking Platonic cave of memory.

Swayze, who built Henderson's house firmly with nuclear fallout in mind, argued that things like views and air wouldn't be necessary, or even desirable in the future, and it was best for humankind to create their own environment from whole cloth. In this case I suppose it was the anxiety in the air–the Berlin blockade, the Cuban missile crisis–that led Henderson underground; how being underground then informed his life, I can only speculate. But it's hard to imagine it not leading to a more sinister, apprehensive view of the world above.

The interesting thing is that once the move into energy-efficient housing began going strong, Swayze changed his sales pitch from having one's own domestic bunker to helping to cut one's heating and cooling costs.

This is all a long way of saying I think that building forms spring out of historical contingencies–but, given enough time, they may create their own form of subjectivity. Witness the erection of new "lofts" in urban, and even suburban, areas that have nothing to do with the very specific manufacturing needs that gave rise to them.

Or to use a more trite example: I live in a former church and, since doing so, I've found myself drawn to Renaissance-era sacred music. Would this have happened if I had moved into a former factory?

I'd even suggest that the city's subterranean property boom has yet to reach its most interesting stage—which will be when private underground complexes can be purchased independently of the houses standing above. Combine this with the redefinition—if not outright elimination—of underground property lines, and perhaps someday the multibillionaire scion of an international media conglomerate will move to the city, buy up underground property in various neighborhoods...and then set about connecting them all together into a labyrinth at Knossos for the modern day.

DERINKUYU, OR THE ALLURE OF THE UNDERGROUND CITY

The premise of Alan Weisman's best-selling 2007 book *The World Without Us*—though it very frequently drifts away from this otherwise fascinating idea—is: what would happen to the Earth if humans disappeared overnight? What would humans leave behind—and how long would those remnants last?

At one point, such questions lead Weisman to discuss the underground cities of Cappadocia, Turkey, which, he says, will out-survive nearly everything else humans have constructed here on Earth. Manhattan will be gone, Los Angeles gone, Cape Canaveral flooded and covered in seaweed, London dissolving into post-Britannic muck, the Great Wall of China merely an undetectable line of minerals blowing across an abandoned landscape—but there, beneath the porous surface of Turkey, carved directly into tuff, there will still be underground cities. Of course, I'm not entirely convinced by Weisman's argument here: Turkey is quite a seismically active country, for instance, and it seems unlikely that it won't be ground to dust by the friction of tectonic plates. But that's something for another conversation.

Weisman writes:

No one knows how many underground cities lie beneath Cappadocia. Eight have been discovered, and many smaller villages, but there are doubtless more. The biggest, Derinkuyu, wasn't discovered until 1965, when a resident cleaning the back wall of his cave house broke through a wall and discovered behind it a room that he'd never seen, which led to still another, and another. Eventually, spelunking archeologists found a maze of connecting chambers that descended at least 18 stories and 280 feet beneath the surface, ample enough to hold 30,000 people—and much remains to be excavated. One tunnel, wide enough for three people walking abreast, connects to another underground town six miles away. Other passages suggest that at one time all of Cappadocia, above and below the ground, was linked by a hidden network. Many still use the tunnels of this ancient subway as cellar storerooms.

I was excited to read that these subsurface urban structures were even acoustically sophisticated. In other words, using "vertical communication shafts, it was possible to speak to another person on any level" down below. There were even ancient microbreweries down there, "equipped with tuff fermentation vats and basalt grinding wheels."

However, the discovery of Derinkuyu also brought to mind another scene from the novel *Foucault's Pendulum*, where we read about a French town called Provins. A deluded ex-colonel from the Italian military has come into Milan to meet with two academic publishers. Touching his moustache, the ex-colonel explains that "something" has been in Provins "since prehistoric times: tunnels. A network of tunnels—real catacombs—extends beneath the hill."

> Some tunnels lead from building to building. You can enter a granary or a warehouse and come out in a church. Some tunnels are constructed with columns and vaulted ceilings. Even today, every house in the upper city still has a cellar with ogival vaults—there must be more than a hundred of them. And every cellar has an entrance to a tunnel.

"Room after room," he adds, "deep in the earth, covered with ancient graffiti." The editors press for more details here, looking for evidence of what he claims. But the colonel parries and forges on. After all, he's an ex-Fascist; he'll say what he likes. As he continues, his story gets stranger: in 1894, he says, two Chevaliers went to visit an old granary in Provins, where they asked to be taken down into the tunnels.

> Accompanied by the caretaker, they went down into one of the subterranean rooms, on the second level belowground. When the caretaker, trying to show that there were other levels even farther down, stamped on the earth, they heard echoes and reverberations. [The Chevaliers] promptly fetched lanterns and ropes and went into the unknown tunnels like boys down a mine, pulling themselves forward on their elbows, crawling through mysterious passages. [They soon] came to a great hall with a fine fireplace and a dry well in the center. They tied a stone to a rope, lowered it, and found that the well was eleven meters deep. They went back a week later with stronger ropes, and two companions lowered [one of the Chevaliers] into the well, where he discovered a

THE FREEZE WALL

Like something out of Nordic mythology—Asgard, snowbound castle of the gods, gone geo-tectonic—Anglo-Dutch oil firm Shell has apparently decided to construct a monumental underground wall of ice stretching across several oil shale deposits in Colorado, Utah, and Wyoming. They call it the "freeze wall." The weirdly exhilarating project falls somewhere between avant-garde earthwork, pagan theology, and the hi-tech petro-economic wet dreams of tomorrow. So what exactly is it?

As the *Denver Post* informed us on October 22, 2006, in order to reach what could be up to 800 billion barrels of oil stuck in subterranean layers of shale, flattened under the central Rocky Mountains:

> Shell is spending $30 million to create and test a massive "freeze wall" that would extend from the surface to 1,700 feet below the ground. The walls would be 30 feet thick in a shape 300 feet wide by 350 feet long. It is designed for a dual purpose: to keep groundwater from infiltrating Shell's oil-shale wells, and to prevent produced oil from contaminating nearby groundwater.

To construct the wall, Shell's engineers will need "about 18 months for the adjacent water and rock to freeze to minus 60 degrees Fahrenheit."

But huge, underground castles made of ice! A new Great Wall of China made from artificial tundra. What could Rem Koolhaas do with this sort of thing—or Zaha Hadid, or Buckminster Fuller, or Sam Jacob? How long before we start using ice walls in our architectural design studios?

big room with stone walls, ten meters square and five meters high. The others then followed him down.

Reading all this, I can't stop thinking about the fact that some of the underground cities in Cappadocia have yet to be fully explored; I also can't help but assume that more than 2,000 years' worth of earthquakes might have collapsed some passages, or shifted whole subcity systems, so that they are no longer accessible from the surface—and, thus, no longer known. Could some building engineer one day shovel through sand and topsoil only to find a previously unknown subterranean city—or might not some archaeologist, scanning the Turkish hills with ground-penetrating radar, stumble upon an anomalous void, linked to other voids, with those voids leading to more voids... and it's yet another long-lost city? Perhaps *Foucault's Pendulum 2* might have a few chapters set in Cappadocia.

THE MINE HIJACKERS

The gold mines of Johannesburg, South Africa, "are veritable underground cities," Fred Bridgland wrote in a 2006 article for the *Scottish Sunday Herald*. Indeed, these gigantic mines have "tunnels winding for hundreds of miles, more than two miles below the surface of the Earth."

To counter the subterranean temperatures, which often reach above 105°F, mine operators "continuously pump down refrigerated air into the subterranean cities where miners and other workers wear special jackets packed with ice to counter temperatures so high that the rock itself is hot to the touch." At Johannesburg's famed Tau Tona mine—"the deepest and biggest [mine] in the world with more than 500 miles of tunnels"—"miners will be working in temperatures as high as 50°C [122°F], requiring cooling systems of enormous power and sophistication with capacities more [than] three million times that of a domestic refrigerator." These "capacities" include the production of at least "20,000 tons of ice a day, which is crushed and pumped along pipes that run down through the mine tunnels and galleries. As the iced water warms up it is pumped back to the surface to be re-frozen." Rig several dozen of these up to a small nuclear power plant, and you could gradually freeze your way to the center of the earth.... That, or construct an artificial glacier outside Cape Town.

Glaciers are the future of landscape architecture.

The most fascinating aspect of this whole story for me, by far, is the fact that, down in these "disused shafts and tunnels" beneath the city of Johannesburg, whole illegal communities have been established. Mineral smugglers—or people who carry

All photographs by Stanley Greenberg, taken from his 2003 book *Waterworks: A Photographic Journey through New York's Hidden Water System*. Courtesy of Gitterman Gallery, New York.

Top: City Tunnel No. 3 beneath Brooklyn, New York.

Center: City Tunnel No. 3 beneath Queens, New York.

Bottom: The spillway at Downsville Dam, Pepacton Reservoir, New York.

web.mac.com/greenbergstanley1

WALKING OVER A VALVE CHAMBER NEAR THE BROOKLYN ACADEMY OF MUSIC

Photographer Stanley Greenberg got in touch with BLDGBLOG in the spring of 2006 to discuss his book *Waterworks: A Photographic Journey through New York's Hidden Water System.* Over the course of a long e-mail exchange, I asked him about the origins and intentions of the project.

"I started photographing the city's infrastructure in 1992," he explained, "after working in NYC government in the 1980s. I felt that the water system was being taken for granted, partially because the government is so secretive about it. Places that were built as parks and destinations were now off-limits to everyone—especially after 9/11. I went back and forth over several years, sometimes being allowed in, other times being a pariah (and a threat to national security, according to the city, since I knew too much about the system). For some reason, though, in 1998 I was given almost total access."

The secrecy that now surrounds New York's aquatic infrastructure, however, is "really just an acceleration of a trend," Greenberg suggested to me over e-mail:

City Tunnel No. 3, the new water tunnel, has been under construction since 1970, and its entryways are: 1) well hidden, and 2) built to withstand nuclear weapons. While there were always parts of the system that were open to the public, there were other parts that became harder and harder to see. Even worse, I think, is the idea that we don't deserve to know about the system; it's that much easier to privatize it (as Giuliani tried to do). The Parks Department here just signed a contract with a private developer to turn part of Randall's Island into a water park, which will not only take away public space, and probably be an environmental disaster, but will also institute an entrance fee for something that was free before. We don't know how well our infrastructure is being taken care of—and we're not allowed to know because of "national security." So how do we know if we're spending too little money to take care of it?

In Greenberg's work, the metropolitan water supply reveals itself to be a constellation of negative spaces: trapezoidal culverts, spillways, and tunnels. His subject is *terrain that is no longer there.* As Greenberg writes: "The water system today is an extraordinary web of places—beautiful landscapes, mysterious structures, and sites where the natural meets the man-made in enigmatic ways." Drained of their water, these excavations would form a networked monument to pure volume, inscribed into the rock of Hudson Valley.

"While the work is not meant to be a comprehensive record of the system," Greenberg pointed out, "it is meant to make people think about this organism that stretches 1,000 feet underground and 200 miles away." Quoting from his e-mail:

> It got to the point where I could sense a water system structure without actually knowing what it was. My friends are probably tired of my telling them when they're walking over a valve chamber, or over the place where City Tunnels 1, 2, and now 3 cross each other (near the Brooklyn Academy of Music), or some other obscure part of the system.

It's easy to imagine, in fact, reading such tales of hidden topology, that pedestrians might hear slight echoes in the ground beneath New York Cty's sidewalks—little trembles of resonance as you and your friends walk by. The next time the ground you're walking on sounds hollow, perhaps it is.

Photographs by Stanley Greenberg, courtesy of Gitterman Gallery, New York.

Top: City Tunnel No. 3 beneath The Bronx, New York.

Bottom: The spillway at Neversink Reservoir, New York.

web.mac.com/greenbergstanley1

TRANSBORDER MAZES

As Bryan Finoki explores on his blog *Subtopia*, there is an underground world of illegally excavated tunnels weaving back and forth across the U. S./Mexico border. These form what he calls "transborder mazes" used to smuggle goods, drugs, and people; they are part of "a thriving subterranean landscape" that worms its way through the soils of Westphalian sovereignty, with police patrols standing insecure over unregistered excavations in the desert. The very idea of the nation-state is undone here by topology: territories sewn one to the other like points on a Klein bottle, in a new kind of economic and political adjacency with no true government in sight.

As Finoki explained in a telephone interview:

From a landscape perspective, it's fascinating to see how even superpowers like the United States were completely stymied by the tunnel systems of the Vietcong or the N.V.A., and how the Nazi regime was compromised by several tunnels dug under the Berlin Wall to escape into West Germany. Of course, militaries have used border tunnels for their own purposes, as well. But the United States is the largest military superpower in history, with one of the longest undefended borders in the world, and it just can't stop the flow of drugs or people. There, border security has become more like a spectacle— a symbolic show of power on the surface—while you've got all these tunnels going on below. To me, they're the most liquid form of landscape—an asymmetric counter-landscape— showing how *space* will ultimately circumnavigate *power*. Border tunnels can come in any shape and go in any direction. They've even become meta-phors for the success of any illicit activity that can go

below, around, and over—if not through—border walls.

Increased militarization has turned the entire border region into a kind of anti-imperial game space—a literal subtopia—where well-funded border agents, armed with remote control drone airplanes and experimental laser-detection networks, fight faceless invaders who pop up at all hours of the day before disappearing from view once again.

You've got people offsite, watching the border through remote surveillance cameras on their laptops and following specific people with joysticks. Ask any border patrol agent and they'll even *tell you* it's a game: There are guys who will run over here to distract you while they run drugs across the border over there, and they'll use a totally different distraction technique to move their clients in an opposite direction somewhere else.

Randal Archibold covered these same spaces in a December 2007 article for the *New York Times* called "Smugglers Build an Underground World." One border tunnel in particular traveled 1,300 feet from the inside of an otherwise unremarkable shipping container in the California desert into the basement of "a sky-blue office building" located in northern Mexico. "Three or four feet wide and six feet high," Archibold writes, "the passageway is illuminated by compact fluorescent bulbs (wired to the Mexican side), supported by carefully placed wooden beams and kept dry by two pumps. The neatly squared walls, carved through solid rock, bear the signs of engineering skill and professional drilling tools."

It's the subterranean DIY architecture of armed black market libertarianism—the world of *narco-spatiality*. It is space that bulges. As a San Diego-based immigra-

tion and customs enforcement agent explained to Archibold, trying to control these tunnels is "like squeezing a balloon": you shut down one tunnel, and another just pops up two miles away. From Archibold's article:

Most of the tunnels are of the "gopher" variety, dug quickly and probably by small-time smugglers…. But more than a dozen have been fairly elaborate affairs like this one, with lighting, drainage, ventilation, pulleys for moving loads and other features that point to big spending by drug cartels. Engineers have clearly been consulted in the construction of these detailed corridors.

In May 2006, Reuters reported on a group called the Tunnel Task Force, with "expertise honed in the hunt for Osama bin Laden," that usually gets the job of raiding these tunnels. Reuters describes how, "with the help of rogue mining engineers," the "longest, deepest, and boldest drug smuggling tunnel found to date" was dug; but state-sponsored engineers simply use ground-penetrating radar, seismic equipment, and even magnetometers to scan the earth "for 'discreet voids' left by man-made tunnels" in the earth. They then call in the Tunnel Task Force, who raid those voids.

Amazingly, a Task Force member remarked: "It's getting to a point where we are planning to build our own tunnels to different depths and specifications to perfect the technologies that we are using to hunt for [the smugglers]…" This suggests a surreal vision of police training schools set in simulated drug tunnels built far underground in the desert. People train there for years. They grow beards. Then a recession sets in and they're all laid-off—so they put their skills to work, smuggling drugs across the border….

subtopia.blogspot.com

pieces of the Earth's surface illegally across borders—"live for up to a year at a time belowground without surfacing, mining illicit gold estimated to be worth nearly £400 million a year for three international criminal syndicates."

The *Sunday Herald* goes on to outline what sounds like the plot of a blockbuster military-horror film. For instance, we read about "unlawful miners" who have gone down into the earthly darkness to "'hijack' closed-off sections of legitimate mines." They become "rogue gold-diggers," selling their metal on the black market. The article quotes a police explosives expert: "They work there, they sleep there, they eat there. It is hot and dark, and they age very quickly. They even smoke down there, which is very dangerous because of the methane gas present in mines, which can explode as a result of the slightest spark." The mine hijackers "face death by suffocation and even insanity in the appallingly nightmarish conditions in which they live." Finally, we read that a special police team, trained in the art of subterranean invasion, has begun a series of raids on the mines, dodging "beer bottle 'grenades' stuffed with explosives and iron waste shrapnel" on the way down.

GEOLOGY IN THE AGE OF THE WAR ON TERROR

A few months after the attacks of September 11th, the *New York Times* published a kind of geological look at the War on Terror. In a short article from November 26, 2001, author Kenneth Chang describes how ancient landscape processes and tectonic events came together to form the interconnected mountain caves in which Osama bin Laden was, at that time, hiding. He would sit there in the darkness, rubbing his grenades, complaining about women, Jews, and homosexuals.

"The area that is now Afghanistan started to take shape hundreds of millions of years ago," Chang writes, "when gigantic rocks, propelled by the immense geological forces that continuously rearrange the earth's landforms, slammed into the landmass that is now Asia." This caused rocks "deep inside the earth" to "flow like taffy." And I love this next sentence.

Just like the air masses in thunderstorms, the warmer rocks rise and the cooler ones sink, setting up Ferris wheel–shaped circulations of magma that drag along the crust above them.

Over time, these forces broke several pieces off the southern supercontinent of Gondwanaland—an ancient conglomeration made from what we now know as South America and Africa—and carried them north toward Asia.

Geology is a kind of slow weather system inside the earth.

Of course, Afghanistan—like most of the Earth's surface—was once entirely under water. Beneath the warm waves of the Tethys Seaway, over millions of years, aquatic organisms "were compressed into limestone." Limestone is less a rock than a biological side effect—something the living can become. These massive and shuddering tectonic mutations continued:

> Minerals from the ocean floor, melted by the heat of the interior, then flowed back up near the surface, forming rich deposits of copper and iron (minerals that could someday finance an economic boom in Afghanistan). The limestone along the coasts of Asia and India buckled upward, like two cars in a head-on collision. Water then ate away at the limestone to form the caves. Though arid today, Afghanistan was once warm and wet. Carbon dioxide from decaying plants dissolved into water to form carbonic acid, and in water-saturated underground areas, the acid hollowed out the limestone to form the caves, some several miles long.

The story gets particularly interesting at this point, where the CIA meets geology.

What happened was that Osama bin Laden, in hiding after 9/11, started releasing his famous videotapes—but those tapes included glimpses of cave walls and rocky hillsides behind him. When John F. Shroder—a geologist specializing in the structure of Himalayan Afghanistan—saw those tapes, he tried to interpret their setting and background, looking for mineralogical clues as to where bin Laden might be. Like a scene from Francis Ford Coppola's classic film *The Conversation*, Shroder pored over the tapes, fast-forwarding and rewinding, blowing up images, scanning for signs. It was the surface of the earth via TiVo.

"Afghanistan's fighters find shelter in the natural caves," the *New York Times* continues. But, of course, "[t]hey also make their own, often in the mountains of crystalline rock made of minerals like quartz and feldspar, the pieces of Afghanistan that were carried in by plate tectonics. 'This kind of rock is extremely resistant,' Dr. Shroder said. 'It's a good place to build bunkers, and bin Laden knows that.' Dr. Shroder said he believed that Mr. bin Laden's video in October was taken in a region with crystalline rocks like those south of Jalalabad"—all of which makes me think that soldiers heading off to Afghanistan could do worse than to carry bulletproof copies of Jules Verne's novel *Journey to the Center of the Earth* along with them. As another *New York Times* article, also published on November 26, 2001, put it:

> Afghanistan is a virtual ant farm of thousands of caves, countless miles of tunnels, deeply dug-in bases and heavily fortified

MOLE MEN

The story of William Lyttle—the infamous Mole Man of Hackney—seems to return to the top of the Internet news cycle once every two or three years. In April 2008, the BBC reported that Lyttle had been fined nearly £300,000 for digging an extensive network of tunnels beneath his dilapidated east London rowhouse; and in August 2006 the *Guardian* wrote:

No one knows how far the network of burrows underneath 75-year-old William Lyttle's house [might] stretch. But according to the council, which used ultrasound scanners to ascertain the extent of the problem, almost half a century of nibbling dirt with a shovel and homemade pulley has hollowed out a web of tunnels and caverns, some 8 meters (26 feet) deep, spreading up to 20 meters in every direction from his house.

One neighbor joked that Lyttle might, at any point, "come tunneling up through the kitchen floor," and another—with the unreal surname of Bunker—was quoted by the *Guardian* in 2001, saying: "I once asked him what he was doing. He replied, 'I'm building a swimming pool as part of a health club for ladies.'"

Subterranean ladies health club or not, it was all too much for the neighborhood. Nearby residents began to fear that their houses—indeed the very streets themselves—might soon collapse into a planet made hollow by unsanctioned excavation. "There has been movement in the ground," a council surveyor complained. The *Guardian*'s 2001 article goes on to point out that a series of X-ray surveys in the 1990s had failed to detect the sum total of Lyttle's digging, and so structural engineers were asked to "descend into the dark labyrinth to gauge the full extent of the damage."

The "full extent" of this damage reached into Lyttle's house itself, which had been subject to nearly four decades of endless tinkering. According to the *Times*, in April 2008, there was a kind of general porosity to Lyttle's domestic life:

Inspectors discovered that parts of the house were supported by nothing more than household appliances and that ceilings had fallen in as a result of his extensive "home improvements."

Mr. Lyttle also dug out holes around his home, in which he placed a range of items including cars and boats.

Perhaps the urge to tunnel is something that crosses both class and nationality. For instance, I was reminded of the Mole Man by a September 15, 2008, article in the *New Yorker* profiling German tunneling entrepreneur Martin Herrenknecht. Herrenknecht's firm, "the largest maker of tunneling machines in the world," is currently engaged in the extraordinary task of carving a new automotive tunnel through the Alps. That tunnel, 35 miles in length, "crosses nine geological zones, none of them fully understood. It cuts through granite and quartz, along fault lines and beneath a sugarlike layer of dolomitic marble—a sand trap to anything going through it." Amazingly, in a geological region near Sedrun, we read, "the marble is so finely ground and under such terrific pressure that it came surging up through the test shafts like seltzer."

Herrenknecht's machines come in all shapes and sizes. On the one hand there are behemoths like the *Mixshields* line of excavators—used "for multi-layered, complex geologies," according to Herrenknecht's website—and, on the other, there are what the *New Yorker* calls "micro-tunneling machines." These can "slip under city streets," like something out of *Spiderman 2*, and they can be "steered by remote control." It's hard not to wonder what the Mole Man of Hackney would have done with equipment like this, micro-tunneling his way throughout south England with the assistance of remote-controlled "ripper chisels," all while sitting firm in the (gradually undercut) safety of his own home.

To put this another way, if the Mole Man ran an international geotechnical services firm, perhaps he would be Herrenknecht's closest competitor. After all, one of them might be an English eccentric, alone with his homemade pulley in the underworld, and the other a well-funded German engineer, but the Mole Man and Herrenknecht seem to share a vision of the Earth's surface. From the *New Yorker*:

To see a map of [Herrenknecht's] projects is to envision the planet as a porous thing—a cosmic loofah—inhabited by an increasingly hive-like humanity. At any given moment, close to a thousand Herrenknecht worms are burrowing under mountains, rivers, and cities on almost every continent. They have tunneled along the San Andreas Fault, under the Yangtze River and beside the Bosporus, through catacombs in Rome and petrified pilings in Cairo. "We are changing the world," Herrenknecht told me. "We are putting it in tunnels. That is my vision."

In the end, the Mole Man gets the best line of all. When faced with the relentless negative media coverage—and the psychological pressure of a police investigation—as if it was the most obvious thing in the world, he simply said: "Tunneling is something that should be talked about without panicking."

herrenknecht.com

bunkers. They are the product of a confluence of ancient history, climate, geology, Mr. bin Laden's own engineering background—and, 15 years back, a hefty dose of American money from the Central Intelligence Agency.

Bin Laden et al., could thus "take their most secret and dangerous operations to earth," hidden beneath the veil of geology. And there you have it: the forensic geology of the War on Terror, as evidenced through terrorist videotapes.

THE DESCENT

I'm reminded of Jeff Long's 1999 novel, *The Descent*, in which a kind of war on terror is declared against a monstrous subhuman race that lives beneath the surface of the earth. Long's book involves nuns and the U.S. military and some Himalayan mountaineers—as well as a rogue branch of the human species, a parallel sub-race that literally went underground many tens of thousands of years ago, and is only now coming back into the light. They're called *Homo hadalis*. Get it? They're from Hades, "the planet within their planet," as Long calls it—where *their* refers to the military men who find themselves confused and under attack by this brand-new enemy confronting the world from below.

More and more of these literally hellish nonhumans start pouring up from the bowels of the earth, killing men, women, and children—even kidnapping a few—before disappearing again into unlit caverns. The militaries of every nation in the world plan a subterranean campaign. Armed with machine guns, hydroponic agriculture, UV lights, and lots of instant concrete, they head downward.

They begin the descent.

Vast caverns are soon mapped. Tunnels stretching clear across the Pacific seafloor are discovered—and, from there, cobwebs of subsidiary tunnels, weaving off into the void. As one of the novel's characters states:

> The abyss beneath the Pacific is basalt, which gets attacked every few hundred years by huge plumes of hydrogen-sulfide brine, or sulfuric acid, which snakes up from deeper layers. This acid brine eats through the basalt like worms through an apple. We now believe there may be as many as six million miles of naturally occurring cavities in the rock beneath the Pacific, at an average depth of 6,100 fathoms.

The earth, in other words, is *hollow*. There are thousands of tiny tunnels, like capillaries, but they're big enough to walk

THE TOPOGRAPHY OF HELL
Even Jesus Christ was curious about Hell. In the New Testament is something now known as the "Harrowing of Hell," which the *Catholic Encyclopedia* describes as Christ's "triumphant descent" into the planetary abyss between crucifixion and resurrection.

But it would be interesting here to create a kind of design survey of the landscape architecture of Hell—its topography and geographical forms, perhaps even its subsurface geology. Could we assemble a catalog of landscape metaphors and geographical analogies writers have used over the centuries to describe this hellish underworld? It's not hard to imagine some obscure papal academy in Rome publishing tract after tract on the exact geotechnical nature of the Inferno. *Is it made of granite?* scholars ask. *Is it slate? Is it ringed by rivers of uranium tailings?*

Hopeful priests and theology scholars take whole courses in the literary-cosmological subgenre of Hell descriptions. They interview engineers and take tours of abandoned gold mines with Catholic priests. They visit nuclear waste entombment sites.

Then BLDGBLOG publishes its own prophecy, that the anti-Christ will arrive when the pope is an ex-mining engineer, trained in the ways of the underworld.

through—and there is one massive one, a geological super-highway spiking east from the Mariana Trench. It angles toward a nest of smaller caves on the surface as far away as Peru. "A profusion of tunnels shoots throughout the Asian plate systems," we read, "giving access to the basements of Australia, the Indonesian archipelago, China, and so on. You name it, there are doorways to the surface everywhere."

There are doorways to the surface everywhere—and the traffic moves both ways. Things come up; things go down. Soon the Army Corps of Engineers gets involved. "They were tasked to reinforce tunnels, devise new transport systems, drill shafts, build elevators, bore channels, and erect whole camps underground. They even paved parking lots three thousand feet beneath the surface. Roadways were constructed through the mouths of caves." It takes days at a time to get anywhere; people move between underground base camps and vast instant cities further on. These are full of klieg lights, ringed with landmines, and thriving behind walls of sandbags and fortified machine gun nests. There are outbreaks of "tropical cave disease" and claustrophobia—and there is something else down there, that enemy twin of the human race, hiding in the darkness. Everywhere the descending soldiers find "evidence of primitive occupation at the deeper levels," down amidst overwhelming pressures beneath both continents and the sea.

Of course, the novel's surface-dwellers want to explore; they want to see where the tunnels lead—to go out to the edges of the Earth by going *into* the Earth.

> Suddenly, man no longer looked out to the stars. Astronomers fell from grace. It became a time to look inward.

I'm tempted to quote Nietzsche. With all this talk of entering into unexplored realms of pressure and darkness—looking into a void that perhaps looks into us, in turn—the obvious final question is: Are we prepared for what we'll find? ⊗

Four of Gustave Doré's classic 1892 illustrations for Dante's *Inferno*, a guided landscape tour of Hell.

The Possibility of Secret Passageways: An Interview with Patrick McGrath

The novels of Patrick McGrath are most often described as "Gothic." They unfold across foggy moors and brackish marshes dotted with rotting houses and dead trees. There are swamps and London graveyards, crumbling barns and basements. It is the *settings*, in other words, of McGrath's novels that led me to speak with him for the following interview.

A question I've often asked on BLDGBLOG is: What do novelists, artists, and filmmakers want from the built environment? More specifically, how can architecture assist a writer as he or she constructs a novel's story line? Are certain types of buildings more conducive to one kind of plot than to another? What about landscape? How does landscape lend itself to literary effect—and could landscape architects actually learn something about the drama of designed space by turning to a novel instead of to a work of theory? To the work of Patrick McGrath, for instance?

BLDGBLOG: On the most basic level, what makes a landscape "Gothic"? Is it the weather, the landforms, the isolation, the plant life…?

Patrick McGrath: Not an easy question to answer! As you point out, a landscape could be tropical—or it could be Arctic, and it could still have those qualities that we consider Gothic. It's hard to know just what these landscapes have in common. I suppose we have to go back to the origins of Romanticism, and to Edmund Burke's book on the sublime, and look at his notions of the horrid and the terrible. There were landscapes that emotionally aroused the people of that time—but because of their what? Their *magnificence* in some way. The sheer scope and grandeur of the high mountains—the Alps, which Mary Shelley described very powerfully in *Frankenstein*—or the eastern European landscape in Bram Stoker's *Dracula*: the loneliness and the remoteness of those

mountains, the density of the forests, the fact that there are very few human beings there. Nature dwarfs humanity in such landscapes. And that will arouse the sense of awe that is made particularly dramatic use of in Romantic and Gothic literature.

Then, at the other end of the scale, we have a tropical landscape such as Conrad's Congo in *Heart of Darkness* where it's almost the reverse: It's the constrictiveness and the fecundity of nature, the way it presses in on all sides. Everything is decaying. And decay, of course, is a central concept in the Gothic. So when you have tropical vegetation, you do have a sense of ooze and rot—of swampiness.

BLDGBLOG: You say that certain landscapes were "emotionally arousing" for the people of the era—but this implies that what makes a landscape *emotionally arousing* can change from generation to generation. If that's the case, might something altogether different be considered Gothic or Romantic today? Have you noticed a kind of historical shift in the types of landscapes that fit into the Gothic canon?

McGrath: My first thought is, not so much of *landscape*—but, let's say, in the view of *the city*. My second novel, *Spider*, was inspired by a book of photographs by Bill Brandt. Brandt captured the seedy, ill-lit character of the East End of London of the 1930s in such powerfully human character—illicit liaisons on wet cobbled streets; toothy barmaids in grotty pubs, pulling pints for sardonic men in cloth caps—that I was at once inspired to find a story there. But I do think the Victorian slum—the dark, rather shadowy streets that have a sort of sinister and threatening feel to them—could be replaced by the blandness of a suburb.

I'm thinking of what David Lynch did in *Blue Velvet*, with a scene of apparent utter normality. Think of the opening scene where a man is watering his garden and everything seems, well, *perfect* in that neat and orderly suburban way, and yet his camera then goes beneath the grass and we see all sorts of forms of life that are slimy and grotesque and that aren't apparent in that hygienic world above. So there may be something in that: the suburb as the most Gothic of sites. Think of the work, say, of Gregory Crewdson.

BLDGBLOG: That raises the question of what sorts of architecture pop up most frequently in Gothic literature: usually English manor houses, church ruins, forgotten attics, and so on. Why are certain types of buildings more conducive to one type of story and not others?

McGrath: I think you'd have to say that there are two questions here. There's the conventional, stereotypical Gothic site, which tends to be a lonely house high on a hill, probably Victorian, with turrets and the possibility of secret passageways and cellars and attics—places of obscurity, places where the past somehow resides. You know, houses of secrets.

These sites, in turn, would have grown out of the more traditional Gothic architectures—basically the ruins of monasteries and abbeys and convents and such, which dotted the British landscape in the 18th century, after the Reformation. Those first aroused the taste for ruins, and that was the origin of the Gothic. It's basically medieval architecture—in ruins because of what Henry VIII did to the English church in the 16th century. So those were the places where people like Horace Walpole set their fiction, because the buildings were in such a state of decrepitude. I think anything that sort of relates to these large, broken down, dilapidated structures would arouse the Gothic effect.

BLDGBLOG: Interestingly, in the work of J. G. Ballard, you get the same sort of psychological atmosphere—of perversion, violence, and dread—from a totally different kind of built environment: Instead of crumbling manor houses, you have corporate office parks in the south of France and even British shopping malls.

McGrath: Absolutely—and that was going to be the second part of my answer. There is what you might call a *new* Gothic, where the particular trappings of the old Gothic, the particular stylistic characteristics, are not necessary to produce the same sorts of effects—the feelings of dread, constriction, obscurity, transgression. You can get those from inner-city projects, for example, or even a little neat row house.

There was an early Ian McEwan novel, *The Cement Garden*, where all sorts of perverse wickedness was going on in a very unmemorable little house, in a street of very similar houses, none of which would particularly smack of evil. Although I did notice, when I was rereading it, that he uses a little crenellation detail in the architecture of one of these absolutely anonymous little houses. He's just touching in this faint hint of the Gothic—as though to say: This is a child of something out of Ann Radcliffe, some decaying monastery in which an aristocrat pursues a maiden in the depths of the night.

BLDGBLOG: Do you have any real buildings in mind as you describe places like Drogo Hall? Put another way, could someone ever do a kind of Patrick McGrathian architectural tour, or heritage walk, visiting sites that have inspired your fiction? Where would that tour take them?

McGrath: [*laughs*] Good question. I don't quite know where I get them from. In part from the imagination, in part from books—with photographs or paintings of buildings, some of which I've observed and remembered.

There's a house called Crook in my first novel, *The Grotesque*. I found a lovely little book in a secondhand bookstore in New York called *The Manor Houses of England*, and I simply leafed through it, picking up details here and there—not only architectural details, but verbal details. The way that aspects of architecture are described—the sorts of terms that are used—can be as much a part of the creation of a building in fiction as a clear, purely visual picture in your mind. You catch a nice phrase that's used to describe, I don't know, a Jacobean staircase or a particular piece of detailing or masonry—and you fling it in because it sounds good, rather than just because it evokes a particular image. For example, in prisons and asylums you will always have the doors opening outwards so that whoever is incarcerated behind that door won't be able to blockade themselves inside the room. Little details like that give the character of an institution and can be very evocative on the page.

But I don't think there's a pattern. They're usually curious amalgams that I put together in my imagination.

BLDGBLOG: I'm also curious about the weather. For instance, a wet climate—with thunderstorms, humidity, and damp—seems to play a major, arguably indispensable, role in the Gothic imagination. Your own novels illustrate this point quite well: from rain-soaked country homes to the Lambeth marshes, from coastal fishing towns to Central American swamps. But can *aridity* ever be Gothic? In other words, if the constant presence of moisture contributes to a malarial atmosphere of decay, mold, infestation, and disease, might there be a whole other world of psychological implications in a climate where things don't decay—where there is no mold, where bodies turn to leather and everything can be preserved? Is *indefinite preservation* perhaps a Gothic horror of its own?

McGrath: Aridity does interest me. It's an unusual application of the Gothic mood. You usually think of northern European or North American climates and landscapes, but that's merely because, traditionally, that's where these sorts of stories have been set. But I can very well imagine aridity being a place, or a site, for such a story.

I think you could safely say that one of the themes of the Gothic is the sins of the father being visited upon the sons—in other words, there is no escaping the past. The past will always haunt the present. And this is certainly true of Gothic stories that are set in crumbling old houses: There's always some piece of evil that has occurred in a previous generation that will work itself out on the current generation. So that continuation—or *persistence*—of the past is what you're expressing: It's the skeleton that can't be disposed of.

But I'm trying to think if I know of a Gothic tale set in a desert, and the only thing I can come up with is an Erich von Stroheim movie called *Greed*. There's a man who has, somehow or another, wound up handcuffed to his companion—and the companion has died. This is in the quest for gold. Somehow or another their greed has got them into an impossible situation: They're handcuffed, the companion has died, and so we have a man crawling across the desert handcuffed to a corpse. It being a desert, of course, he's doomed. But that's a very powerful image of an utterly arid landscape.

In the spirit of a new Gothic, one that isn't dependent on very particular types of landscape or architecture, you could certainly exploit an arid landscape in order to create a condition of extreme thirst, extreme solitude, extreme desperation—all of which would be appropriate states of mind for a Gothic story.

BLDGBLOG: One of the most striking images I've read is your character Hugo Coal, from *The Grotesque*, assembling his dinosaur skeleton in the family barn. I'd love to hear your thoughts about what went into that—but also what you think about the human encounter with what I'll call *prehistoric monstrosity*: with dinosaur bones, and marine fossils, and the utter strangeness of the Earth's inhuman past.

McGrath: What interested me there—before I'd even thought through aspects of deep time, and what that means—was that a man could go to Africa and collect a bunch of bones and crate them up and bring them back, and then spend the rest of his life trying to see what fitted where. This may be completely implausible, in terms of paleontology, but I just liked the notion of Sir Hugo sitting there in his barn—year in, year out—trying to make a pattern, to make a structure—and continuing to get it wrong. It seemed, somehow, very much in the spirit of human endeavors to discover the truth, or to figure out how nature works—or even, within that book, to get an answer to the mystery of who killed Sidney. It was to do with the fallibility of knowledge that was contained within this enterprise of getting the bones to fit—and they won't! [*laughs*] There's always a bit left over, or something that won't go where it's supposed to go. So that was the aspect, the epistemological aspect, of reconstructing a skeleton that first fascinated me.

Then there was the notion of this thing coming from deep in the past and being now extinct—from so deep in the past that it no longer had any place on this Earth—and the suggestion that Sir Hugo, in a sense, was the same. He, too, was a dinosaur; his day, as a representative of a certain social class, was past. But this was also a carnivorous creature. This wasn't a gentle herbivore Hugo's got there. This was a creature of enormous violence and absolute rapacity, capable of tearing its prey to pieces, and I wanted to suggest that those sorts of implicit violent energies were now swirling about this old country house.

BLDGBLOG: In some ways, I might suggest that contemplating the Earth's biological past lends itself well to the Gothic mood—but contemplating, say, the Earth's *geological* past simply doesn't have the same psychological impact. For some reason, rocks aren't very Gothic!

McGrath: Well, I remember the way that Conrad handles the river in *Heart of Darkness*: He speaks of the journey that Marlow takes to get to Kurtz as being a journey through, or deeper into, the geological history of Africa. I forget how he does it, but he gives you the sense that, as the boat moves up the river, it is also descending through eons of time. So there is almost a sense of a *geological regression* occurring as Marlow moves toward a man who has committed an act of enormous *moral* regression. Everything is about a movement downwards in that book. I'd say that he employs geological descent to mirror a moral descent.

BLDGBLOG: Of course, there's also Hugo Coal's surname: *coal*, a geological product.

McGrath: There you are. Absolutely. That was no accident. Again, I'm referring to deep layers of what once had been wood, and that now, through the operation of time and pressure, has become something quite different.

Edinburgh

In a (very) short story called "The Antipodes and the Century," author Ignacio Padilla describes "a great Scottish engineer, left to die in the middle of the desert, [who] is rescued by a tribe of nomads."

Upon recovery, the engineer inspires his saviors "to build an exact replica of the city of Edinburgh in the dunes."

There, "amidst the rocks of the Gobi," Kirghiz nomads are taught "the exact height that Edinburgh Castle must attain, the precise length of the bridge that connects the High Street with Waverly Station, the correct calculations necessary to establish the perimeter of Canongate Cemetery, [and] the true distance between the two spires of St. Giles' Cathedral."

With that knowledge—and with lots of rocks—they construct "an elephantine fortress of streets, bridges, and windows." It is "a shimmering haze of towers," we read, and it blends in architecturally with the mirages of the desert horizon. Until it is buried by a sandstorm, this replicant Edinburgh functions as "a kind of global map in the very heart of the Gobi Desert."

Edinburgh (2002) by Jim Webb.

snacksize.com

Where Cathedrals
Go to Die

When large container ships can contain or ship no more, they're sent halfway around the world to so-called breaking yards, to be dismantled by torch and hand. Their metal is salvaged, their intact structures, down to cabin doors and toilet seats, put back onto the global market. Today, these breaking yards tend to be in Bangladesh or India—but the location is just a factor of cheap labor and nonexistent environmental regulations. After all, it's toxic work.

In his book *The Outlaw Sea*, author William Langewiesche visits the Alang ship-breaking yard in Gujarat, India. He describes it as "a shoreline strewn with industrial debris on the oily Gulf of Cambray, part of the Arabian Sea." Camera-like, Langewiesche wanders through the scene: "Dawn spread across the gargantuan landscape," he writes, and he sees that "Alang, in daylight, was barely recognizable as a beach."

It was a narrow, smoke-choked industrial zone six miles long, where nearly two hundred ships stood side by side in progressive states of dissection, yawning open to expose their cavernous holds, spilling their black innards onto the tidal flats. . . . Night watchmen were swinging the yard gates open now, revealing the individual plots, each demarcated by little flags or other markers stuck in the sand, and heavily cluttered with cut metal and nautical debris.

He then visits a hull rerolling mill where "perhaps a hundred emaciated men moved through soot and heavy smoke." Like a vision from the early poems of William Blake, they are "feeding scrap to a roaring furnace leaking flames from cracks in the side. The noise was deafening. The heat was so intense that in places I thought it might sear my lungs. The workers' clothes were black with carbon, as were their hair and their skin. Their faces were so sooty that their eyes seemed illuminated."

As Langewiesche's own, vaguely Homeric language implies, there's something mythological in the sight of humans standing amidst the debris of a structure they have disassembled. They are surviving—barely—on the scraps of a First World that has sent its waste elsewhere, in this raw and displaced landscape of rare metals, forming poisonous deltas that leach out across the sand into the sea.

But such scenes also lead me to wonder what might happen if architectural structures weren't destroyed by wrecking balls, or by bulldozers, or even by well-placed explosives—if they were instead uprooted in their entirety, packed onto Panamax cargo ships and dropped on a beach somewhere in a Pacific archipelago. Complete, still intact, and ready for salvage. Half a dozen old stone cathedrals lined up in the mist at dawn, their arches ready for cutting, naves open like the hulls of derelict ships; behind them stand American football stadiums. On another island, skyscrapers tilt at dangerous angles, sinking six floors deep at high tide. Saltwater washes through elevator shafts, establishing tide pools in the former offices of offshore accounting firms.

Notre Dame is too expensive to maintain? Chartres has irreparable structural damage? Ship them to the islands, to the building-breaking yards, where buttresses, arches, and colonnades are stacked all around like an inland reef. Strapped to the flatbeds and cargo holds of unregistered ships, the Houses of Parliament go floating by. Recognizable chunks of famous architecture litter the island shores of a barely visited archipelago.

Perhaps declaring war will no longer mean military invasion—it will mean shipping entire enemy cities off to the beaches of tropical islands, with their residents still inside.

European cathedrals overgrown with palm trees, half-buried in sand, their crypts exposed, stained glass catching every sunset. Windblown bank towers tip to one side, covered in creeper vines and home to bats. The floors of ritzy Fifth Avenue high-rises, with their familiar rooms and corridors intact—complete with chandeliers—are now infested with crocodiles and half-singed by wildfire.

National Geographic sends its top photojournalist to document the landscape; she walks, stunned, through the python-infested arches of what was once Westminster Abbey.

↑ previous page
Shipbreaking No. 11, Chittagong,
Bangladesh (2000) and *Shipbreaking
No. 27 with Cutter*, Chittagong,
Bangladesh (2001). Both photographs
by Edward Burtynsky. Images copy-
right Edward Burtynsky, courtesy
Charles Cowles Gallery, New York/
Nicholas Metivier Gallery, Toronto.

edwardburtynsky.com

Shipbreaking No. 8, Chittagong,
Bangladesh (2000), by Edward Burtynsky.
Image copyright Edward Burtynsky,
courtesy Charles Cowles Gallery, New
York/Nicholas Metivier Gallery, Toronto.

edwardburtynsky.com

Crimes Against Architecture

In his book *The Destruction of Memory: Architecture at War,* Robert Bevan describes how specific buildings—and whole cities—have been targeted, damaged, or destroyed by war. He writes of the "violent destruction of buildings for other than pragmatic reasons," claiming that "there has always been [a] war against architecture." This war is fought through the deliberate "eradication" of an enemy's built environment—that is, "the *active* and often systematic destruction of particular building types or architectural traditions."

Some of Bevan's examples sound less like warfare, however, than a peculiar and highly violent kind of architectural ritual, played out over centuries between rival governments and religions. This trans-civilizational clash includes the "repeated demolition or adaptation of each other's buildings," where retaliation often takes generations. The site of the cathedral in Córdoba, Spain, for instance, "started out as a Roman temple" before it was destroyed by Christian Visigoths:

> A subsequent church on the site was replaced by a mosque following the Arab conquest of the early eighth century. Some seventy years later this was itself demolished to create the first stage of a massive new mosque. The Christians recaptured Córdoba in 1236 and consecrated the building as a cathedral. (…) It is said that the mosque's lamps were melted down to make new bells for the Cathedral of Santiago de Compostela, 800 km to the north. This probably seemed only fair, since the lamps had themselves been made from Santiago's original bells: when the Moors had conquered the city in 997 they had dragged the bells to Córdoba and melted them down into lamps.

Bevan also describes how the Bastille, after being stormed in 1789, was reduced to a heap of stones—but these stones were then "broken up and sold as souvenirs," in a "commodification process repeated with the fragments of the Berlin Wall 200 years later." Architectural destruction becomes souvenirized, so to speak; ruins are something that people will pay money not only to see but to have.

Synagogues burned to the ground in both Poland and Germany; Loyalist mansions dynamited by Irish Republican militias; the destruction of the World Trade Center; Armenian monasteries reduced to foundation stones (as, even today, they continue to be dismantled and reused to build houses in eastern Turkey); archaeological sites destroyed during the 2003 U.S. invasion of Iraq—these, among many, many other such examples, are all, Bevan says, "crimes against architecture."

More intriguingly, when Bevan points out that "the bulldozed remains of the Aladza mosque" were "dumped" by Serbian troops into a nearby river, and that those ruins were only "identified by the mosque's distinctive stone columns," it occurred to me that fragments like these are now so numerous that you could probably use them to assemble whole buildings elsewhere. You could construct a whole city from fragments of buildings destroyed by war. All the gravel, dirt, and foundation stones from ruined buildings and cities around the world could be dropped into shallow waters off the western coast of Greece—to form the in-filled base of an artificial island, as large as Manhattan, on which to build your memorial to the architectural victims of war.

You draw up plans with a local architecture school, plotting a whole new island metropolis constructed from nothing but pre-existing pieces of annihilated architecture—fitting arches with arches and floors with floors. Within a decade you've covered the island in a maze of Chicago tenement housing, Russian churches, Indian temples, and Chinese hutongs; Aztec walls and pillars stand inside reconstructed Romanian opera houses. Then most of pre-WWII Europe begins to appear, together with shattered Welsh border castles, North African villages, and the weathered masonry of pre-Columbian South America, all the buildings merging into one another, indistinct, with Mayan rocks and Kurdish roofing joined together atop bricks from Köln and Dresden. You lay out paths with gravel taken from Hiroshima and Nagasaki. Another decade and the island-city is complete. There are no cars and no electricity—in fact, no one lives there at all. It sits alone in the waters, covered in wild herbs and home to songbirds, casting shadows onto itself, eroding a bit in the occasional rainstorm. Documentaries about it soon appear on CNN and the BBC. Only ten people are allowed on the island at any given time; most of them just take photos, draw sketches, or write letters to loved ones as they wander, awestruck, through the narrow streets of total desolation, deciphering architectural cacophonies of extinct building types and lost statuary—towers of churches destroyed by bombs—hardly able to conceive how all of these buildings could have been destroyed by human conflict.

Tourists brush the dust of structures off their shoes as they board the boat to go home, looking back at the sun setting a brilliant orange behind the island's almost pitch-black silhouette.

The Birds

The Campaign for Dark Skies, an anti-light-pollution organization based in the United Kingdom, republished this account on their website of the *Tribute in Light*, those blazing towers of floodlit sky and clouds that Manhattan used to memorialize the fallen World Trade Center:

> The beams were visibly filled with birds for their entire height, looking like clouds of bugs. Their twittering was audible. There were so many birds, it was impossible to track any one individual for any length of time. I did see one bird that circled in and out of the uptown beam six times before I lost track.

The birds had been fatally mesmerized, often spiraling to the ground—or into the windows of nearby buildings. They formed a kind of bird tornado.

The circular disorientation of birds—winged animals thrown athwart by the optical effects of architecture—also makes an appearance in W. G. Sebald's novel *Austerlitz*, albeit on a much smaller scale. Here, the narrator recounts a friend's visit to the new Bibliothèque Nationale in Paris:

> The four glazed towers themselves, named in a manner reminiscent of a futuristic novel …make a positively Babylonian impression on anyone who looks up at their facades and wonders about the still largely empty space behind their closed blinds. (…) And several times, said Austerlitz, birds which had lost their way in the library forest flew into the mirror images of the trees in the reading-room windows, struck the glass with a dull thud, and fell lifeless to the ground.

Could this serve as a new form of avian predation? Conversely, of course, the birds might obliterate the city. Hitchcock's revenge. I'm reminded of the beautifully descriptive title of an old (and fairly awful) song by Coil: "Red Birds Will Fly Out of the East and Destroy Paris in a Night." But, as a bulwark against those murderous flocks, Paris deploys a mirrored library.

Slums and Other Rogue Micro-Sovereignties: An Interview with Mike Davis

In his influential 1990 book *City of Quartz*, Mike Davis explores the militarization of space in Los Angeles, from the impenetrable "panic rooms" of Beverly Hills mansions to the shifting ganglands of South Central. Not only, we read, does the Los Angeles Police Department use "a geo-synchronous law enforcement satellite" in its literal oversight of the city, but "thousands of residential rooftops have been painted with identifying street numbers, transforming the aerial view of the city into a huge police grid." In Los Angeles today, Davis suggests, "carceral structures have become the new frontier of public architecture."

The following interview took place after the publication of Davis's *Planet of Slums*. There, Davis writes that we are now at "a watershed in human history, comparable to the Neolithic or Industrial revolutions. For the first time the urban population of the Earth will outnumber the rural." This "urban" population will not find its home inside *cities*, however, but in horrific megaslums where masked riot police, food shortages, human sewage, toxic metal-plating industries, armed militias, and emerging diseases all violently coexist with literally billions of human beings. What, then, is the future of the city on our planet of slums? This, as Davis explained in the following interview with BLDGBLOG, "in a way, is the most interesting—and least-understood—dynamic of global urbanization.… [I]t's not well-studied. The census data and social statistics are notoriously incomplete."

BLDGBLOG: Your book suggests that the real academic question now is how to study the slums—who and what to ask, and how to interpret the data.

Mike Davis: At the very least, it's a challenge of information. Interestingly, this has also become the terrain of a lot of Pentagon thinking about urban warfare. These non-hierarchical, labyrinthine peripheries are what many Pentagon thinkers have fastened onto as one of the most challenging terrains for future wars and other imperial projects. After a period in which the Pentagon was besotted with trendy management theory—using analogies with Wal-Mart and just-in-time inventory—it now seems to have become obsessed with *urban theory*—with architecture and city planning. This is happening particularly through things like the RAND Corporation's Arroyo Center, in Santa Monica. I wouldn't be at all surprised if there's a great leap forward in our understanding of what's happening on the peripheries of Third World cities because of the needs of Pentagon strategists and local military planners. For instance, Andean anthropology made a big leap forward in the 1960s and early 1970s when Che Guevara and his guerrilla fighters became a problem.

I think there's a consensus, both on the left and the right, that it's the slum peripheries of poor Third World cities that have become a decisive geopolitical space. That space is now a military challenge as much as it is an epistemological challenge, both for sociologists and for military planners.

BLDGBLOG: One of the things I found most interesting in your other recent book, *Monster at Our Door*, is the concept of "biosecurity." Could you explain how biosecurity is, or is not, being achieved on the level of urban space and architectural design?

Davis: I see the whole question of epidemic control and biosecurity being modeled after immigration control. That's the reigning paradigm right now. Of course, it's a totally false analogy—particularly when you deal with something like influenza, which can't be quarantined. You can't build walls against it. Biosecurity, in a globalized world that contains as much poverty and squalor as our urban world does, is impossible. There is no biosecurity. The continuing quest will be to achieve the biological equivalent of a gated community, with the control of movement and with regulations that just enforce all the most Orwellian tendencies—the selective creation and provision of vaccines, antivirals, and so on. But, at the end of the day, biosecurity is an impossibility—until you address the essence of the problem, which is public health for the poor and the ecological sustainability of the city.

In *Monster at Our Door*, I cite what I thought was an absolutely model study, published in *Science*, about how breakneck urbanization in western Africa is occurring at the same time that European factory ships are coming in and scooping up all the fish protein. This has turned urban populations massively to bush meat—which was already a booming business because of construction crews logging out the last tropical forests in West Africa—and, presto: You get HIV, you get Ebola, you get unknown plagues. I thought the article was an absolutely masterful description of inadvertent causal linkages, and the complex ecology—the environmental impact—that urbanization has. Likewise, with urbanization in China and Southeast Asia, the industrialization of poultry seems to be one of the chief factors behind the threat of avian flu.

As any epidemiologist will tell you, these are just the first new plagues of globalization—and there will be more. The idea that you can defend against diseases by the equivalent of a gated community is ludicrous, but it's exactly the direction in which public health policy is being directed.

I did a lot of calculator work on the UN data, from *The Challenge of Slums*, calculating urban densities and so on, and this is the Victorian world writ large. Just as the Victorian middle classes could not escape the diseases of the slums, neither will the rich, bunkered down in their country clubs or inside gated communities. The whole obsession now is that avian flu will be brought into the country by—

BLDGBLOG: —a Mexican!

Davis: Exactly: It'll be smuggled over the border—which is absurd. This ongoing obsession with illegal immigration has become a one-stop phantasmagoria for everything. Of course, it goes back to primal, ancient fears: The Irish brought typhoid, the Chinese brought plague. It's old hat.

BLDGBLOG: What would a biosecure world actually look like, though, on the level of

architecture and urban design? Further, do you see any evidence that the medical profession is being architecturally empowered, so to speak, and thus influencing the design of "disease-free" public spaces?

Davis: Well, sure. It's exactly how Victorian social control over the slums was defined as a kind of hygienic project—or in the same way that urban segregation was justified in colonial cities as a problem of sanitation. Everywhere these discourses reinforce one another. What really has been lacking, however, is one big epidemic, originating in poverty, that hits the middle classes—because then you'll see people really go berserk. I think one of the most important facts about our world is that middle-class people—above all, middle-class Americans—have lived inside a historical bubble that really has no precedent in the rest of human history. For two, three, almost four generations now, they have not personally experienced the cost of war, have not experienced epidemic disease—in other words, they have lived in an ever-increasing arc not only of personal affluence but of personal longevity and security from accidental death, war, disease, and so on. Now if that were abruptly to come to a halt—to be interrupted by a very bad event, like a pandemic, that begins killing some significant number of middle-class Americans—then obviously all hell is going to break loose.

The one thing I'm firmly convinced of is that the larger, affluent middle classes in this country will never surrender their lifestyle and its privileges. If suddenly faced with a threat in which they may be made homeless by disaster, or killed by plagues, I think you can expect very, very irrational reactions—which of course will inscribe themselves in a spatial order, and probably in spectacular ways. I think one thing that would emerge after an avian flu pandemic, if it does occur, will be a lot of focus on bio-security at the level of domestic space.

BLDGBLOG: Duct tape and plastic sheeting.

Davis: Sure.

BLDGBLOG: Shifting focus a bit, do you see any intentional, organized systems of self-government emerging in the slums? Is there a slum "mayor," for instance, or a kind of slum city hall? In other words, with whom would a non-military power negotiate in the first place?

Davis: Organization in the slums is, of course, extraordinarily diverse. In the same city—for instance, in a large Latin American city—you'll find everything from Pentecostal churches to *Sendero Luminoso,* to reformist organizations and neoliberal NGOs [nongovernmental organizations]. Over very short periods of time there are rapid swings in popularity from one to the other and back. It's very difficult to find a directionality in that, or to predict where things might go.

But what is clear, over the last decade, is that the poor—and not just the poor in classical urban neighborhoods, but the poor who, for a long time, have been organized in left-wing parties, or religious groups, or populist parties—this new poor, on the fringes of the city, have been organizing themselves massively over the last decade. You have to be struck by both the number and the political importance of some of these emerging movements, whether that's Sadr, in Iraq, or an equivalent slum-based social movement in Buenos Aires. Clearly, in the last decade, there have been dramatic increases in the organization of the urban poor, who are making new and, in some cases, unprecedented demands for political and economic participation.

The other part of your question concerns the *politics* of poor cities. I'm sure that somebody could write a book arguing that one of the great developments of the last 10 or 15 years has been increased democratization in many cities. For instance, in cities that did not have consolidated governments, or where mayors were appointed by a central administration, you now have elections, and elected mayors—like in Mexico City. What's so striking, in almost all of these cases, is that even where there's increased formal democracy—where more people are voting—those votes actually have little consequence. That's for two reasons: One is because the fiscal systems of big cities in the Third World are, with few exceptions, so regressive and corrupt, with so few resources, that it's almost impossible to redistribute those

resources to voting people. The second reason is that, in so many cities—India is a great example of this—when you have more populist or participatory elections, the real power is simply transferred into executive agencies, industrial authorities, and development authorities of all kinds, which tend to be local vehicles for World Bank investment. Those agencies are almost entirely out of the control of the local people. They may even be appointed by the state or by a provisional—sometimes national—government.

This means that the democratic path to control over cities—and, above all, control over resources for urban reform—remains incredibly elusive in most places.

BLDGBLOG: Has this transformed our conceptions of sovereignty, territory, and even citizenship?

Davis: That's a very interesting question. Clearly, though, what's happened with globalization has *not* been the transcendence of the nation-state by the corporation, or by new, higher-level entities. What we've seen is much more of a loss of sovereignty on some levels—and the reinforcement of sovereignty on others.

Obviously, the whole process of Structural Adjustment in the 1980s meant the ceding of much local sovereignty and powers of local government to the international bodies that administer debt. The World Bank, for example, working with NGOs, creates networks that often dilute local sovereignty. A brilliant example of this problem is actually what's happening right now in New Orleans: All the expert commissions, and the oversight boards, and the off-site authorities that are being proposed will basically destroy popular government in New Orleans, reducing the city council to a figurehead and transferring power back to the traditional elite. And that's all in the name of fighting corruption and so on.

But whether you'll see new kinds of supranational entities emerge depends, I think, on the country. Obviously some countries are strengthening their national positions—the state remains all important—while other countries have effectively lost all sovereignty. I mean, look at an extreme case, like Haiti.

Untitled, Bay Bridge (2007) by Alexis Tjian. alexistjian.com

BLDGBLOG: And how are these shifts being accounted for in the geopolitical and military analyses you mentioned earlier?

Davis: The problem that military planners, and some geopoliticians, are talking about is actually something quite different: that's the emergence, in hundreds of both little and major nodes across the world, of essentially autonomous slums governed by ethnic militias, gangs, transnational crime, and so on. This is something the Pentagon is obviously very interested in, and concerned about, with Mogadishu as a kind of prototype example. The ongoing crisis of the Third World city is producing almost feudalized patterns of large slum neighborhoods that are effectively terrorist or criminal mini-states—rogue micro-sovereignties. That's the view of the Pentagon and of Pentagon planners. They also seem quite alarmed by the fact that the peri-urban slums—the slums on the edges of cities—lack clear hierarchies. Even more difficult, from a planning perspective, there's very little available data. The slums are

kind of off the radar screen. They therefore become the equivalent of rain forest, or jungle: difficult to penetrate, impossible to control.

I think there are fairly smart Pentagon thinkers who don't see this so much as a question of regions, or categories of nation-states, so much as *holes*, or enclaves within the system. One of the best things I ever read about this was actually William Gibson's novel *Virtual Light*. Gibson proposes that, in a world where giant multinational capital is supreme, there are places that simply aren't valuable to the world economy anymore—they don't reproduce capital—and so those spaces are shunted aside. A completely globalized system, in Gibson's view, would *leak space*—it would have internal redundancies—and one of those spaces, in *Virtual Light*, is the San Francisco Bay Bridge.

But, sure, this is a serious geopolitical and military problem: If you conduct basically a triage of the world's human population—where some people are exiled from the world economy, and some spaces no longer have roles—then you're offering up ideal opportunities for other

people to step in and organize those spaces
to their own ends. This is a deeper and more
profound situation than any putative conflicts
of civilization. It is, in a way, a very unexpected
end to the 20th century. Neither classical
Marxism, nor any other variety of social theory
or neoliberal economics, ever predicted that
such a large fraction of humanity would live in
cities and yet basically outside all the formal
institutions of the world economy.

You'll never reconquer these parts of the city
simply through surveillance, or military invasion,
or policing—you have to offer the people some
way to reconnect with the world economy. Until
you can provide resources, or jobs, the danger is
that this will worsen. People are being thrown
back onto tribal and ethnic clientelism of one
kind or another as a means of survival—even as
a means of excluding other poor people from
these already limited resources. Increasingly,
new arrivals in the city—the sons and daughters
of the urban poor—are being pressed by tighter
housing markets, and by the inability to find
cheap—certainly not *free*—land. Where cheap
land *does* exist, it only exists because the land
is otherwise undevelopable. It's too dangerous.
You're just wagering on natural disaster. In fact,
the end of this frontier of squattable land is one
conclusion of *Planet of Slums*.

Another conclusion is that almost all the
research on informal urban economies has
shown that informality is simply not generating
job ladders. Sure, some microentrepreneurs
go on to become minientrepreneurs—but the
larger fact is you're just subdividing poverty.
You're getting more and more people competing, trying to pursue the same survival strate-
gies in the same place. Those are the facts that
darken this book the most, I think. They're
also what darken the horizon of research on
the city in general, even more than questions
of sanitation and so on. What the World Bank,
what the NGOs, what all the apostles of neoliberal self-help depend on is the availability
of cheap, squattable land, and the existence of
entrepreneurial opportunities in the informal
sector. If you exhaust those two, people will
be driven to the wall—and then the safety
valves won't work. Then the urban poor will
run out of resources for miracles.

The Museum of Assassination

Leaving aside the question of whether or not it was the real deal, the window through which JFK was assassinated was purchased on eBay for more than $3 million. "The starting price was just $100,000," Justin Webb of the BBC reported back in February 2007, "but bidding was brisk, and the item eventually fetched $3,001,501." Why was it available for purchase at all? Well, apparently, "the window of the Dallas building was removed shortly after the assassination because people were stealing bits of it." They presumably took those bits home as macabre souvenirs—latter-day relics, perhaps enshrined in secret temples to American history next to devotional photographs of Elizabeth Taylor and Marilyn Monroe.

No one is entirely sure, however, if this particular window is authentic; for instance, the BBC mentions a few "conspiracy theorists" who say that it cannot possibly be the real window—after all, they claim, "a man from Tennessee bought the building years ago and

took the window with him when he left town." No one knows what he did with it next—which just adds to the mystery. Perhaps you've even looked through it while visiting your parents' neighbors in Memphis; or perhaps you saw a man with a Tennessee accent hanging out at a gas station in New Mexico, and he was transporting a large window in the back of his minivan. Looking closely, you saw that it was secured with several padlocks—and the man was carrying a stun gun... Perhaps this mysterious dealer in architectural fragments is actually amassing items for a museum of his own—a Museum of Assassination—in which pieces of architecture, historical documents, and associated weaponry will all be put on display. A complete, hyperrealistic simulation of Dealey Plaza is being constructed out back.

But what all of this actually made me think of was New York artist Gordon Matta-Clark and his project "Bronx Floors." To produce these artworks, Matta-Clark "would chainsaw large circles or other shapes in abandoned buildings and exhibit both a photograph of the building after the operation *and the parts that had been removed,*" William Zimmer wrote in

the *New York Times* [emphasis added]. In other words, many of the "objects" that Matta-Clark displayed in New York City art galleries were actually decontextualized fragments of existing buildings—including, of course, several Bronx floors. These mobile pieces of real architecture—a fever of walls and floors on the loose in New York City—became instant works of sculpture, somewhere between a ready-made object, archaeological remains, and a new kind of found architecture.

What's interesting about the JFK window, at least in this context, is that it seems to have become a Matta-Clark "building cut" if there ever was one. Perhaps we might even find that Gordon Matta-Clark never died of cancer—in fact, he moved to Tennessee, only to purchase, years later, a certain building in Dallas, Texas…

On the other hand, the auctioning off of JFK's fatal window also opens up the possibility that we could chainsaw, chisel, or otherwise reclaim—in other words, steal—historically important bits of architecture, removing them from their original contexts and exhibiting them elsewhere. The balcony over which Michael Jackson dangled his baby in Berlin;

the terrace from which Juliet addressed Romeo; the windows through which administrators were defenestrated in Prague. Perhaps we could even reassemble these architectural fragments into a complete, if eclectic, and quite controversial new building—add the JFK window as the *coup de grâce*, and you've got a 21st-century version of Sir John Soane's Museum. But, of course, archaeology is full of such acts of structural burglary. Whole temples and friezes and doorways and rooms have been removed and transported elsewhere. Just ask Lord Elgin—or, for that matter, ask the Getty.

In light of all this, then, are we witnessing some new Lord Elgin of the 21st century, raised on the novels of J. G. Ballard, as he or she begins a new quest to collect pieces of architectural morbidity? The sale of JFK's window would thus be the opening salvo in this death-obsessed archaeology of tomorrow.

↑ previous page
Parking Lot 1 (2007) by Emiliano Granado.

↑ this page
Parking Lot 2 (2007) by Emiliano Granado.

emilianogranado.com

The Cloud

I found myself sitting outside one day in Los Angeles, intrigued by a huge brown cloud that seemed to hover there, more or less stationary, above the parking lot beside me. The cloud was totally alone, surrounded on all sides by perfectly blue sky, as if a thunderstorm had rolled in only to change its mind and drift off, leaving part of itself behind, atmospherically orphaned in the sunlight. After all, there was no rain. The cloud didn't appear to be moving. I began to expect an earthquake.

"Is there a fire or something?" I asked a guy wearing sunglasses as he walked past me on the sidewalk. It occurred to me, though, absurdly, even as I heard myself asking it, that perhaps the cloud would be impossible to see through his sunglasses: its color would be visually filtered out by the glass's brown tint and so he wouldn't even know what I was talking about. Instead, he just nodded and said, "Uh huh," walking off past Radio Shack.

Noticing at that point that not a single other person was looking up into the sky at what seemed, at least to me, to be a very obvious and possibly threatening brown cloud, I decided that people here really must be so blasé and over-trustful of the world that even a menacing, oily blur above their heads could simply be perceptually filed away as some weird but harmless fluke: It'll go away—it won't be here tomorrow—so you can just forget it ever happened.... Don't think about it and it won't harm you.

Which is when I remembered the "airborne toxic event" from Don DeLillo's 1985 novel *White Noise*.

About a third of the way through that book, there is a train derailment somewhere outside a small American college town. The accident releases a toxic cloud into the sky: "the smoke was plainly visible," we read, "a heavy black mass hanging in the air beyond the river, more or less shapeless." One of the characters says it resembles "a shapeless growing thing. A dark black breathing thing of smoke."

Families close to the accident are almost immediately asked to evacuate—"Abandon all domiciles," an amplified voice calls out, broadcast from a truck that drives around through cul-de-sacs—while "medical problems" that might develop upon "personal contact with the airborne toxic event" are discussed on the radio. One of these problems is apparently déjà vu.

The source of the cloud, meanwhile, is being buried by snow machines, in the weird hope that this will thermochemically contain its spread; and so an artificial winter begins to erupt as rogue flakes blow on contaminated winds through the suburbs.

At one point the drifting cloud becomes an all-out military spectacle:

A few minutes later, back on the road, we saw a remarkable and startling sight. It appeared in the sky ahead of us and to the left, prompting us to lower ourselves in our seats, bend our heads for a clearer view, exclaim to each other in half finished phrases. It was the black billowing cloud, the airborne toxic event, lighted by the clear beams of seven army helicopters. They were tracking its windborne movement, keeping it in view. In every car, heads shifted, drivers blew their horns to alert others, faces appeared in side windows, expressions set in tones of outlandish wonderment.

The enormous dark mass moved like some death ship in a Norse legend, escorted across the night by armored creatures with spiral wings. We weren't sure how to react.

Returning to that bench in Los Angeles where I sat, looking up at a brown cloud that seemed oddly rooted in place there above a parking lot—with no one else visibly concerned, no one else appearing to wonder what on earth it was that had come to visit us that day, there in the atmosphere, shadowing us, perhaps some strange and voidlike aerial inversion set to suck away the very oxygen we breathed—I learned that the whole thing was just the downwind result of a fire in the Hollywood Hills, an event I had otherwise managed to miss seeing entirely, not being a local news follower.

So much for the sublime or the inexplicable or the mysterious. I went back to reading, and the cloud blew away.

The Military Sublime:
An Interview with
Simon Norfolk

As photographer Simon Norfolk claims in the following interview, his work documents an international "military sublime." His photos reveal half-collapsed buildings, destroyed cinemas, and depopulated urban ruins in diagonal shafts of morning sunlight—from Iraq to Rwanda, Bosnia to Afghanistan—before venturing further afield into more distant, and surprising, landscapes of modern war. These include the sterile, climate-controlled rooms of military command centers, and the gargantuan supercomputers that both design and simulate nuclear war.

Norfolk himself writes:

These photographs form chapters in a larger project attempting to understand how war, and the need to fight war, has formed our world: how so many of the spaces we occupy; the technologies we use; and the ways we understand ourselves, are created by military conflict.

He reminds us that "anybody interested in the effects of war quickly becomes an expert in ruins."

Norfolk's written work delivers crisp and often stunning insights about urban design and historical landscapes. Also on Norfolk's website we read:

What these "landscapes" have in common—their fundamental basis in war—is always downplayed in our society. I was astounded to discover that the long, straight, bustling, commercial road that runs through my neighborhood of London follows an old Roman road. In places the Roman stones are still buried beneath the modern tarmac. Crucially, it needs to be understood that the road system built by the Romans was their highest military technology, their equivalent of the stealth bomber or the Apache helicopter—a technology that allowed a huge empire to be maintained by a relatively small

army, that could move quickly and safely along these paved, all-weather roads. It is extraordinary that London, a city that ought to be shaped by Tudor kings, the British Empire, Victorian engineers, and modern international finance, is a city fundamentally drawn, even to this day, by abandoned Roman military hardware.

Simon Norfolk: All of the work that I've been doing over the last five years is about warfare and the way war makes the world we live in. War shapes and designs our society. The landscapes that I look at are created by warfare and conflict. This is particularly true in Europe. I went to the city of Cologne, for instance, and the city of Cologne was built by Charlemagne—but Cologne has the shape that it does today because of the abilities and non-abilities of a Lancaster Bomber. It comes from what a Lancaster can do and what a Lancaster can't do. What it *cannot* do is fly deep into Germany in the middle of the day and pinpoint-bomb a ball-bearing factory. What it can do is fly to places that are quite near to England, that are five miles across, on a bend in the river, under moonlight, and then hit them with large amounts of high explosive. And if you do that, you end up with a city that looks like Cologne—the way the city's *shaped*.

So I started off in Afghanistan photographing literal battlefields—but I'm trying to stretch that idea of what a battlefield *is*. Because all the interesting money now—the new money, the *exciting* stuff—is about entirely new realms of warfare: inside cyberspace, inside parts of the electromagnetic spectrum: eavesdropping, intelligence, satellite warfare, imaging. This is where all the exciting stuff is going to happen in 20 years' time. So I wanted to stretch that idea of what a battleground could be. What is a landscape—a surface, an environment, a space—created by war?

BLDGBLOG: Which led you to photograph supercomputers?

Norfolk: Those supercomputers—IBM's BlueGene, in particular—are battlegrounds. BlueGene is designing and thinking about a space that is only about 30 cm across and

exists for about a billionth of a second, and that's an exploding nuclear warhead. BlueGene is thinking about and modeling that space very intensely, because what happens there is very complicated. That computer is as much a battlefield as a place in Afghanistan is, full of bullet holes.

BLDGBLOG: Your photos are usually unpopulated. Is that a conscious artistic choice, or do you just happen to be photographing these places when no one's around?

Norfolk: Well, part of this interest of mine in the sublime means that a lot of the artistic ideas that I'm drawing on partly come out of the photography of ruins. When I was in Afghanistan photographing these places—photographing these ruins—I started looking at some of the very earliest photojournalists, and they were *ruin* photographers: Mathew Brady's pictures of battlefields at Gettysburg, or Roger Fenton's pictures from the Crimea. And there are no dead bodies. Well, there *are* dead bodies, but that's very controversial—the corpses were arranged, etc.

But a lot of those photographers were, in turn, drawing upon ideas from 17th-century and 18th-century French landscape painting—European landscape painting. Claude Lorrain. Nicolas Poussin. Ruins have a very particular meaning in those pictures. They're about the folly of human existence; they're about the foolishness of empire. Those ruins of Claude Lorrain's: it's a collapsed Roman temple, and what he's saying is that the greatest empires that were ever built—the empire of Rome, the Catholic church—these things have fallen down to earth. They all fall into ivy eventually. So all the empires they could see being built in their own lifetimes—the British empire, the French empire, the Dutch empire—they were saying: Look, all of this is crap. None of this is really permanent. All of these things rise and fall and, in the long run, all of this is bullshit.

I wanted to try to copy some motifs from those paintings—in particular, that amazing golden light that someone like Claude Lorrain always used. Even when he does a painting called *Midday*, it's bathed in this beautiful, golden light. To do that as a photographer, I can't invent it like a painter can; I have to take the photographs very early in the morning. So they're all shot at 4 a.m.

It is partly because of that that people aren't there—but it's also…for me, I think people kind of gobble up the photograph. They become what the photograph *is*. For me, the people just aren't that important; it's about this panoptic process, it's about this kind of eavesdropping, it's about this ability to look into every aspect of our lives. And I think if you put people into these pictures, I don't know—it would draw viewers away. It would draw viewers into the story *of the people*. It's not about, you know, Bob who runs the radar dome; it's about this thing that looks inside your e-mail program, and listens to this phone call, and listens to every phone call in the world in every language, and washes it through computer programs. And if you say *plutonium nerve gas* bomb to me over the telephone, in an instant this computer is looking at what Web pages you've been to recently, it's looking at your credit card bills, it's looking at your health records, it's looking at the books you check out of the library. That's what frightens me—it's not about: here's *Dave, he works on the computer systems for Raytheon.*

BLDGBLOG: In fact, it often seems like the most interesting thing about these sites is exactly what *cannot* be photographed.

Norfolk: Absolutely—absolutely. That's why, whenever you see warfare now, it's photographed in that same dreary, clichéd way: it's metal boxes rolling across the desert. Every time you switch on CNN, or buy a newspaper, you see guys in metal boxes—because that looks good. These photojournalists, and these TV crews, they don't explain the process: they show things that look good on TV. A satellite orbiting in space doesn't look good. A submarine—you know, the greatest platform we've ever built for launching nuclear weapons and for surveillance—has no presence whatsoever in how most people understand what the military does today.

The same is true of electromagnetic stuff—information warfare, cyber-warfare—and I wonder what photojournalists of the future are going to photograph? Are they still going to photograph guys with guns, shooting at each other? Because quite soon there aren't going to *be* guys with guns shooting at each other. We're getting to the era of unmanned aerial vehicles, and people aren't even going to know what shot them—and there will be nothing to photograph.

Look at the way the war in Afghanistan was photographed: what you got was a guy on a ridge in a turban watching a very, very far away explosion. That was war photography! That was the way the Afghan war was covered. What worries me is that, if these wars become invisible, then they will cease to exist in the popular imagination. I'm very worried that, because these things become invisible—people don't seem to be bothered.

But, you know, wouldn't it be amazing to have a series of portraits printed of missile systems, but you photographed them the way you'd photograph a BMW? [*laughter*] You get them straight off the production line in the factory, and then you polish them, and you wax them—so they're just beautiful—and then you light them the way you would an Audi TT, with a black background, and you shoot them on a big camera. Just gorgeous—sculptural. Then the caption says, you know: *Predator Drone. Hellfire Missile. Nuclear Warhead.*

↑ page 108

Top: The Mare Nostrum supercomputer sits inside a deconsecrated chapel in Spain.

Bottom: A semi-destroyed cinema in Kabul, Afghanistan, shows the very visible traces of war.

↑ pages 110-111

Top left: King Amanullah's Victory Arch in Kabul, built in 1919 to celebrate independence from the British.

Top right: Norfolk's travels have taken him to Ascension Island, in the South Atlantic, from which the global ECHELON surveillance system, run by the United States, is partly operated. Strange antennas dot the landscape of this sparsely populated volcanic island.

Bottom left: A "victory arch" constructed by the Northern Alliance in Afghanistan. In the distance can be seen the caves that once housed the giant Buddha statues of Bamiyan—statues destroyed by the Taliban in 2001.

Bottom right: Ascension Island.

↑ pages 112-113

Top left: Rashid Street in Baghdad, photographed in April 2003.

Top right: The Ministry of Planning in Baghdad, photographed in April 2003.

Bottom left: TERA-1 supercomputer.

Bottom right: "Modeling physics inside an exploding nuclear warhead."

All images by Simon Norfolk, courtesy of the photographer.

simonnorfolk.com

REI

The Northern Lights in Iceland, photographed by Örvar Atli Þorgeirsson.

pbase.com/orvaratli
flickr.com/photos/orvaratli/

3

ESIGNING THE SKY

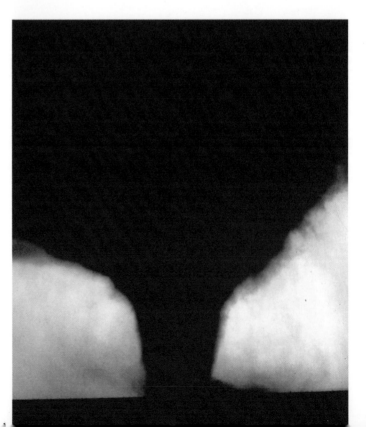

Images courtesy of the NOAA Photo
Library, NOAA National Weather Ser-
vice (NWS) Collection, and the NOAA
Central Library; OAR/ERL/National
Severe Storms Laboratory (NSSL).

Top left: A waterspout off the Florida
Keys, photographed by Steve Nicklas
(1969).

Top right: Tornado south of Dimmitt,
Texas, photographed by Harald
Richter (1995).

Bottom: Tornado in Seymour, Texas,
photographed by D. Burgess (1979).

photolib.noaa.gov

WHEN CITIES RUN OUT of ways to attract new residents, perhaps they'll turn to *weather control*: producing storms on demand or clearing the skies of clouds. Rain will be as easy to schedule as a weekend football game. Vast dehumidifiers on the roofs of Manhattan high-rises will turn even muggy summer nights into pleasant evenings out. In an attempt to emulate Jupiter's famous Great Red Spot, perhaps some rogue adventure tourism firm will set up a series of repurposed airplane engines and start a permanent storm deep in some distant mountain valley. Tourists will come from all over the world. If we can have designer landscapes and designer buildings—not to mention designer clothes and designer cuisines and designer prosthetic organs—then how far away can we be from *designer climates*? It's often said in architectural circles that the space between buildings is too quickly overlooked; that those spaces are disregarded as mere landscapes, best left to urban design. But the space between buildings is also *the weather*. The space between buildings is where *climate* takes place. Climate is thus open to architectural design.

For your 50th birthday, your finally appreciative children hire the hottest thing in town: a climatologist. He takes ten days to set up, but then there you are, grilling red meat and peppers on the back patio, while patented cloud forms take shape in the sky above you. The climatologist stands in front of what appears to be a theremin, waving his hands around as if to hypnotize something—and suddenly there is snow falling on your hamburger buns. You laugh—and say, *stop it, that's good bread, and you should remember who's paying you.*

We saw this in Beijing, for instance, when the 2008 Olympics took on the character of a *Gesamtkunstwerk*—a total work of art in which even the television commentators joked that every minute of good weather and sunlight had been brought to you by the Chinese government. *We can already change the weather*—sometimes intentionally, though mostly accidentally and with disastrous results. But perhaps all weather will soon be planned. Perhaps we will formally declare war on the atmosphere, like some long-lost Greek myth. Perhaps we might even win.

THE WEATHER BOWL

In the fall of 2006, I attended a talk at the MAK Center in West Hollywood. The MAK Center is a house designed in 1922 by Rudolf Schindler, with surprisingly low ceilings, and it's become something of a touchstone for midcentury California modernism. Now run by a private foundation based in Austria, the MAK is part gallery, part gathering place, part architectural museum that exhibits itself.

Architect Karl Chu was there as part of the day's panel discussion, and in the midst of his talk he explained that he was not interested in constructing mere buildings—he wanted to design whole continents and weather systems, artificial climates and storms.

Which got me thinking.

Given time, some digging equipment, a bit of geotechnical expertise, and loads of money, could you turn the entirety of greater Los Angeles into a *weather bowl*? It could be dedicated to the re-creation of famous storms—a new spectacle. Millions of people would get together each year to watch historical re-creations of old weather. You'd install some wind tunnels and rotating fans around Silver Lake, build some deflection screens in the Hollywood Hills, scatter smaller fans and blowers throughout Culver City or Burbank, and amplify the natural sea winds funneling in over Long Beach. You could thus reenact the most notorious weather systems of the 19th century or even earlier: bring back, for one night, the Mediterranean storm that killed Shelley.

Weather control is the future of urban design. Engineering the climate is how we'll make our cities interesting again.

Consult your table of weather histories, choose your storm, and lo! Fans deep in hillsides start turning, wind tunnels roar, and the exact speed and direction of Hurricane Andrew is unleashed. Then you rewind and start again—creating Cyclone Nargis midway through. Storm after storm, atmospherically mixed by a DJ in the skies above Los Angeles. Seed the clouds a bit and reprogram the fans, and you can precisely re-create the skies from the night William Blake was born. Or the ice storm that leveled electrical gantries outside Montreal in the mid-1990s, now whirling in a snow-blurred haze through Echo Park. Internet use plummets; people just watch the sky.

Competing weather colosseums could be built in London, San Francisco, Tokyo, and Beijing. Every night new storms are reenacted, moving upward in scale and complexity. The storm Goethe saw as a 19-year-old, contemplating European history, kills a family of six outside Nanking. This is then blurred imperceptibly into the tropical storm Charles Darwin once saw raging offshore in the Galapagos—and weather interpreters, a

URBAN ATMOSPHERES

It was reported in 2006 that Chinese authorities had become worried about the hundreds of new, video game-like skyscrapers being constructed in Shanghai; the buildings, it seems, had begun to produce and concentrate high winds. Warming to the role of architecture critic, government figures actually "identified skyscrapers as one of the biggest potential threats to the city," according to a report in *CRI News*. The article went on to explain that Shanghai city planners have suggested that more trees should be planted "to block part of the winds," and that "the walls of the buildings should be fortified while notice signs are put up to signal potentially dangerous areas." Engineering an urban microclimate through landscape architecture.

THE STORM ROOM

Instead of TV, you can watch 3D reconstructions of ancient storms (in surround-sound). It's the immersive, weather-reconstructive home cinema of the future. In May 2007, *New Scientist* reported that researchers—and burgeoning home storm aficionados—will one day "be able to visually recreate past typhoons, hurricanes and cyclones, then stand in the middle and watch as the weather pattern swirls around them." It's the *storm room*: a "simulator that crunches real storm data and turns it into 3D images that can be viewed with virtual-reality goggles." A new kind of teenage rebellion breaks out in the suburbs of middle America: angry 16-year-olds program tropical storms onto the walls of their bedrooms. Parents faint with vertigo.

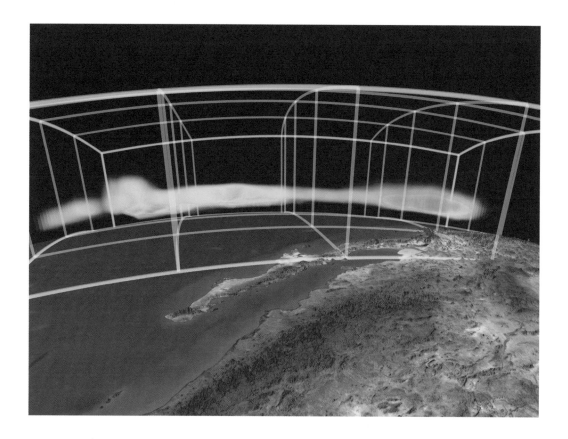

The geometry of thunder as a storm
approaches Southern California:
Image courtesy of NASA/JPL–Caltech/
GSFC/Goddard Scientific Visualization
Studio. According to the website *Earth
Observatory*, "NASA's Atmospheric
Infrared Sounder instrument is able
to peel back cloud cover to reveal
3-D structure of a storm's water vapor
content, information that scientists
can use to improve weather forecast
models."

svs.gsfc.nasa.gov
earthobservatory.nasa.gov

new class of media pundit, immediately realize that something is being said here about the intellectual history of Western humanism.

It gets to the point where no one trusts the real weather. One day, the Weather Bowl is down for maintenance, but a dust storm rolls through…and people run out into the streets, cheering. They love it. The stock market soars. Don DeLillo writes a novel about it and wins the National Book Award. Had everyone known that it was natural, no one would have cared.

Then thirty-three days in a row of spectacular, cloudless weather hits San Francisco, and a mysterious note shows up on the mayor's door: *This weather brought to you by Climate Services. Pay up or we'll bring back the fog.*

Soon we get Weather Olympics, and a new Pritzker Prize for Best Weather Effects. Cities try to attract new residents by hosting storm festivals every summer, colliding hurricanes with blizzards like a gladiatorial tournament in the sky above the heads of amazed crowds—who have purchased anti-hail insurance along with their family-price tickets. Subsidiary storm economies grow. The Super Bowl is cancelled for lack of interest.

AURORA BRITANNICA

Manipulating the weather to serve up tourist entertainment is one thing; but what about *space weather*? Perhaps we could control that, too.

For instance, the northern lights are on the move: "The Earth's north magnetic pole is drifting away from North America so fast that it could end up in Siberia within 50 years," the BBC reported in December 2005. "The shift could mean that Alaska will lose its northern lights, or auroras, which might then be more visible in areas of Siberia and Europe"—including, of course, in cities, where the northern lights might soon be coiling above cathedrals, bus routes, and sidewalk cafes, visible through stained glass, reflecting in the windshields of parked cars.

Auroras have already been spotted as far south as Rome, crackling above the Pantheon; following these recent, accelerating movements of the earth's magnetic field, Roman auroras may soon occur every night. Hotel rates will skyrocket. Like the old moon-viewing platforms mentioned in medieval Japanese poetry, we'll have aurora rooms where hammocks sway gently beneath crackling tides of green light.

It'd be interesting, then, as an architectural project, if you could build a tower of some sort, or a superstadium full of ring magnets, that would attract—and trap—the Earth's north magnetic pole. The pole would be permanently anchored there

MAN TRAINS FOR BIG NIGHT; THINS AIR IN HOUSE
According to the December 25, 2006, issue of *Sports Illustrated*, Gilbert Arenas of the NBA "hired a company to reduce the oxygen content in his house." This will allow him to "train under high-altitude conditions similar to those in Colorado." Interviewed by the *Washington Post*'s sports blog, Arenas claimed "that 'at least 14 players' have contacted him about having the same simulated conditions" installed in their houses—and this includes "the whole Chicago Bulls team," who now want "to get that in their homes." But ESPN's headline says it best: ARENAS SORRY FOR TEAM USA VENT; THINS AIR IN HOUSE. What I want to know is: If you did this to someone without them knowing, would it be illegal? And what would such a crime be called? Aerial larceny? Nonconsensual atmospheric alteration?

by this superstadium; its terrestrial migration—and ultimate reversal—would stop. The stadium would hum quietly, and all compasses would point toward it. Massive sheets of auroral light would torque downward every night at high speed—breaking away at the last minute to fold off toward the suburbs. You could stand on your roof and drink beer with your mates. Forget fireworks.

And it's not impossible. For instance: "Powerful radio waves beamed up into the sky have created artificially enhanced auroras visible to the naked eye," *New Scientist* wrote in February 2005.

> Todd Pedersen from the Air Force Research Laboratory in Massachusetts and Elizabeth Gerken of Cornell University in Ithaca, New York, have created emissions of "unprecedented brightness," using pulses of radio waves sent from a base station in Alaska. "The beam is more like a flashlight than a laser," says Pedersen. "The total power is about the same as large shortwave transmitters like the BBC's."

They just need to attach some radio transmitters to the tops of London's tallest skyscrapers, and every night the city's skyline will be bathed in swirling auroras.... Crackling wisps of a green-and-blue—and orange-and-red and yellow-and-white—ionized atmosphere will form snakelike rolling arcs and curtains between the mirrored outer walls of bank towers; ships at sea will see a city gone haloed and prismatic. The International Space Station floats over an Earth of urban auroras—London, Shanghai, Cairo...

It's the *Project for a New North Pole*.

THE AEOLIAN REEF

On the other hand, we needn't always *create* new forms of weather; we can also prevent certain climates from happening at all. We could pinpoint certain meteorological events and stop them. And we could do it through architecture.

In December 2006, a tornado swept through northwest London: "At least six people were injured and hundreds left homeless," the *Guardian* reported, "when the tornado swept through Kensal Rise at around 11 a.m., tearing the roofs and walls off houses. Eyewitnesses said it lasted for up to 40 seconds; one man said he heard a sound 'like standing behind a jetliner.'" It was a "genuine twister," the *Times* wrote. And though tornadoes of this kind are surprisingly frequent in the UK, the event should be taken as a "warning," the *Guardian* suggests, "that such weather events are likely to increase in frequency because of global warming." For instance:

AIRBORNE GEOLOGY
One of many interesting things in Alan Weisman's book *The World Without Us* is his rhetorical approach to the industrial burning of fossil fuel. He refers to burning oil and coal as a way of "tapping the Carboniferous Formation and spewing it up into the sky." Industrially produced CO_2 is "carbon we have mined from the Earth and loaded into the air." Fossil fuels thus undergo their own secular ascension. Because of this unintentionally aero-geological project, Weisman writes, "[a]mong the human-crafted artifacts that will last the longest after we're gone is our redesigned atmosphere." After all, that atmosphere now has a very large chunk of the Earth's surface in it, storing sunlight and heat. It's as if, Weisman implies, humans have achieved something both dangerous and extraordinary: the installation of a geological formation in the sky.

TROPOSPHERIC RIVERS

According to a 2003 report by Robert A. Nelson, *tropospheric rivers* are "huge filamentary structures" in the sky, a kind of fluted cobwebbing of intercontinental air pressure. Apparently discovered 10 years earlier by MIT's Reginald E. Newell, tropospheric rivers act as "preferable pathways of water vapor movement in the troposphere (the lower 10-20 km of the atmosphere) with flow rates of about 165 million kilograms of water per second. These 'atmospheric rivers' are bands from 200 to 480 miles wide and up to 4,800 miles long, between 1 to 2 kilometers above the earth. They transport about 70% of the fresh water from the equator to the midlatitudes, [and] are of great importance in determining the location and amount of winter rainfall on coastlines." Moisture-trapping towers and vast air wells could thus be built to tap into these rivers, turning the sky itself into an aquatic reservoir. Fog, Scotch mist, and monsoon storms become available on demand.

In July last year, a tornado in Birmingham damaged 1,000 buildings, causing millions of pounds of damage, while a tornado was reported just off Brighton, on the Sussex coast, this October. A mini tornado swept through the village of Bowstreet in Ceredigion, west Wales, last Tuesday. Terence Meaden, the deputy head of the Tornado and Storm Research Organization, said the UK has the highest number of reported tornadoes for its land area of any country in the world.... He added that the UK was especially susceptible to tornados because of its position on the Atlantic seaboard, where polar air from the north pole meets tropical air from the equator.

In which case, I suggest they build the *London Tornadium*: an architectural tornado-attractor. Combining urban design; arched viaducts; smooth, valved walls; steel pipes; and complex internal cavitation like a conch shell, the Tornadium will be a kind of urban-architectural sky-trumpet built for the cancellation of storms.

Warm winds and water vapor from the tropics will hit Arctic fronts outside Ireland, then move down toward the city—where the Tornadium, located perfectly at the vertex of converging streets, will suck storms toward it, defusing their energy (and perhaps even acting as a wind-power plant). It's anti-storm architecture. Could a perfectly engineered great wall of specialty high-rises outside the city—each structure a honeycomb of

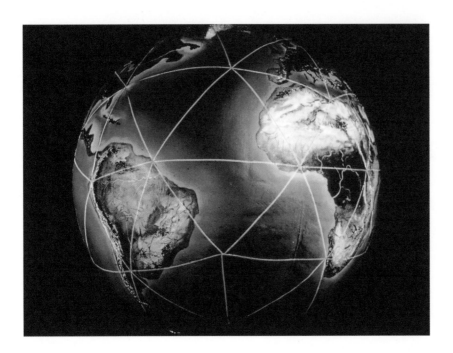

Global satellite triangulation images
from NOAA's Geodesy Collection,
courtesy of the Office of NOAA Corps
Operations (ONCO).

photolib.noaa.gov

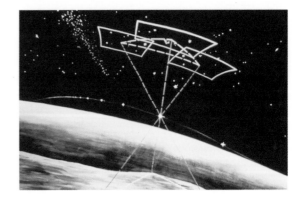

WIND CAVE

On a cross-country drive with my brother in the summer of 1996, we stopped off at Wind Cave in South Dakota.

According to the U.S. National Park Service, before the cave was even found to be a cave at all, it was known by local Native American tribes simply as a "hole that breathes cool air." But then "Cowboys came across [the] breathing hole in 1881 and the exploration of Wind Cave began." These cowboys were brothers Tom and Jesse Bingham: "Jesse reported that it was the sound of the wind coming from the entrance that caught his attention. According to legend he and Tom looked into the hole and the wind coming out was strong enough to blow Tom's hat off of his head." Within six years, the entrance had been widened, explorations had begun, and "by 1887 the cave was said to be 3 miles long and 'no bottom found.'"

Wind Cave is now thought to be the fourth longest cave system in the world—and, at one point, its only visible (or, really, audible) surface feature was a small breathing hole, barely wide enough to fit an arm through, rustling the wild grasses outside.

valved passages—prevent all storms from reaching London...? It'd be a Thames Barrier for the sky: the public infrastructure of airborne defense. After all, urban design can help to create certain atmospheric conditions as much as it can also stifle pre-existing climatic tendencies. Add purpose-engineered architecture to the mix, and you have a city that controls its weather.

After Hurricane Katrina hit New Orleans in September 2005, for instance, I found myself remembering a few lines from Virgil's *Aeneid*, where we read about something called "Aeolia, the weather-breeding isle":

> Here in a vast cavern King Aeolus
> Rules the contending winds and moaning gales
> As warden of their prison. Round the walls
> They chafe and bluster underground. The din
> Makes a great mountain murmur overhead.
> High on a citadel enthroned,
> Scepter in hand, he mollifies their fury,
> Else they might flay the sea and sweep away
> Land masses and deep sky through empty air.
> In fear of this, Jupiter hid them away
> In caverns of black night. He set above them
> Granite of high mountains—and a king
> Empowered at command to rein them in
> Or let them go. (*Book 1, Lines 75–89*)

In other words, King Aeolus stores the major winds of the world deep within well-controlled reservoirs in the rocky bowels of an island—like an atmosphere in reserve, a gaseous pet, domesticated.

Why not build something like this today? It'd be a kind of offshore geotechnical sousaphone, full of vaulted tubes, valves, and twists—metal walls vibrating with the captured winds of tropical storms. A modern-day Aeolia, like an atmospherically active oil derrick, would *negate storms*. It would be a "weather-canceling isle." If you built hundreds of these things, with complex and well-calculated curves in riveted steel, perhaps you could even prevent hurricanes from forming. An entire archipelago of anti-hurricane islands, absorbing proto-storms before they ever leave their low-pressure home.

You'd need, in other words, an *Aeolian Reef.*

The Aeolian Reef would consist of platform-islands built in climatologically influential patterns throughout the Gulf of Mexico and the larger, equatorial Atlantic. The Reef would:

- Trap and redirect high-speed tropical winds, thus preventing hurricanes from forming;

- Provide atmospheric observation platforms far out at sea—including, perhaps, good places to send poets on residential writing fellowships; and

- Be readily exportable to other countries and climates—for instance, to be used as land-based anti-tornado clusters outside London.

The Aeolian Reef would use architecture, or landscape architecture, as a way to influence, change, and redirect the climate. It would be *landscape climatology*.

THE WEATHER EMPERORS

For the most part, climate change is unplanned, uncontrolled, and unpredictable—as are its effects. For instance, one of the most interesting, if unexpected, side effects of global climate change is that the Alps are growing taller. Per the August 19, 2006, issue of *New Scientist*, warmer temperatures have been causing those mountains to "shed the weight of their glaciers," with the result that "the unburdened crust beneath them is rebounding, causing the mountain range to rise slowly." Mont Blanc, for instance, "where the melting is fastest, is growing by as much as 0.9 millimeters per year due to climate change." Less than one millimeter per year doesn't sound like much—but these deep and shuddering geological adjustments are already having big effects elsewhere, such as increasing the rate of seismic activity throughout the Alpine region (with parts of the mountains themselves literally shattering as old faults decompress). Amazingly, this Alpine growth spurt has also begun to alter wind patterns flowing across the greater European landmass—but, then, the tectonic birth of the Himalayas, with India grinding north into Asia, also affected the global climate. There has even been conjecture that the water-heavy winds of the southeast Asian monsoon season actually *slow down the earth's rotation* when they collide with the Himalayas, like wind trapped in a giant sail. In other words, augmented by these Super Alps, the weather will begin to change even faster—feeding back yet more and changing the very tectonic structure of the continent.

Meanwhile, one of the more interesting—if commonsensical—discoveries of recent years has been that cities are substantially hotter than the surrounding countryside, often by as much as 10 degrees. The built environment simply absorbs more heat than the natural landscape, with roads, parking lots, roofs of buildings, etc., all baking slowly in the afternoon sunlight. Add to that the mechanical systems of buildings and the

TO MAKE THE WIND CHIMES IN YOUR BASEMENT RING

One day I began playing around with the windows in my car and noticed that, when the passenger window was down, air coming in on the driver's side became more violent, whipping through the car and joining the wind on the other side—but when both back windows were open, air coming through the driver's window actually *decreased*, as air pressure was distributed among all the windows equally. (This made it easier to hear the radio.) So what if I drove past another car that had all *its* windows down but in different positions: What would happen to the wind blowing into my car?

I've seen the same thing inside houses: you leave a window in the bathroom open and closet doors nearby slam shut. Again, it's all air pressure. But then, if you open up the windows on the opposite side of the house, some sort of air tunnel develops, because different doors move, cupboards stay closed, and a free home-ventilation system is in effect for the whole afternoon.

An infinite experiment could ensue: Open up some windows in combination with other windows (vary until exhausted), leave certain doors in the house open, others closed (vary as necessary), and soon you'll be caught up in a huge architectural pneumatics experiment. You could even hang wind chimes at select points in the house and see what combinations of windows and doors need to be open or closed, and in what order, to get your wind chimes to jingle. Or you could hide wind chimes in the attic, or down in the basement, and have a contest: Whoever figures out the right combination of windows and doors (you could even include the chimney and strategically placed rotating fans) that jingles the attic wind chimes wins.

What if your next-door neighbors (who live upwind, of course) are mucking about with their own windows and doors, affecting the speed and direction of the wind in your experiment? And don't forget that your neighbors have neighbors, and *their* neighbors have neighbors—and, if you live near a highway, maybe you will need to consider all of this.

Maybe you discover that the only way to make the wind chimes in your basement ring is for a neighbor who lives within 200 feet of your house to have his upstairs windows open (as well as his front door), the little fan in your living room to be turned on, an 18-wheeler on a nearby highway to be driving by at 65 miles an hour, and a large bird to flap its wings within 10 feet of the truck's windshield. Then, and only then, can you make the wind chimes in your basement ring.

MACHINE WEATHER

In April 2007, *New Scientist* reported that "shape-shifting 'smart dust' may explore alien worlds." Thousands of miniscule wireless sensors, or "smart dust," could one day be used to explore other planets. These individual pieces of "smart dust" will "navigate by shape-shifting," drifting in artificial clouds of nanotechnology. The implications are that machines may someday form entire weather fronts, with their own microclimates and atmospheric effects—someday there might be a summer storm on Mars formed entirely by machines.

engines of countless cars, and the temperature difference is not hard to account for. This is the appropriately named *urban heat island effect*—and urban heat islands can strongly impact the local weather. Not only can they increase the moisture content and intensity of thunderstorms, they can affect climates even dozens of miles downwind. Chicago can affect the weather in northern Indiana, and Miami can affect the weather out at sea. So if it's raining in your hometown tonight, perhaps you should blame the nearest city.

But this also leads me to wonder if there is a particular patch of sea somewhere outside New York City where the winds are stronger, or the waves more violent, or the rain more extreme—all due to the complex downwind effects of Manhattan. If New York has a *climatic presence* in the north central Atlantic, then the city should be rethought as a kind of storm valve, changing the weather for distant ships. The Department of Public Works could even go so far as to attach wind mirrors to every building in the city, thus producing an artificial microclimate…and then rearrange them all so that high-powered, hurricane-like winds blow northeast, destroying Halifax and grounding planes at London's Heathrow. You could rig sailing contests. Neutralize rainstorms. Assist sunbathers perturbed by the insolence of a cloudy atmosphere. Intentional climate manipulation again reveals its use for at least three ends: increasing quality of life, protecting against adverse weather, and acting as a weapon of international aggression.

Perhaps we could build something, then, a structure or device that would take advantage of both Alpine growth and excessive urban heat. If we combined these stories, for instance, a new kind of military tactic might take shape: You could build strange, fortified, geologically monumental weather-affecting landscapes all over the world—and then destroy distant targets downwind. The Thames Estuary could be lined with a series of heated platforms—large towers, like ovens—pointed toward Europe. This artificially generated microclimate would then be weaponized and run by the British military, who would lay claim to the weather itself. Amsterdam could be blown away in a fortnight, Paris flooded by rain for years. Or perhaps an armada of heated ships could be sent to the South China Sea: Beijing becomes servant to the Queen. China's soldiers are blown over and umbrellas are inverted throughout the country as the nation's stock of nuclear missiles is redirected north into the thawing wastes of Siberia. It would be the world's first *air weapon*, shooting bad weather on demand.

I'm reminded here of a story I once heard about an Australian man who began to notice strange flowers growing in his garden. These were flowers he'd never seen before—and that he'd certainly never planted—and it turned out that a drought on the other side of the country, coupled with unseasonably strong winds, had led to a thin layer of dirt, seeds, and bits of soil being blown all over Australia, some of which landed in this man's garden. As a result, strange flowers bloomed. This man was a victim of the weather, botanically vandalized—his local environs a record of distant landscape events.

Perhaps, then, instead of unleashing storms upon distant opponents, you could convert your air weapon to a more useful, peacetime purpose: horticulture. Grow gardens at a distance. Throw exotic seeds into gathering breezes—and, within weeks, distant hillsides color and bloom with breadfruit and roses, berries and genetically modified knotweed. Shift the direction of the wind, and a hundred miles of orange trees take root, forming orchards; shift the wind again, and uncountable acres of lavender, mint, rosemary, white pine, and birch appear, as you reforest the world from afar.

So, as the Alps grow taller and continental wind systems shift, perhaps we'll find the balance of power in Europe shifting *upward*. There, on the slopes of snowless mountains, strange ovens in towers will blow both weather and seeds over the horizon of nations below. Amidst angled platforms and wind-ramps, a new breed of rulers grows strong, distributing gardens and thunderstorms upon the countries they now dominate. The Weather Emperors, ruling Europe from above.

Until a small group of irritated gardeners, congested with allergies and choking on seeds, begins to climb up the Alpine front, intent on liberating their countrymen from this artificial weather. They haul themselves through rocky passes, eating rare Peruvian potatoes that now grow freely in Swiss crevasses. They pull each other up toward the storm machines, those great chimneys spewing unwanted landscapes upon the flatlands of central Europe.

The rebels approach the nearest tower, hammers raised.

THE SKY WAR

Weaponizing the earth's atmosphere, in however minor a way, was the subject of a long and fascinating article by James R. Fleming, published in the Spring 2007 issue of the *Wilson Quarterly*. Fleming discusses what he calls "unilateral climate modification"—asking what might happen if deliberate and controlled climate change does in fact become, or perhaps is already, possible. Fleming writes that "weaponized weather manipulation" means nations might someday "alter the global climate for strategic purposes." This could take the form of aggressive cloud-seeding, causing thunderstorms and snow over enemy airfields—and thus preventing their air force from

ATMOSPHERIC WEAPONRY

"Someday the U.S. military could drive a trailer to a spot just beyond insurgent fighting," author Sharon Weinberger posited in the January/February 2006 issue of *Defense Technology International*, "and, within minutes, reconfigure part of the atmosphere, blocking an enemy's ability to receive satellite signals, even as U.S. troops are able to see into the area with radar."

Lightning strikes the Eiffel Tower (1902). Image courtesy of NOAA's National Weather Service (NWS) Collection.

photolib.noaa.gov

A lightning storm over Boston (1960s). Image courtesy of NOAA's National Weather Service (NWS) Collection.

photolib.noaa.gov

The crew of the USS *Pittsburgh*
watches a waterspout off the coast
of China. Photo by the United States
Navy, courtesy of NOAA's National
Weather Service (NWS) Collection.

photolib.noaa.gov
navy.mil

OLYMPIC CLIMATOLOGY

Compare this, for instance, to China's own *Regulations on Administration of Weather Modification*, signed by Premier Zhu Rongji and put into effect on May 1, 2002. Article 7 of these regulations—and there are 22 such Articles—says the following: "The State encourages and supports scientific and technological research of weather modification and extended application of advanced technologies thereof." However, Article 10 points out that "[p]ersons engaged in weather modification operations may not implement such operations until they have received training"—after all, Article 20 adds, there might be "extraordinarily serious safety accidents" associated with handheld weather modification technologies—and so, Article 15 points out, "[r]ocket launchers, shells and rockets used for weather modification operations shall be manufactured according to the relevant compulsory technical standards and requirements of the State." I could go on and on. Article 16: "The transportation and storage of anti-aircraft guns, rocket launchers, shells and rockets used for weather modification operations shall be subject to the laws and regulations of the State on the administration of weaponry and explosives." Rogue weather separatists in the wastelands of Xinjiang Province send black storm clouds racing toward Beijing. Weather modification as a subset of the war on terror. "What are you in Guantánamo for?" someone asks. "Who, me?" you say. "Storm clouds."

taking off—or it could even mean decimating whole cities and military camps with strategically redirected hurricanes. Indeed, Fleming notes, with spectacular deadpan: "Hurricanes were also fair game for weaponization."

The article goes on to describe a "paramilitary rapid deployment force" armed with its own "perfectly accurate machine forecast" of global weather systems, using specially assembled equipment that might "provide the capacity to disrupt storms before they formed, deflect them from populated areas, and otherwise control the weather." He quotes General George Churchill Kenney, commander of the U. S. Strategic Air Command during WWII: "The nation which first learns to plot the paths of air masses accurately and learns to control the time and place of precipitation will dominate the globe."

Incredibly, it wasn't just the time and place of precipitation that was at issue here; it was also *what was precipitated*. In other words, there was talk of using rain and snow as delivery mechanisms for chemical and biological agents—anthrax snowing down upon enemy populations, disguised as a thin white powder on the windshields of parked cars. Weapons of Mass Precipitation.

And this was no mere armchair speculation. Fleming describes Operation Popeye:

> Operating out of Udorn Air Base, Thailand, without the knowledge of the Thai government or almost anyone else, but with the full and enthusiastic support of presidents Lyndon B. Johnson and Richard M. Nixon, the Air Weather Service flew more than 2,600 cloud seeding sorties and expended 47,000 silver iodide flares over a period of approximately five years at an annual cost of some $3.6 million.

With weather control and climate security being understandably touchy subjects, the U. S. State Department explains, "the Senate adopted a resolution in 1973 calling for an international agreement 'prohibiting the use of any environmental or geophysical modification activity as a weapon of war…'" This agreement was signed in 1977 and enacted in 1978.

Referred to now as the Convention on the Prohibition of Military or Any Other Hostile Use of Environmental Modification Techniques, Article 1 of that Convention reminds the world that each of its signatories "undertakes not to engage in military or any other hostile use of environmental modification techniques having widespread, long-lasting or severe effects as the means of destruction, damage or injury to any other State Party." Article 2 further defines these "environmental modification techniques" as being "any technique for changing—through the deliberate manipulation of natural processes—the dynamics, composition or structure of the Earth, including its biota, lithosphere, hydrosphere and atmosphere, or of outer space." Changing the "structure of the Earth"! Certainly one of the boldest examples of such interventions is a present-day plan by physicist Lowell Wood. According to Fleming, Wood would like to create "an engineered Arctic ice sheet"—that is, an artificial glacier in the Canadian north—that could be used to regulate global temperatures. I've said earlier in this book that glaciers are the future of landscape architecture—a future test-structure for winter design seminars—but perhaps that future is already here.

Of course, this discussion adds military urgency to the question of climate change. If all those automobile factories in rural China suddenly turn out to be adversely affecting growing conditions in California's Central Valley, or London's urban heat island effect proves to be disastrous for its European neighbors, who's to say that these aren't deliberate acts of undeclared war? They could be heavy industry—or clandestine atmospheric operations. Perhaps both.

"Assume for a minute," Fleming writes, "that climate control were technically possible."

Who would be given authority to manage it? Who would have the wisdom to dispense drought, severe winters, or the effects of storms to some so that the rest of the planet could prosper? At what cost, economically, aesthetically, and in our moral relationship to nature, would we manipulate the climate?

Latent in such questions is the idea that a whole new class of international "sacrifice zones"—as sites in the United States used for the testing of nuclear weapons are now called—could arise, a new type of landscape park in which all of the world's bad weather will be confined. Perhaps you could build a dystopian franchise of ultramax prisons there, surrounded perpetually by blizzards, tornadoes, or a permanent drought.

Out there somewhere in a valley in central Africa—or Utah, or Rajasthan—an unending storm begins swirling, brought to you by the U. S. military, overseen by an unelected and corrupt weather control board. Meteorology grad students can buy time there to run experimental storm fronts, about which tenure-winning theses will be written.

These militarily engineered storm parks will compete with the Los Angeles Weather Bowl for public interest—until a crazed, *Pruned*-reading James Bond villain hijacks them and city-destroying climatological hijinks ensue....

HOW TO GROW A GLACIER

One hint for how glaciers might be grown comes to us from the mountains of northern Pakistan, where "glacial grafting" has been practiced now for centuries. In February 2008, *New Scientist* author Ed Douglas introduced us to the local techniques. These include the use of carefully planned layers of rocks, charcoal, sawdust, wheat husks, cloth, and, of course, snow, to grow artificial glaciers. Small gourds of water are placed within this matrix so that, when the gourds break beneath the pressure of mounting snow, cold water spills out and freezes, forming a kind of glacial glue. Then, "[w]hen the mass of rock and ice is heavy enough," Douglas writes, "it begins to creep downhill, forming a self-sustaining glacier within four years or so."

I can't help but speculate here about the possibilities awaiting avant-garde landscape artists looking to break into the ice market. Columbia University could run a winter design studio in the mountains of Pakistan, where students assemble custom structures of ice. At the end of the project, they leave the glaciers in place; fifty years on, the still-growing remnants of these architectural experiments trigger a minor Himalayan ice age.

SCI-FI REGIONALISM

The world is already becoming radically unlike itself, altered in some cases beyond all recognition. The Earth, you could say, is becoming unearthly.

Answering the question of whether or not these changes can be mapped, in the summer of 2007 climate experts Stéphane Hallegatte, Minh Ha-Duong, and Sebastian Kopf produced a new map of Europe. Their map relocated twelve European capitals according to what their climates might be like in the year A.D. 2071. While the map is initially quite confusing, it shows that, in 2071, London will have the climate of Lisbon; Berlin, incredibly, will have the climate of today's Algiers; and Oslo will feel like Barcelona (and so on). These are those cities' future "climate analogues." Think of them as climatological sister-cities in the future possible tense.

As Hallegatte explained to the *Guardian* on May 15, 2007, the map was meant to "help architects and officials who plan buildings, streets, and services to adapt to the likely impacts of global warming. 'If you look at the map you see that Paris moves to the south of Spain. It's scary that just a few degrees rise will make such a difference. Paris is currently designed to deal with a very different climate, which means designs in future will have to be very different.'" For example: "Houses and buildings in northern Europe typically have windows to the west to make the most of meager winter sun.... 'But in warmer countries you will never find windows to the west because the sun just pours in all afternoon during the summer.'" What he doesn't mention, however, is that architecture will have to change *gradually*, decade by decade, even year by year; after all, it would be inappropriate, not to mention presumptuous, to get rid of all west-facing windows today—and it still might be premature to do so in 2030. But, by 2071, perhaps all west-facing windows will have been phased out. Or skylights, or rain catchment systems, or winter insulation, or whatever. Either way, you'll be able to track changes in the European climate based on what styles of architecture still exist, and where. As Stockholm gradually takes on the architectural characteristics of a Mediterranean port city, you'll know that climate change is in full effect.

On a related note, I've often thought it would be interesting to travel around southern Europe with some graph paper and a box full of GPS devices, mapping zones of desertification. The new cartography of aridity: tracking the inevitable northward spread of the Sahara, complete with statistics on where people are dying of thirst. France, Italy, Greece, Spain, Portugal. Whoever finds the northernmost point of desert—some strange and growing patch of dust outside Oslo—wins something. Whether or not such a project ever happens, the minute any place,

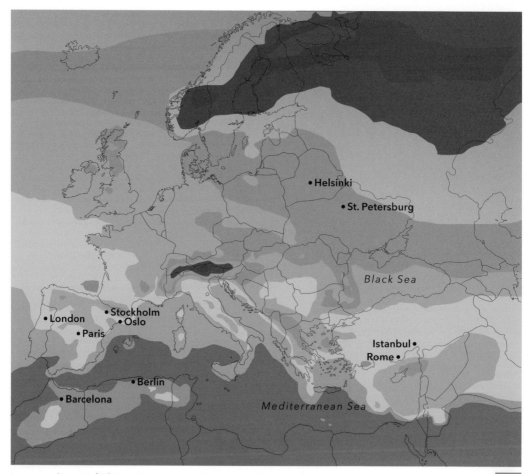

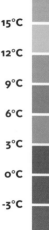

In 2071, as this map of "climate analogues" shows, London could have the climate of coastal Portugal—and Berlin might feel similar to Algiers. Based on a map by Sebastian Kopf, Minh Ha-Duong, and Stéphane Hallegatte of CIRED, for a paper published in August 2008 by the journal *Natural Hazards and Earth System Sciences*.

As the authors point out in their paper, "according to one simulation, Paris could have at the end of the 21st century a climate similar to Vieste Aero near Rome. (. . .) However, according to another simulation, Paris could also have the climate of the city of Badajoz in Southern Spain." The data presented here is inherently limited, they add:

> An integrated assessment of the impact of future climate change on urban areas would require a systematic consideration of a large number of heavily interwoven urban attributes which affect the adaptation process, such as architectural styles, transport infrastructure and cultural

lifestyles. Defining a convincing reference scenario under these conditions, together with a consistent vision of economic and cultural drivers of the adaptation process, is a daunting task. Predicting the consequences of climate change on human settlements accurately seems not feasible at this point.

It is also important to note, then, that my own interpretation of this map is not necessarily endorsed by the map's creators. In a brief e-mail exchange, Kopf emphasized that this map and its variants give "only a limited impression of the uncertainty in climate projections." In other words, the exact future climates of European cities are still only a matter of speculation.

centre-cired.fr

21°C
18°C
15°C
12°C
9°C
6°C
3°C
0°C
-3°C

anywhere in Europe is officially named part of the Sahara Desert will be a very surreal moment, indeed.

So can architects somehow account for these wild fluctuations in both weather and climate? Is there a way to prepare for unpredictable and extreme changes in regional climate—and to do so through architectural design? And what happens to the new, modern, glass-walled housing stock of Berlin when it finds itself baking in Algiers-like desert temperatures?

In architectural circles today there is much talk of a "new regionalism," in which architects pay more attention not only to a region's climate but also to its historically established vernacular building traditions. But what such a "new regionalism" doesn't account for is radical future changes in climate. In other words, we need a real new regionalism, one that builds for future transitions so out of the ordinary that they verge on science fiction. It's *sci-fi regionalism*—architectural design in an era of global climate change.

THE MUSEUM OF THE SKY

In December 2005, Australian "environmental philosopher" Glenn Albrecht coined a term: *solastalgia*. According to Albrecht, solastalgia is the deep sense of mourning that sets in when one's everyday, familiar environment becomes unrecognizable because of things like climate change. As he wrote on his blog much later, in March 2007:

> The factors that cause solastalgia can be both natural and artificial. Natural disasters such as drought, fire, and flood can be a cause [of] solastalgia. Human-induced change such as war, terrorism, land clearing, mining, rapid institutional change, and the gentrification of older parts of cities can also be causal agents. The concept of solastalgia has relevance in any context where there is the direct experience of negative transformation or desolation of the physical environment (home) by forces that undermine a personal and community sense of identity, belonging and control.

Science writer Clive Thompson picked up on the term, elaborating on it in the December 2007 issue of *Wired* magazine. "Albrecht believes that this is a new type of sadness," Thompson wrote.

> People are feeling displaced. They're suffering symptoms eerily similar to those of indigenous populations that are forcibly removed from their traditional homelands. But nobody is being relocated; they haven't moved anywhere. It's just that

the familiar markers of their area, the physical and sensory signals that define home, are vanishing. Their environment is moving away from them, and they miss it terribly.

"In a world that's quickly heating up and drying up," he adds, "you can't go home again—even if you never leave."

Controlled climate change here would be something like an act of *nostalgia*: preserving the climate of the place in which you live so that you can *always* go home again. The weather itself would be a psychological projection, an expression of culture—an indefinitely preserved abstract model of a region's past. It would be climate, subject to historic preservation.

And the opposite? Deliberately changing the climate so that you can forget your own or your culture's past? Perhaps the psychiatrists of the future will need degrees in meteorology. ⊗

A house flooded by the April 1, 1946,
earthquake and tsunami on Unimak
Island, Alaska. Image courtesy of the
University of California, Berkeley, and
the NOAA/NGDC Natural Hazards
Photo Archive.

ngdc.noaa.gov

Trapped Iceberg–East Greenland, August 2006, by Camille Seaman.

camilleseaman.com

4

MUSIC SOUND NOISE

From the *Blackboards* series by
Meggan Gould. "In this series I
photograph the ever-shifting landscapes of erased blackboards,"
the photographer writes, "where
layers of communication and time
build up, accumulate, and are
systematically obliterated."

meggould.netfirms.com

"VENICE HAS GOT A VERY different sound," Austrian musician and sound artist Christian Fennesz explained in a May 2004 interview with the *Wire*. "It's very interesting, when you're there—you always hear some kind of hum, like from far away, but also people talking, and you never know if it's in the next apartment or if it's 400 meters away, because the *labyrinth* of the houses works as an amplifying system somehow." The city's unique acoustics have as much to do with what Venice lacks—the internal combustion engines of tens of thousands of cars—as with what the city has: a *complicated* network of waterborne streets that reflect and break sounds at odd angles.

Meanwhile, Cairo, according to the *New York Times*, has grown so loud that its residents have to shout simply to be heard over the sound of other people shouting; combine this with the raw noise of endless cars and the city is more like a stationary airplane engine, a deafening roar on the deltaic fringe of the northern Sahara.

But what of the sonic qualities of other spaces, other landscapes—even other planets, perhaps? How often do people make travel plans based on the way their chosen destination *sounds*? You'll go somewhere because of how it looks in the travel brochure—but why not because of what it sounds like when you look out your hotel window, go for walks at night, or eat lunch? What is the acoustic side of space—and how can we best explore it?

As Allen Ginsberg once wrote in his journals: "[S]omewhere in the middle of all these buildings is a place where you can clap your hands and be heard in heaven." So how do we find that place?

AUDIO ARCHITECTURE

The company known as Muzak claims to provide "audio architecture" for its clients. The phrase *audio architecture* sounds quite wonderful; it conjures up images of cathedrals made from noise—whole buildings connected by bridges of music—but, in the world of Muzak, it means something altogether less exciting. Audio architecture, Muzak writes, is "the integration of music, voice, and sound to create experiences designed specifically for your business." In other words, audio architecture is about making you feel comfortable—so that someone else can sell you things.

The "power" of audio architecture, Muzak's website continues, "lies in its subtlety." These subtle sounds, played incessantly in the background, can "bypass the resistance of the mind and target the receptiveness of the heart." It is thus almost literally *subliminal.* "When people are made to feel good in, say, a store, they feel good about that store. They like it," the company claims. "Audio architecture builds a bridge to loyalty. And loyalty is what keeps brands alive." If there is a connection between background sounds and customer loyalty, then perhaps sound could also inspire a kind of *urban* loyalty—where the sound of a certain city plays its own subtle role in making a place feel more habitable. Like Muzak, the city's ambient sounds would make residents "feel good"—which "builds a bridge to [urban] loyalty."

Of course, this would not be the first time someone has suggested that cities have a certain sound, unique to them, or that cities should learn to cultivate these sonic qualities. More than thirty years ago, for instance, the World Soundscape Project called for the "tuning" of the world. Cities would be treated as vast musical instruments: certain sounds would be eliminated altogether; others would be promoted or even subtly redesigned. The World Soundscape Project was about *sonic improvement*, making the world sound better, one city—one building—at a time. Where the Project went wrong, however, and where it began to be a bit like Muzak, was when it thought it had a kind of sonic monopoly over what sounded good. Industrial noises would be scrubbed from the city, for instance, and a nostalgic calm would be infused in its place. Think church bells, not automobiles. But where would this sensory cleansing leave those of us who enjoy the sound of factories?

We could still have some fun with the World Soundscape Project, designing alternative sonic futures for the cities of the world, if we turned, ironically, to the techniques of Muzak itself. Muzak *imitates.* Rock, jazz, blues, Mozart—even Muzak itself: Anything at all can be absorbed, replaced, and reproduced by Muzak. So why not a Muzak version of the street sounds of Amsterdam—played on a continuous loop in the supermarkets

THE SKY ORCHESTRA
Artist Luke Jerram's ongoing Sky Orchestra project aims to explore "how one can perceive an artistic experience" while sleeping. To do this, Jerram has "develop[ed] music specifically for sleeping people which is delivered out of the sky." Quoting from the artist's own website:

> Seven hot air balloons, each with speakers attached, take off at dawn to fly across a city. Each balloon plays a different element of the musical score creating a massive audio landscape.

> *"Like whales calling in the ocean, the same sounds may be heard in succession passing from one balloon to another across the sky..."*

Many hundreds of people experience the Sky Orchestra event live as the balloons fly over their homes at dawn. The airborne project is both a vast spectacular performance as well as an intimate, personal experience. The music is audible, both consciously and subconsciously, to all those in the balloon's flight paths.

Wired covered the project, writing: "If you're lulled awake by electronic music at daybreak, look up. The tune may be coming from the seven hot-air balloons in artist Luke Jerram's Sky Orchestra as it bumps '80s-synth-style ambient tracks from the heavens." The *Telegraph* jumped in at that point, reporting that "residents of Stratford-upon-Avon awoke yesterday to find a flotilla of hot air balloons drifting over their roofs serenading them with ambient music and readings from Shakespeare." Last but not least, of course, way back in 2004 the *Guardian* claimed that residents of Birmingham had been "helplessly lulled into deeper sleep at dawn yesterday morning, by specially composed music played from a flight of hot air balloons drifting over the dozing city....The flutes and oboes, bird song and whale calls, were based on scientific research to promote deeper and sweeter dreams."

Of course, it'd be interesting to see if something like this could be abused for political purposes, whispering subliminal messages into the sleeping, predawn brains of the local electorate. But it also raises an interesting paranoid-philosophical question: If you experience a particularly good night's sleep, and you live alone in the countryside somewhere, with neither witnesses nor neighbors, how do you know whether the Sky Orchestra has not come floating through?

I'm reminded of an article from *New Scientist*, published on October 30, 2003, where we read that the Big Bang sounded not like an explosion at all, but "rather like a large jet plane flying 100 feet above your house in the middle of the night." Perhaps it was really a cosmic Luke Jerram.

lukejerram.com

of London? The sounds of yesterday could be replayed today, transformed into Muzak—and Muzak versions of your old phone conversations could be broadcast over the radio, with laughter replaced by synthesizer trills. University lectures and books on tape could be replaced with Muzak, pushing us toward a post-verbal society. There could be a Muzak version of BLDGBLOG, playing constantly, at low volume, in the basement.

Or perhaps we should just forget Muzak altogether and simply swap urban soundtracks, cities imitating cities to sound entirely unlike themselves. In the elevators of the Empire State Building, you'd hear the elevators of the Eiffel Tower. The sounds of the Paris Métro are replaced with the sounds of the Beijing subway, complete with squeals from overworked brakes and the metallic thud of sliding doors. If you don't like Rome, you can make it sound like Dubai.

Recording the everyday noises of, say, Oslo, as if Oslo is an ongoing symphony—and then replaying that symphony through hidden speakers in San Francisco—perhaps even transforming it into Muzak—should certainly be the next artistic step.

It would be a question of acoustic urban design—of true *audio architecture*.

In his 1964 novel *Nova Express*, William Burroughs described a series of elaborate, hallucinatory, assemblages of tape recorders and microphones that can be carried from city to city. Borderless, these roving sound installations, with their capacity for instant playback, would blur the line between your own thought processes and the sounds of the city around you. Like Muzak, Burroughs's legion of rogue microphonists would "bypass the resistance of the mind," installing a soundtrack where there once had been thought. Or, in *Naked Lunch*, Burroughs writes: "I know this one pusher walks around humming a tune and everybody he passes takes it up. He is so grey and spectral and anonymous they don't see him and think it is their own minds humming the tune." Replace that "pusher" with the sounds of a city, and you've got a new kind of audio architecture, subliminally indistinguishable from thought.

SOUNDTRACKS FOR ARCHITECTURE

Midway through David Toop's excellent book *Ocean of Sound*, a survey of "sonic history" focusing on ambient music, Toop quotes a short review by composer Paul Schütze. "Recently listening to Thomas Köner's *Permafrost*," Schütze writes, "I found that by the end of the disc my sense of aural perspective was so altered that the music seemed to continue in the sounds around me. Tube trains passing beneath the building, distant boilers, the air conditioning, and the elevator engines had been pulled into the concert. This effect lasted for about forty minutes during which I could not get anything to return to its 'normal position' in the 'mix' of my flat."

But what if Schütze had been wrong? What if the disc *had still been playing*—and Schütze didn't live anywhere near the Tube, nor did his building have elevators? What if those subtle and distant architectural sounds had actually been part of the CD? This would be *music as the illusion of architecture.*

You move into a house without a basement—but you purchase this CD, or download these tracks, and you achieve the uncanny sonic effect of having more floors below you. Or perhaps you want an attic, or even a next-door neighbor.

You would buy *soundtracks for architecture*: producing the illusion of architecture through nothing but sound.

Think of the Francisco López album, *Buildings. Buildings* is "a work composed entirely of sound fragments López procured while wandering around big buildings in NYC," recording the "sounds of elevators, air conditioning systems, cables, pipes, air ducts, boilers, clocks, thermostats, video cameras, and so on."

So instead of an addition, or a home renovation, perhaps you should commission a new piece of ambient music: For as long as that music is playing, your house has several thousand more square feet…and a Tube line nearby…and distant boilers….

Elsewhere in Toop's book he quotes composer Brian Eno at great length on the connections between landscape, sound, time, and the city. "There's an experiment I did," Eno tells us; it was "a good exercise that I would recommend to other people."

I had taken a DAT recorder to Hyde Park and near Bayswater Road I recorded a period of whatever sound was there: cars going by, dogs, people. I thought nothing much of it and I was sitting at home listening to it on my player. I suddenly had this idea. What about if I take a section of this—a 3½ minute section, the length of a single—and I tried to learn it? So that's what I did. I put it in *SoundTools* and I made a fade-up, let it run for 3½ minutes and faded it out. I started listening to this thing, over and over. Whenever I was sitting there working, I would have this thing on. I printed it on a DAT twenty times or something, so it just kept running over and over. I tried to learn it, exactly as one would a piece of music: oh yeah, that car, accelerates the engine, the revs in the engine go up and then that dog barks, and then you hear that pigeon off to the side there. This was an extremely interesting exercise to do, first of all because I found that you can learn it. Something that is as completely arbitrary and disconnected as that, with sufficient listenings, becomes highly connected. You can really imagine that this thing was constructed somehow: "Right, then he puts this bit there and that pattern's just

SOUNDING ROOMS

You've been living in an apartment for almost a year, one of three separate apartments in an otherwise unremarkable building on a street somewhere in the city. You know the building fairly well; you've had brief glimpses inside the other apartments; and, with buildings directly on either side, there should be no major architectural surprises in store. But one day somebody new moves in—and the acoustics of the building begin to change. Suddenly you're hearing people walk up and down a staircase whose position in the house should be impossible, and you're picking up fragments of conversations that sound as if they're taking place in rooms that simply cannot be there—voices coming through the walls of the closet, or down through the ceiling of a room that's supposed to have no rooms above it.

What is going on? Have your new neighbors simply begun using one or two rooms that the previous tenants had left empty—or have they stumbled on some strange and unexpected system of rooms that no one else had known about? If so, should they pay more rent? Or perhaps someone has moved into an apartment in the building next door—only it acoustically overlaps with yours in unpredictable ways.

So you begin an investigation. You record brief snippets of these murmuring conversations to see if the voices match those of your new neighbors—after all, you've spoken to them in the building's foyer, and you don't remember them sounding anything like this.

Then, one night, a TV seems to be playing—from behind a wall in your bedroom.

It's too much.

You soon notice that many of the walls in the house, particularly down in the entry hall, are actually sealed-over doorframes—not walls at all—and some of the doors in your apartment had simply been hammered right through the old walls. The interior of the house has been rearranged several times, in other words—but, of course: how else convert a single-family house into a three-apartment complex? You even find trace evidence in the back of the kitchen cupboard of a staircase that's no longer there.

But you can't be hearing ghosts; you don't believe in ghosts. So is some weird new acoustic effect being demonstrated? It is the rainy season, your best friend points out; maybe all that moisture in the air has somehow changed the way that sounds travel through the building. You should talk to an architect, he says, or just dig up old plans of the house. Phone your landlord.

Instead, you start knocking on walls and tapping for hollow spots. You tell yourself after work each day that you'll stop by the hardware store to buy some sort of stud-finder—some technical way to peer through walls, looking for adjacent spaces. But you never do; you're too tired, and a stud-finder sounds expensive.

You start daydreaming about radar: You will turn around slowly in the center of your bedroom holding a machine in both hands, recording the electro-acoustic presence of unknown rooms around you. It'll be like that scene in *Aliens*, you joke to yourself, except you'll be detecting space. Perhaps you'll even find a room that moves, you think, a distant but invisible void, approaching.

But then it stops. The sounds go away. The mysterious conversations cease. There is no more radio hum or TV chatter. When your neighbors come home from work each night it sounds the way it did before. There are no more hidden stairways. No more unexpected rooms.

And so you think it's all over—till you're hanging a picture one day. Your hammer goes through the drywall, revealing what appears to be a newly furnished room, just sitting back there in the darkness.

at the exact same moment as this happening. Brilliant!" Since I've done that, I can listen to lots of things in quite a different way. It's like putting oneself in the role of an art perceiver, just deciding, now I'm playing that role.

All of which is interesting already—but it makes me wonder if a band could then reproduce the sounds on Eno's tape, as a kind of cover song, live in concert. Godspeed You! Black Emperor plays the sounds of Bayswater in their closing set, a perfect rendition. Instead of another Led Zeppelin cover band, you book a Times Square cover band for your daughter's Bat Mitzvah; they play the traffic, voices, and horns of a typical Times Square day, and they go for hours. Even lifelong Manhattanites can't tell the difference. Or an International Space Station cover band plays you live, acoustic versions of the Station's lonely clicks and whirs. A St. Louis Arch cover band—the St. Louis Arches®—reproduces the sounds of Eero Saarinen's structure on stages around the world. "It's just like being there," the *New Yorker* reports. "The effect is uncanny." Alexanderplatz, acoustically reproduced on guitar, in a small room outside Tokyo. The sounds of Death Valley—live, at the Hollywood Bowl.

Or a man tunes the infrastructure of his building till it sounds exactly like the hotel he once stayed in in Paris. The air ducts rattle in just the right way, and the door hinges creak…. He then hires a band to reproduce those sounds at the office Christmas party.

What is the future of *abstract karaoke*?

Tuning out these background sounds—or, more specifically, turning them off—is the subject of another short anecdote from Toop's book.

For an installation of fifty specially made "sound creatures"— little interactive robots, Toop explains, "inspired by the communication eco-system of frog choruses"—experimental musician Felix Hess insisted that there be no "extraneous sounds" in the concert hall. That is, Hess's miniature sound performance required *absolute silence*, or else the machines would not *function properly*. Toop quotes a lengthy description of the creatures' setup:

We had imagined that the foyer, on an afternoon when nothing was being held there, was extremely tranquil, but not even one of them began to call out in response to any of the others. So first we turned off the air conditioner in the room, and then we turned off the one on the second floor. Then we turned off the refrigerator and the electric cooking equipment in the adjoining cafe, the power of the multi-vision in the foyer, and the power of the vending machine in a space about ten meters away. One by one we took away these continual noises, which together created a kind of drone there.... Hess was very interested in this and said things like, "From now on maybe I should do a performance of turning off sounds."

It's amazing to think, of course, that anything could pick up, and even respond to, sounds that subtle; but it's also quite incredible to imagine one's own acoustic awareness of architecture as a process of subtraction.

You could even turn it into a game:

1. You are sitting on a stage, wearing a blindfold.
2. Every electrical device in the building around you is on.
3. Suddenly, you detect a slight difference, a vague change in sonic pressure somewhere, as if an extremely distant mosquito has been swatted—a spot of silence, as it were, has appeared in the room.
4. "Toaster, fourth floor!" you call out—and you're right: someone just turned off a toaster on the fourth floor.
5. You win a trip to France.

It's easy to imagine Hess and his assistants finding this process much more difficult than they'd imagined it would be. At one point in the afternoon, then, with only hours to go before the doors open, they have to step across the street and turn off the appliances in a nearby high-rise—and then go next door, to a block of flats, and then down the road to the neighborhood hospital, turning off all machines as they go. Still nothing. The sound creatures sit there silently.

Gradually Hess goes on to turn off the whole world, street by street, city by city, in an ever-expanding ring of total silence. The world becomes a sonic sculpture from which sources of background sound are continually removed. Finally, 25 years from now, as the very last radio is unplugged in a distant house in Tanzania, the sound creatures sitting with Felix Hess on stage begin singing.

ROGUE SOUND CITY: AN INTERVIEW WITH DJ /RUPTURE

Where the individual sounds of certain cities come from seems beyond our ability to calculate. Endless maps could be made just to trace each sound to its source—every voice, bird, and car horn. Spaces bleed into one another through sound.

But is it the physical city itself we hear—the steel and glass, wood and stone, bricks and aluminum siding—or something altogether less tangible than that?

ANDEAN THUNDERDOME

According to a September 2008 article in *New Scientist*, the ancient temple ruins at Chavín de Huántar, in the Peruvian Andes, were once a complicated acoustic device—a kind of earth-trumpet, or mountain reverberatorium—used for nearly a thousand years by power-hungry priests.

Archaeologist John Rick, with the assistance of acoustician Jonathan Abel, has put forward the controversial idea that "the priests gradually learned to manipulate their temple's acoustics to create the illusion that they channeled the power of the gods, or that they themselves could turn into gods."

For Rick, the clincher came in 2001, when he discovered 20 identical trumpets, made from a type of conch shell called a strombus, in one of Chavín's underground chambers. The trumpets were highly decorated, indicating a ritualistic use. Measurements of the chambers' dimensions, and recordings Rick made of how various noises sound in the chambers, seemed to show that these were no ordinary rituals: the complex network of galleries was designed specifically to turn the trumpet blasts into a truly otherworldly experience.

The temple priests were "sophisticated sound designers," Rick suggests, and the site itself "evolved by design to become ever more suited to inducing disorientation." Indeed, "together with the dark, maze-like networks of tunnels that lead to the chambers, and the strong evidence for the use of hallucinogenic drugs in Chavín rituals, it all adds up to a visceral, perhaps terrifying experience."

I'm reminded of another project by Francisco López. In the liner notes of a 1998 CD that documented his ongoing study of rain forest acoustics, López pointed out that when we refer to the sound of the *wind* in the forest we are most likely referring to the sound of *plants*: the whispering rustle of leaves and branches. This reversal of foreground and background—which also brings to mind Walter Murch's famous line from the book *The Conversations* by Michael Ondaatje: "If I go out to record a door-slam, I don't think I'm recording a door-slam. I think I am recording the space in which a door-slam happens"—becomes immediately relevant here with the switch of just two terms. When we refer to the sound of *cities*, we most often mean the sound of *culture*: people, surrounded by materially specific examples of the built environment. Not cities, you could say, but the spaces within which culture happens.

For at least half a decade I have been listening to mixes by DJ /rupture, Jace Clayton, a New York–based musician who writes an excellent blog called *Mudd Up!* One day I decided to get in touch: Jace had just returned to the United States after more than half a decade living in Barcelona, where he'd been performing at a variety of gigs, concerts, and festivals throughout Europe and North Africa, and his blog was full of sharp insights about cities, history, geography, and the sounds of cultural migration. I realized he would be an excellent person with whom to discuss the cultural nature of urban acoustics.

BLDGBLOG: Certain cities literally sound different than others—but where does that difference come from? The Djemaa el Fna in Marrakech sounds very different than Times Square, for instance—which sounds different than Hampstead Heath. So what is it that shapes a place's sound?

DJ /rupture: It's funny—it's actually hard to talk about the sound of cities without talking about the sound of cars. I feel like for a city to have a sound you need to be able to *hear* that sound, on a very basic level. So a lot of the denser, less trafficked cities are the ones that have the most sonic personality.

When I think of sounds and cities I immediately think of Barcelona. There are a lot of motorcycles, because cars are expensive and gas is not as subsidized as it is in the United States, so there are all these young guys out on motorcycles all the time. It's incredibly loud—just motorcycles and construction. Whereas in New York City—in Brooklyn, in particular—it's more like you don't really hear the cars, you hear the people's sound systems, instead. You'll be walking down the street and you'll hear this bass approaching from around the corner, you know, like a hip-hop song or an R&B song—and it's really, really loud, like moving loudspeakers coming down the street.

There are certain cities that are particularly good to do field recordings in, or that have a specific spot that sounds good. You mentioned the Djemaa el Fna, which is sort of this spectacle space: it's loud, open, raucous. Sounds just drift up into the air. That puts all the people—the storytellers, magicians, and acrobats—into a really heavy sonic competition with each other, just to find an audience.

In terms of a citywide level of sound, that's more difficult to talk about; the terrain within any city is just so varied. Again, in Brooklyn, if you're thinking about the music, and the sound you get in the streets, and the languages you hear—that changes. That changes from neighborhood to neighborhood as the cultures shift. Even the *volume* of the neighborhood changes.

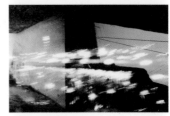

BLDGBLOG: To some extent, it seems like that's a factor of the actual built materials of the city—how different materials absorb or reflect sounds. Does the physical architecture of a city change that city's acoustics?

Rupture: Yeah, yeah—absolutely. To put it in pretty straightforward terms, if you're in a dense, modern city, with a lot of concrete, glass, steel, and cars, then there's a very bright, almost brittle, sound. There's a lot of noise, a lot of dynamics. In a lot of Mediterranean cities, the buildings are older and a lot less regular, in terms of layout, and in terms of building material, so sound becomes softer, more refracted. It's *absorbed* in a way. But every space has its own acoustic quality. That's why certain high-end recording studios are really in demand, and why some people like to perform in churches with all that natural reverb.

So—absolutely. I think that walking the streets of Marrakech, in the medina, is fantastic, because there are no cars. There's just that whole nature of city life. A woman is killing a chicken in the street—and that's not the kind of sounds or urban life you get in New York! [*laughs*] You know, I do a lot of field recordings. I've got these nice binaural microphones. They look like headphones—one goes in each ear—so you get delicate, nicely spatialized recordings. But it's really difficult in a noisy, industrial city like New York. For a while I lived right by an aboveground subway in Williamsburg, and there were so many huge amplitude shifts. There's a train—and everything goes distorted. The levels go out of control. But something beautiful happens. If nothing else, those recordings document how hard it is to capture the decibel range of a loud city—and how much abuse your ears get just by traveling in or near a subway or a busy street.

BLDGBLOG: What impact do things like pirate radio stations, local recording studios, specific nightclubs, and so on have on the sound of a city—on a city's musical identity?

From *Morocco Double-Exposures*
(2002) by Geoff Manaugh.

Rupture: I think radio actually has a lot to do with it. Radio is very local. I think a city like London can be sort of a generative crucible for new music in all these different forms: jungle, garage, grime, dubstep. Those all pretty much burst out of London in a short period of time. But London also has a long history of pirate radio: It's dense and congested enough for people—whole neighborhoods—to get competitive with each other, and for crews to get competitive with each other. People can go on the air and give shout-outs. It's this amazing sort of feedback machine for accelerating the culture and for making people feel like they're *in* that place, and that place is now the center, and let's represent, and play these tunes, and really push it. A lot of those scenes pretty much rode on the backs of pirate radio stations.

Especially music like grime—this futuristic rap music from London. Because there are all these racist fears and acts of violence—fears of guns or some other problem—I think it's often hard to have a grime party in London. So this music exists on the radio and in a few shops and in passing cars—but it doesn't really have a physical location in the city.

But I do often wonder how all this musical evolution happened in London. It's not just the pirate radio scene—though that's been a huge help. It wasn't just John Peel pushing these sorts of sounds from a very mainstream position. It was all of those factors plus a long history of Jamaican immigrants coming to London, with the sound system culture—which brings in music and dubplate culture and all that—but then it still steps beyond. There's always this kind of intangible aspect, I feel, to really have a city hopping, the way London is.

BLDGBLOG: Your description of London reminds me of a paper by architectural theorist Stefano Boeri. Boeri suggests that, for all the talk today about rogue nations, there are also *rogue cities*: cities like Pyongyang where space is organized and experienced differently than in a modern, Western city. But are there *musical rogue cities*—cities with totally unique and unexpected music scenes—and, if so, what cities might you think of?

Rupture: When you say *rogue*, that implies going against the norm—when a musical culture is vibrant but noncanonical.

So the first two cities that came to mind are Rennes, France, and Bristol, in the United Kingdom. Both of those cities have had a long history of electronic music. Or, to put it bluntly, some of the craziest parties I've been to, with the most nonstandard, difficult music, have been in those two places. I remember in 2001, I had to play in Rennes—I had never heard of it before!—and I showed up and there were 2,000 people at this party, and there was all this music: very, very noisy techno, breakcore, and just straight noise. And I was like, oh man, something very strange is going on here! [*laughter*] But Rennes has a reputation for a series of ridiculous parties that have happened there and for a network of shops that support that.

The same with Bristol. It's a bit less extreme than Rennes, but every time I go there I'm shocked by all the music happening and the fact that it's not… it's not like London. The thing with London is that it is very creative. On the one hand, there is a lot of ground-up culture there, and a lot of musical styles, but London is also a place where music becomes monetized very quickly, almost quicker than any other city. In Bristol, that money aspect is much less prevalent. A lot of the music at underground parties is not at all based on fame—you know, "this DJ has been in *NME* or the *Wire*, or whatever music magazine." It's much more community-based.

BLDGBLOG: Finally, I'm interested in the actual sites where all of this takes place—whether that's at a nightclub, an outdoor market, or a park. Or, as you wrote on your blog, "on southbound boats from Cádiz or Algeciras is where [cultures] meet in fascination and embrace." How do these minor, unofficial spaces on the periphery of the city help to incubate new forms of music?

Rupture: Well, there's still a lot of cultural segregation in the Mediterranean, so these sorts of cultural moments tend to happen at nightclubs, bars, and even bus routes—spots that are very unstable.

For instance, there's an African bar in Barcelona, which, because Barcelona can be a fairly racist city, has a bad reputation and not many Catalans go there—but that's where it's happening. There are a few spots in Madrid—a few nightclubs—that host world music and different types of black music, but it's always kind of edgy. In Barcelona there's a neighborhood called El Raval, which is changing quite rapidly, but there's a little strip with all these bars and they're filled with drunk Muslims and Eastern European and African prostitutes, and there are pimps and pickpockets waiting for the men walking in and out. But because they've all been corralled into this one little street, it's fascinating. There are Moroccan guys dancing together to this weird tape of Algerian rai—and it's these sort of bent spaces where it's happening. It's where cultures go to miscegenate—where people pick up people.

Some of the most amazing moments for me are free public events in Europe catering to Maghrebi music, West African music, or even Arabic music. There are quite a few African and Northern African immigrants in Spain, for example, but they're not in positions of public power—they're very much second-class citizens—but sensitive governments feel as though they should get this free party from time to time. So you go and it's

ACOUSTIC PRESERVATION

A particular intersection in Chicago is found to have utterly unique and surprising acoustics: Whispers come out like shouts, certain resonant tones, like car engines, take on near-deafening reverb, and unpredictable echoes break out, only to continue far longer than expected. Something about the arrangement of buildings, or the materials they're made from—no one quite understands. As a joke people call it Echo Place, then Sound Park, then Echo Park. The name soon sticks.

One day, though, a developer buys the high-rise building on the intersection's southwest corner—and he proceeds to have it dismantled, slowly, removing the windows and doorframes for salvage, and reducing the whole thing floor by floor.

The acoustics of the intersection begin to change. Chicago's Echo Park is under threat.

An extraordinary legal case ensues, followed closely by both the AIA and the National Trust for Historic Preservation. But this is something no one's ever heard of before: Concerned citizens have rallied behind what they call *acoustic preservation*. It doesn't matter what the developer's new building will *look* like, they say, or whether or not it's in keeping with the historic style of the neighborhood; it only matters that, even after the new structure is built, the intersection will *sound the same as before*.

The acoustics must be brought back, they say. This soundmark must be acoustically preserved.

At great expense to the developer, then, bewildering calculations are made—and it's determined that an elaborate series of echo-screens and semi-detached, angled walls like car spoilers will need to be added to the future building.

Architecture critics say that it's the return of the Baroque—in the ornamental service of sound.

an amazing, incredible mix, getting a social equality that isn't present at any other level of Spanish or Mediterranean society. They're fleeting moments—but they do happen, and that's interesting to me. There are Arabic nightclubs, for instance, but they happen outside the major cities; if you want to hear Arabic pop, you don't go to Barcelona, you go to Badalona, this working class city next to it, or to the cities to the north and to the west of it. But you actually have to travel to get there.

That just underscores the casual nature of these encounters: It really is on boats and in bars that people just happen to hear someone doing their thing, and they get a little curious. They're delicate moments, where things cross over, because of the natural curiosity that comes from living next to people you're unfamiliar with.

BLDGBLOG: There's an emotional intensity to the experience of something that new—or to being reconnected to something you've been separated from.

Rupture: That brings me to *rembetika*, actually, which is the perfect example of these types of movements.

When the Greeks invaded Turkey in 1921, they kicked out 2 million Turkish Greeks who had lived in Turkey for multiple generations. These Turkish Greeks were forcibly resettled in Greece as second-class citizens—in camps, slums, and the poorest parts of cities. Their whole way of life had been uprooted, and they had taken their strange Ottoman instruments, Oriental tunings, and songs with them, so this incredibly sad music grew up. The major themes are unrequited love, drug addiction, opium, hashish, jails, and dislocation. It's often just a voice accompanied by strings—and it's heartbreaking, powerful, and mysterious. And it came from utter alienation in one's own country—and from poverty. Music is extremely portable like that, and its edges are evanescent.

AMPLIFIER HOUSE

Joel Sanders, Architect; Karen Van Lengen; and Ben Rubin of EAR Studio took a step beyond "the modernist notion of visual transparency" (i.e., large windows and glass houses) by adding "aural transparency"—acoustic openness—to a project they call the Mix House. As Sanders describes the house on his website:

> Situated on a generic suburban plot, the dwelling is composed of two sound-gathering volumes outfitted with three audiovisual windows. The curved profile of each of these sonic windows is composed of two elements: a louvered glass

window wall that regulates the sound of the air-borne ambient environment, and a parabolic dish that electronically targets domestic sounds and transmits them to an interior audio system controlled from the kitchen island. From this sound command center of the house, occupants are free to design original domestic soundscapes by mixing media sponsored sounds with the ambient noises of the neighborhood.

These "sonic windows"—or *parabolic ornaments*—amplify the audio setting of the house, thus making site and location several orders of magnitude more important than before. In fact, should a house like this really be constructed in the suburbs, as the architects seem to assume? Instead of deep in the woods somewhere, or even on top of a glacier...? Crystalline pressures of melting ice 3,000 feet below you suddenly break, sending cascades of sound shivering upward through the house's foundations. Some days it's impossible to get out of bed, hypnotized by unearthly noises.

The "den/bedroom wing is oriented vertically to capture audio-visual views of the sky," we read, and "the front window wall doubles as a sliding glass door that allows the occupant to hear the sounds of the streetscape." Further: "Located above the bed, the skylight captures sky-borne sounds, as well as signals transmitted through TV and Internet connections." It's architecture as the cure for—or cause of?—schizophrenia.

The artistic possibilities here are endless. One wonders, for instance, if several of these houses could be constructed in the same neighborhood, on the same street—with each one then hooked up to public broadcasting equipment and loudspeakers. Pirate radio. Cul-de-sac FM. The houses play sounds for each other, like instruments, orchestrating the neighborhood's sonic environment—becoming part of, and borrowing, one another's "audio-visual views." Each house—already an outside-in acoustic snapshot of the environment in real-time—then turns sound around to offer a corresponding inside-out anthem for the streets and passersby: The clinking forks and knives of a private dining room are broadcast onto the street. An architecturally outside-inside-out soundtrack for the local neighborhood. Standing at an audio booth in the kitchen, drunk homeowners mix belches with airplane roars.

Someone plays layered tape loops of the sounds of their house from yesterday—and this gets picked up by a neighbor and rebroadcast, with reverb, over the noise of a distant lawnmower. Rival teenagers declare audio warfare, their microphones left open all night long.

Then, in 2017, a particularly well-constructed house, full of weird audio equipment, becomes the sole instrument used to soundtrack Steven Spielberg's final film....

THE AMBIENT WALKMAN

In a multi-authored recap of the best and worst ideas of 2006, the *New York Times* mentioned something called the Ambient Addition, designed by Noah Vawter, then a graduate student at MIT. The Ambient Addition "consists of two headphones with transparent earpieces, each equipped with a microphone and a speaker":

> The microphones sample the background noise in the immediate vicinity—wind blowing through the trees, traffic, a cellphone conversation. Then, with the help of a small digital signal-processing chip, the headphones make music from these sounds. For instance, percussive sounds like footsteps and coughs are sequenced into a stuttering pattern, and all the noises are tuned so that they fuse into a coherent, slowly changing set of harmonies.

This apparently amplifies users' interest in their surroundings by encouraging direct sonic engagement. According to the project's website, for instance, the Ambient Addition's users start "to play with objects around them, sing to themselves, and wander toward tempting sound sources." In other words, they start acting like Teletubbies....

The Mix House by Joel Sanders, Architect; Karen Van Lengen; and Ben Rubin/EAR Studio.

joelsandersarchitect.com
earstudio.com

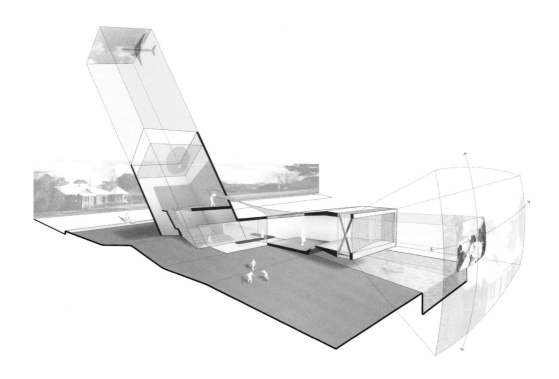

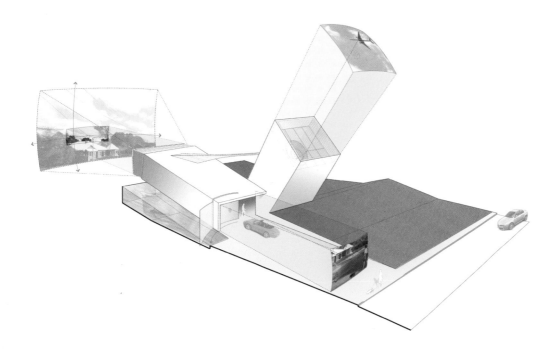

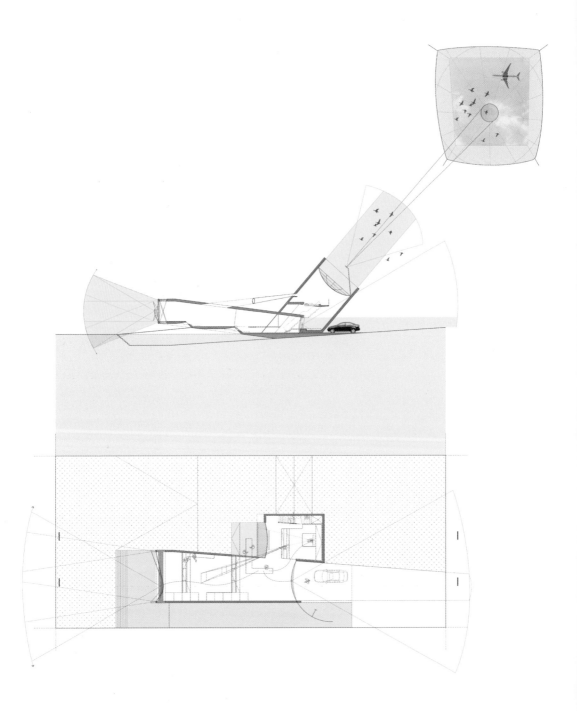

SLEEP LABS OF THE SOVIET EMPIRE

Even Stalin was into weird audio equipment. In the Winter 2007/2008 issue of *Cabinet* magazine, we read how, following the implementation of Stalin's first Five-Year Plan, and in the wake of food rationing and extended work hours, "the shock-troops of Communism were edging perilously close to physical and mental exhaustion: what they needed was rest." Soviet authorities thus "announced a competition to design a garden suburb outside Moscow, where workers could be sent to recuperate from the strains of factory labor."

One detail of the project highlighted by the article was a sort of dream academy, or colosseum of slumber: a purpose-built structure referred to as the "Sonata of Sleep." Designed by Konstantin Melnikov, the building "consisted of two large dormitories either side of a central block," each of which had sloping floors to "obviate the need for pillows."

> At either end of the long buildings were to be situated control booths, where technicians would command instruments to regulate the temperature, humidity, and air pressure, as well as to waft salubrious scents and "rarefied condensed air" through the halls. Nor would sound be left unorganized. Specialists working "according to scientific facts" would transmit from the control centre a range of sounds gauged to intensify the process of slumber. The rustle of leaves, the cooing of nightingales, or the soft murmur of waves would instantly relax the most overwrought veteran of the metropolis. Should these fail, the mechanized beds would then begin gently to rock until consciousness was lost.

While all this certainly sounds ambitious enough, "Melnikov's original impulse had been much more far-reaching." His initial dream had apparently been to create an Institute for Changing the Form of Man. Melnikov's plans encompassed the resurrection of the dead, a house in which residents would feel as if they "were floating in thick golden air," and what *Cabinet* calls a "series of spatial adventures," most notably a building whose oversize interior was "a delirium of gigantic stairways and roller bearings."

SOUND FIELD

The Mix House by Joel Sanders, Architect; Karen Van Lengen; and Ben Rubin/EAR Studio.

joelsandersarchitect.com
earstudio.com

If we can use sound and other stimulants to change "the form of man," why not change the form of agriculture? In 2007, *New Scientist* reported that Korean scientists "identified two genes in rice that respond to sound waves." These "sound-sensitive genes"—or "sound-responsive genes"—"could be attached to other genes to make them respond to sound too."

> The genes rbcS and Ald became more active at 125 and 250 hertz and less active at 50 hertz. As both are known to respond to light, the researchers repeated the tests in the dark and found that the two genes still responded to sound.

Though these results "have been greeted with profound skepticism" by other researchers, if the tests can be repeated, then they would indicate "that sound could be an alternative to light as a gene regulator." It's not photosynthesis, then, but *audiosynthesis*. Geneto-acoustic biology.

> If the researchers are correct, they say their discovery could enable farmers to switch specific crop genes on and off, such as ones for flowering, by blasting sound into the fields.

Which leaves me wondering if, someday, there might be whole warehouses full of hybridized crops growing vigorously in absolute darkness, a thunderous drone roaring from hidden speakers. Somewhere below, in a soundproof lab, scientists subject single seeds to 6,000 hours of shifting frequencies, synthesizing vitamins, coaxing corn into wheat. The new agrialchemy. Someone breaks in one night, unaware of what the building really is, only to switch on his flashlight, terrified by the thunderous roar, and see a thousand stalks of corn vibrating in rows all around him. The ground is shaking and the air is full of pollen.

Will we grow tomorrow's crops inside recording studios?

Or, 10 years from now, you stumble upon vast fields of barley stretching off to the horizon, with weatherproof speakers placed every 300 feet emitting F-sharp—though the exact

PATTERNS OF PLANTS

In 1997, Japanese composer Mamoru Fujieda released a CD called *Patterns of Plants*. According to his record label, the album featured "melodic material" that Fujieda had developed using the "surface-electrical potential" of plant leaves. In other words, he had transformed leaves into sound. Fujieda then played these plant sounds through a combination of "alternate tuning systems (just intonation, Pythagorean) with traditional instruments of China and Japan (*sho, koto* and the ancient 25-stringed zither, the *hitsu*)," creating a "bizarre and fascinating mixture of European Medieval music, the traditions of Asia and modern science."

In fact, Fujieda's musical translation of plant life is similar to work done by composer Yuji Dogane. As the Japanese website *Contemporary Art and Spirits* writes, Dogane is known for creating a device called the Ecological Plantron. Dogane's Plantron "measures the minute electrical changes which flow across the surface of the leaves of plants, and changes them into sounds."

THE SOUND OF EVOLUTION

City birds have begun to sing new songs. As *New Scientist* wrote on March 28, 2008, the constant background sounds of cities—from road noise to airplane engines—are having a biological effect on local bird species. House finches, blackbirds, and even great tits are learning how to adapt. Researchers found that great tits in the city, for instance, now sing "higher-pitched tunes than their forest-dwelling counterpart[s]"—indeed, that these urban birds make entirely different noises because they've been rendered all but deaf at certain frequencies. This could have huge implications:

> If singing and hearing diverge enough, urban birds may be less likely to find the vocals of rural birds attractive, or even to recognize them as members of the same species. These changes could serve to eventually split populations into genetically distinct urban and rural species.

"In the long term," they write, "new species may evolve."

In other words, urban acoustic effects are helping to catalyze the evolution of new animal species—making entire strains of life on Earth the indirect offspring of sound.

sound they're playing has been patented. It is illegal to play it elsewhere; if you do, the RIAA will sue you. Will Monsanto perhaps enter into future contracts with the music industry?

And what about *our* genes, of course, perhaps shaken into new configurations by exposure to the rarest of frequencies—are *we* genetically responsive to sound? Might there even have been a civilization somewhere whose "music" was really a complicated form of genetic stimulation? At every concert you attend, you become something other—acoustically moving through new forms of alteration. While you sit there listening, off in the distance somewhere behind you a group of plants begins to shake, their roots and branches knitting together, a whole new landscape taking shape.

MUSICALIZING THE WEATHER THROUGH LANDSCAPE ARCHITECTURE

Listening to a landscape tends literally to be overlooked in favor of a site's visual impact. It seems quite rare, in other words, for people to pack up the family car and head off to Wales, or through the Green Mountains of Vermont, and it's all so that they can *listen to the hills*. They'll go out to look at autumn leaf colors, or to take photographs of spring wildflowers—but to go all the way to the Adirondacks so that they can hear a particular autumn wind storm come howling through the gorges—specifically going somewhere to *listen to the landscape*—is almost unheard of, if you'll pardon the pun.

One of the most interesting artifacts from World War II are the so-called *sound mirrors* built before the age of radar on the British coast. These acoustic early warning devices were concave concrete structures—resembling ice-cream scoops, satellite dishes, or curving parabolic walls—that faced the

skies above Europe, amplifying the sound of enemy aircraft approaching. Almost instantly obsolete, the sound mirrors now stand abandoned in the fields—rain stained, sometimes covered with graffiti, often sinking into the sand—and have frequently been repurposed for various projects (related to war, British history, or ambient music—sometimes all at once).

But why not build a new series of sound mirrors in a landscape with regular, annual wind phenomena? A distant gully that moans every year in the second week of November due to northern winds from Canada could have its low, droning, cliff-created reverb echoed carefully back up a chain of sound mirrors to supply natural soundscapes for the sleeping residents of nearby towns. The Great November Moan. Or a crevasse that makes no sound at all could have a sound mirror built nearby, which then amplifies and redirects the ambient air movements, coaxing out a tone . . . but only in the first week of March. It's a question of interacting with the earth's atmosphere through human geotechnical constructions. Transforming a landscape into a saxophone—through sound mirrors.

You'd need:

- Detailed meteorological charts of a region's annual wind-flow patterns
- Sound mirrors
- A very large arts grant

You could then musicalize the weather using nothing but landscape architecture.

If we've explored the idea of building storm-generating mechanisms and anti-weather walls, then why not consider turning those same structures into huge musical instruments? Sound mirrors like French horns installed somewhere in the landscape. By precisely arranging sound mirrors atop a mesa, for instance, or deep inside a system of canyons—whether in the Peak District or northwestern Italy—you could transform weather systems into music for two weeks a year, amplifying the sounds of seasonal air patterns. People would come, camp out, check into hotels, open all their windows—and just listen to the landscaped echoes.

TECTONIC SOUND MACHINE

A short article in the August 2004 issue of the *Wire* reviewed the work of sound artist Mark Bain. "Equipped with seismometers," the *Wire* explained, Bain "can turn architectural structures into giant musical instruments and demolish buildings with sound alone." His installations have included "sensing devices, oscil-

BOTANICAL OTOLOGY

Artist Alex Metcalf's *Tree Listening Installation* is a small electronic listening device built for eavesdropping on the inner soundscapes of trees. How does it work? The device—a small and somewhat unassuming metal cone—is placed on a given tree trunk and then connected to as many as ten sets of headphones, which hang down from the tree's canopy. "This allows the public to listen 'live' to the sound of water being pulled up from the roots to the leaves through the xylem tube," Metcalf writes on his website.

As he explained in an interview with the *Guardian* in May 2008: "The technology for this is usually invasive. You bore into the tree and take away a section, then seal in a listening device. The thing about my device is that you don't have to cause any damage, and you can listen to any tree, anywhere, any time—plus you can do it long term. Cutting a hole in a tree means you are wounding and infecting it, which will affect the recording."

Ten years from now, a pirate radio station pops up in the distant suburbs of west London—and it turns out that an old couple living on a plot of wooded land near Windsor Great Park have begun to broadcast their trees. It's soon an international sensation and a great hit with cover bands: You go down to the pub one night to hear music, but the band, visibly drunk, gets lost in a three-hour rendition of the inner sounds of sessile oak trees.

alexmetcalf.co.uk

SONIC LANDMARKS

A few questions arise in this context—for instance, does Stonehenge have a sound? What if it had been built not as an astronomical observation device but as a landscape wind instrument? Five thousand years ago you could be wandering around the Cotswolds, thinking, "Oh my god, we're lost—wait: *I hear Stonehenge...*" You thus locate yourself. Sonic landmarks.

Might there even be a *sonic signature* to the U.S. occupation of Baghdad? Not the rumble of Hummers and airplane engines—but if all those concrete blast walls inadvertently act as sound mirrors, generating sounds during evening windstorms. All the American military bases of Iraq moaning at 3 a.m. in the desert breeze.

What does the occupation of Iraq *sound* like?

lators and the occasional sculptural element"—such as a "six meter high inflatable speaker" called the *sonusphere*.

The sonusphere, formerly installed in the Edith Russ Haus in Germany, gave acoustic shape to the deep movements of plate tectonics. From the gallery's own description of the piece:

Modified seismic sensors pick up the normally unheard movements of the earth [which] are channeled through the entire building until reaching a "crescendo" in Bain's sonusphere. Unique in its purpose and design, the sonusphere is essentially a wired, inflatable ball that fills the entire upper floor and takes signals generated from an acoustic network running through the entire architecture. It acts as a low frequency, 360 degree, acoustic radiator translating the sound to its curved walls as physically pulsating sound pressure.

Bain's work, the *Wire* adds, references "the ideas of maverick engineer Nikola Tesla." Tesla's avant-garde electrical ideas inspired Bain to develop "a system for resonating buildings that allowed him to 'play' structures. 'The multi-resonator system I designed could drive waveforms into buildings,' Bain comments, 'like giant additive synthesis where you get different beatings of frequencies and shifted harmonics. I was basically designing systems that turned a structure into a musical instrument.'"

Writing for the UK sound journal *Earshot* in November 2002, Bain himself described how he could thus destroy architecture through sound. He called these "whole building projects," and examples include his installation at Het Paard, a music venue in the Hague that was, at the time, scheduled for demolition. Somehow convincing the city that they should let him play deliberately ruinous sonic frequencies inside the building before it was torn down, Bain was able to "induce severe damage on some of the thicker walls" of the structure using resonators and sound alone. Sound becomes a weapon that you can turn against architecture.

Inspired, he went on to build "two portable earthquake machines in Holland":

In Gronigen [*sic*], I produced the Angel Machine [which] involved three six-ton earth compacting machines connected together and tuned for earth frequencies. In Tilburg I produced the GeoSite, a portable earthquake which consisted of a 6-meter long steel plate buried in the ground with three large vibronic activators mounted to it. The piece was invisible on the surface of the ground, but when activated induced severe tremors that spread outward to a half a kilometer radius in the surrounding area.

Bain's projects have also included the "activation of large steel trestle bridges" in which massive waves of sound "produced [a] low frequency ringing tone that could be tuned to different harmonics including a frequency that would flake rust off." And, proving that decommissioned pieces of Cold War military architecture can be turned into gigantic musical instruments, Bain even built something called the Live Room. The Live Room "involved a defunct laboratory space that was used originally to develop and test guidance systems for ICBM missiles in the 1960s," he explains.

> This space had a unique suspended floor system that was made of aluminum, with I-beams and a thick plate covering. Underneath the floor panels was a sub foundation made of concrete and sand which was isolated from the surrounding building and contained seven isolation pads which were designed to hold the tilt tables used in the testing of the gyroscopic apparatuses. For this piece, I reversed the original intention of the space (made specifically for isolation from outside vibration) and added six large frequency inducers (vibration exciters) to the underside of the floor which were connected to a control mixer. After the room was reassembled, the instrument was complete and I had a kind of tectonic sound machine which spectators could walk on and feel through their bodies.

This connection between sound and architectural demolition came up again on September 11. Extensive seismic readings were taken by Columbia University as the Precambrian bedrock of Manhattan shook during the collapse of the World Trade Center towers. Perhaps unsurprisingly, Bain transformed this information into audio files—with the result that you can actually listen to the wounded, melancholic howl of Manhattan as its two tallest buildings fall to the ground. In the end, Bain released "a 74-minute recording of the ground vibrations of the World Trade Center's collapse and contiguous mayhem," the *Guardian* wrote on February 13, 2004. All of New York City became Bain's "tectonic sound machine," and the music of September 11 "certainly does not make easy listening," we read.

> The piece begins with a low, disconcerting rumble and proceeds through a range of fluctuating sounds. Bain says the vibration of the towers as they were hit by the hijacked passenger planes sounds like "tuning forks."

He seems quick to add, when asked about the project, that he "sees nothing morally questionable in making an artwork out of the event." In fact, Bain finds acoustic "events" everywhere. In

MUSIQUE CONCRÈTE

Scotland's Rosslyn Chapel, famous for its appearance in Dan Brown's *The Da Vinci Code*, has apparently been hiding a fascinating secret, after all. A father and son duo found that carved stone ornaments affixed to the church's ceiling actually encode a musical score.

From the website of Thomas J. Mitchell, who decrypted the music:

> Rosslyn Chapel holds a musical mystery in its architecture and design. At one end of the chapel, on the ceiling are 4 cross-sections of arches containing elaborate symbolic designs on each array of cubes (in actual fact they are rectangles mostly). The "cubes" are attached to the arches in a musically sequential way.

In the overambitious application of a cryogenics metaphor, Mitchell says that the music has now "thawed out," enabling it to be understood—and heard—by people today.

Whether or not there really is music encoded in the arches of Rosslyn, the implications of this are extraordinary. Will someone detect, for instance, a thousand years from now, a symphony encoded in the runways at Heathrow? Or will the New York City subway system be re-understood as a series of subterrestrial folk songs, themed around a chorus of transportation? Or perhaps the International Space Station will be revealed as an étude of pressurized air tanks, awaiting its musical decryption; three-dimensional music, hovering in space.

tjmitchell.com

his article for *Earshot*, Bain suggests that, with an "unconventional apparatus" he would be able to pick and amplify—even generate—subtle vibrations inside architecture. This apparatus would allow him to "tap into the strange sounds resident within the materials of structures and land sites," a "secret world of micro sound standing right beneath our feet and containing a quality of sublime heaviness."

What might such an apparatus be? A smaller, modified sonusphere? I've often thought that it would be well worth the effort, if—in the same way that Rome has hundreds of free public fountains to fill the water bottles of thirsty residents—London could introduce a series of *audio listening posts*: iPod-friendly masts anchored like totem poles throughout the city, in Trafalgar Square, Newington Green, the nave of St. Pancras Old Church, outside the Millennium Dome. You show up with your headphones, plug them in, and the groaning, amplified howl of church foundations and overused roadways—the city's subterranean soundtrack, reverbed 24 hours a day through contact mics into the headsets of greater London—greets you in tectonic surround-sound, the city an instrument of arches and railway viaducts, Tube tunnels straining under riverine pressures. The unsettling groan of wet masonry. Like the creaking timbers of an old ship, or an architectural iceberg, the city sings its otherwise inaudible music…and you've got your headphones on, plugged into the urban understructure, so that the reverbed shudder of a Georgian terrace house lulls you to sleep in a café. You put sound masts on the Thames foreshore, where you can listen to the passing of underground trains, and then in a ring around the M25, which begins to soundtrack itself with an automotive drone that lasts whole seasons at a time. This is what your city sounds like, you say, handing the headphones to a passerby: the loose wobble of brickwork and glass. Seventy floors of an iron tower humming in the darkness as late winter rain begins to fall.

For that matter, you could drill contact microphones into the surface of Greenland and listen to that terrestrial baritone, the ice a reverberatory—such a strange and haunting sound, like bells shattering, of pure ice heaving beneath your feet, caves and tunnels realigning along audio slip-faults. Someday perhaps we'll eavesdrop on breaking glaciers from within.

SUPER REEF

A "vanished giant has reappeared in the rocks of Europe," the February 2, 1991, issue of *New Scientist* tells us. It was "one of the largest living structures ever to have existed on Earth." This "bioengineering marvel" is actually a fossil reef that spans

Europe in a zigzag from Spain, through France and Switzerland, into Germany, Poland, and down to the Black Sea. It's now believed that parts of the reef have been uncovered as far away as Newfoundland and Russia.

"Despite the scale of this buried structure," *New Scientist* wrote, "until recently researchers knew surprisingly little about it. Individual workers had seen only glimpses of reef structures that formed parts of the whole complex. They viewed each area separately rather than putting them together to make one huge structure."

The reef's history, as relayed by *New Scientist*:

> About 200 million years ago the sea level rose throughout the world. A huge ocean known as the Tethys Seaway expanded to reach almost around the globe at the Equator. Its warm, shallow waters enhanced the deposition of widespread lime muds and sands which made a stable foundation for the sponges and other inhabitants of the reef. The sponge reef began to grow in the Late Jurassic period, between 170 and 150 million years ago, and its several phases were dominated by siliceous sponges.

Rigid with silicate glass, this proto-reef "continued to expand across the seafloor for between 5 and 10 million years until it occupied most of the wide sea shelf that extended over central Europe." Thus, today, in the foundations of European geography, you see the structural remains of a million living creatures, like something out of H. P. Lovecraft.

From *New Scientist*:

> We do not know whether the demise of this fossil sponge reef was caused by an environmental change to shallower waters, or from the competition for growing space with corals. What we do know is that such a structure never appeared again in the history of the Earth.

For whatever reason, reading this story brought to mind a concert by Japanese musician and sound artist Akio Suzuki that my wife and I attended back in 2002, at the School of Oriental and African Studies in London. Suzuki played a variety of instruments that night, including the amazing "Analapos," which he'd constructed himself, and a number of small stone flutes, or *iwabue*.

These flutes were really just rocks, plain and simple, but they had been hollowed out by erosion. Suzuki had chosen the stones because of their natural acoustic properties, their musical playability; he could attain the right resonance and hit the right notes. The "music" they produced was just a factor of geology.

↑ previous spread
Two photographs by Camille Seaman.

Top: Grand Pinnacle Iceberg III–East Greenland, August 2006.

Bottom: Iceberg & Glacier–Antarctic Peninsula, December 2007.

camilleseaman.com

WHEN LANDSCAPES SING

The polar seas are filled with sound: unearthly vibrations that moan almost constantly through near-frozen waters. From a December 2005 issue of *New Scientist*: "'It's like a string orchestra all practicing different tunes at the same time but then suddenly playing together,' says Vera Schlindwein, a geophysicist at the Alfred Wegener Institute for Polar and Marine Research in Bremerhaven, Germany." If you're hoping to stick your head underwater, however, and listen directly to the arctic seas, think again. "The sounds are not usually audible, but can be heard when recordings of seismic signals...are speeded up."

So what are the instruments creating this frozen music? Icebergs, of course. "A spectacular 16-hour 'song' in July 2000 helped pinpoint the cause," *New Scientist* continues, and this was "traced to a 400-meter-high iceberg." As the iceberg scraped along the seafloor, "seawater running through crevasses in the ice would have continued to flow rapidly, causing the tunnel walls [to] vibrate." The iceberg as cello string (or perhaps kettle drum): the internal crystalline pressures of a half-submerged, mobile landscape soundtracking the arctic seas. Tectonics of ice in surround-sound.

They were accidents of erosion—as if rocks everywhere might hide musical instruments inside them.

Putting these together, the idea that there might be a similar flute the size and shape of a vast fossilized reef, stretching from Portugal to southern Russia, suddenly seems like a real possibility. Locked into the rocks of Europe could be the largest musical instrument ever made: awaiting a million more years of wind, rain, and artificial excavation, for the reef to be carved into a flute, or a buried saxophone, made of fossilized glass, pocked with caves and indentations. It will reflect the black light of uncountable eclipses until it erodes from the surface of the earth altogether.

Weird European land animals, evolving 500,000 generations from now, will notice it first: a strange whistling on the edge of the wind whenever storms blow up from Africa. Mediterranean rains wash more dust and soil into the sea, exposing more reef, and the sounds get louder.

The reef looms larger. Its structure, like hollow backbones, frames valleys, rims horizons, and carries all sounds through a reverberating latticework of small wormholes and caves. It is equivalent to 100 million flutes embedded in bedrock per square mile. Soon the reef generates its own weather, forming storms where there had only been breezes; it echoes with the sound of itself from one end to the other. It wakes up animals, who begin howling. Birds imitate it in their unearthly songs.

Then, amidst the last two or three remaining groups of humans—those dying, malnourished tribes who tried to flee the effects of nuclear war and climate change—it's rumored that if you whisper a secret into the reef it will echo there forever; that a person can be hundreds of miles away when the secret comes through, passing from ridge to ridge on Saharan gales.

Of course, if I've implied that reefs might actually be huge musical instruments—barely understood acoustic installations in the rocks and under the sea—it turns out that a group of Scotsmen have been testing that exact hypothesis.

From the April 16, 2005, *New Scientist*:

Stephen Simpson at the University of Edinburgh, UK, and his colleagues set up 24 artificial reefs, each with a speaker system, near Australia's Great Barrier Reef. On six consecutive nights they played recordings of natural reefs at half the sites. A reef that was noisy one night was silent the next and vice versa. Reefs with the audio cue attracted four times as many cardinal fish and nearly twice as many damselfish.

This "audio cue" is later described as the "'frying bacon' sound of snapping shrimps," and it "can be picked up from 20 kilometers away."

All of which is another way of saying that reefs already *are* musical instruments: They are vast landscape saxophones being played by shrimp underwater...

THE B-FLAT RANGE

Another kind of geological instrument could well be forming right now in Antarctica.

Ventifacts are "geologic formations shaped by the forces of wind," Jackie Dee Grom wrote in the Summer 2006 issue of *Cabinet* magazine. "The McMurdo Dry Valleys of Antarctica are home to one of the most extreme environments in the world—a polar desert blasted by ferocious winds, deprived of all but minimal rain, and beset by a mean annual temperature of negative twenty degrees Celsius."

It is there, in the Antarctic Dry Valleys, that "gravity-driven winds pour off the high polar plateau, attaining speeds of up to two hundred kilometers per hour."

> In the grip of these aeolian forces, sand and small pebbles hurl through the air, smashing into the volcanic rocks that have fallen from the valley walls, slowly prying individual crystals from their hold, and sculpting natural masterworks over thousands of years. The multi-directional winds in this eerie and isolated wasteland create ventifacts of an exceptional nature, gouged with pits and decorated with flowing flutes and arching curves.

Part of me, though, can't help but imagine these weird and violent geologies—reduced and abraded by multidirectional Antarctic winds as strong as hurricanes and filled with geologic debris—as *musical instruments* in the making. You *hear* them before you see them, as they scream with polar tempests. Looking at photos of ventifacts, I'm even led to wonder if the entirety of Antarctica could slowly erode over millions of years into an orchestral device. The entire Transantarctic Range carved into flutes and oboes, frigid columns of air blasting off the island's most elevated glaciers like biblical trumpets into the sky. The *B-flat Range*. Somewhere between a Futurist noise-orchestra and a Rube Goldberg device made of well-layered bedrock. Where musical instrument design and landscape architecture collide. Flocks of birds in Patagonia hear the valleys, blaring atonal chords like foghorns for thousands of miles. *The Valve Mountains*. Global wind systems coil through hundreds of miles of ventifactual canyons before coming out the other end. On quiet nights you can hear it in southern Australia, blowing in over the waves.

SPACE IN THE KEY OF B-FLAT
According to NASA, in November
2003: "Astronomers in England
have discovered a singing black
hole in a distant cluster of galax-
ies. In the process of listening
in, the team of astronomers . . .
heard the lowest sound waves
from an object in the Universe
ever detected by humans"—and
they realized that it's singing, yes,
B-flat. As Reuters describes it,
a "particularly monstrous black
hole has probably been humming
B-flat for billions of years, but at
a pitch no human could hear, let
alone sing."

In his ultimately disappointing but still wildly imaginative 1936 novella, *At the Mountains of Madness*, H. P. Lovecraft writes about a small Antarctic expeditionary team that stumbles upon an alien city deep in the south polar continent's most remote glacial valleys. It is a city "of no architecture known to man or to human imagination, with vast aggregations of night-black masonry embodying monstrous perversions of geometrical laws." This city's largest structures are "sometimes terraced or fluted, surmounted by tall cylindrical shafts here and there bulbously enlarged and often capped with tiers of thinnish scalloped disks." Even better, "these febrile structures seemed knit together by tubular bridges crossing from one to the other at various dizzy heights, and the implied scale of the whole was terrifying and oppressive in its sheer gigantism."

Lovecraft describes how the continent's "barren" and "grotesque" landscape interacted with the polar wind:

> Through the desolate summits swept ranging, intermittent gusts of the terrible antarctic wind; whose cadences sometimes held vague suggestions of a wild and half-sentient musical piping, with notes extending over a wide range, and which for some subconscious mnemonic reason seemed to me disquieting and even dimly terrible.

It was the Earth's surface in fugue: the first acoustic trace of the B-flat Range . . . . ⊗

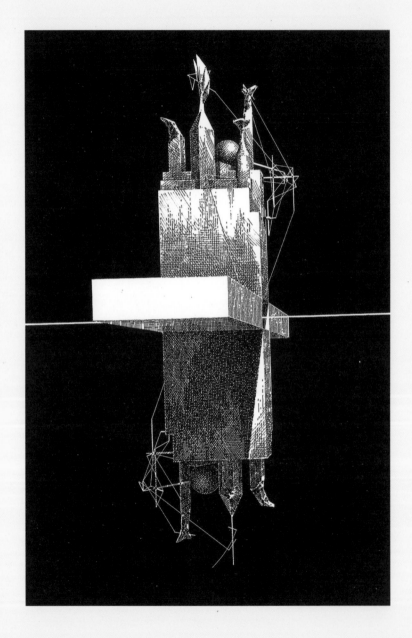

Without Walls: An Interview with Lebbeus Woods

Lebbeus Woods's work is the exclamation point at the end of a sentence proclaiming that the architectural imagination, freed from constraints of finance and buildability, should be uncompromising—always. Architects should radically reconstruct the outermost possibilities of the built environment—if need be, rethinking the very planet we stand on.

One early project by Woods, in particular, just floors me. In 1980, Woods proposed a tomb for Albert Einstein—the so-called *Einstein Tomb*—inspired by Boullée's *Cenotaph for Newton*. But Woods's proposal wasn't for some paltry gravestone or mausoleum hewn out of mountain granite; it was a post-terrestrial space station, sailing through the void. The *Einstein Tomb* struck me as such an ingenious solution to an otherwise unremarkable problem—how to build a tomb for an historically titanic mathematician and physicist—that I've followed his work ever since.

BLDGBLOG: To start with, what was the origin of *Einstein Tomb*?

Lebbeus Woods: Back in 1978–80, I was looking for some philosophical grounding for architecture, other than historical references, and I was very interested in cycles, and the cyclical nature of human life. I was reading—and I had read years before—people like Giambattista Vico, who was a great influence on a lot of people, including James Joyce and W. B. Yeats. I was very involved in this whole idea of the cyclical nature of life rather than the linear historical story of the Enlightenment. That's one side of the story. The other is that I was thinking of Boullée's *Cenotaph for Newton*, a celebration of one of the greatest scientists of that period. I felt there should be something for Albert Einstein, too, because his theories certainly revolutionized our view of nature and our view of the universe.

Einstein wanted his body cremated and the ashes scattered when he died—he didn't want any monuments to commemorate his life. So I was stuck with the problem of how to create a cenotaph to commemorate his thought and his life, yet knowing that he didn't want any such thing. How could I do it and respect his wishes? I realized that the way to do it is to build the cenotaph and then send it out into space where no one would see it. In a sense, we would know that it existed, but we wouldn't be able to visit it, or lay flowers, wreaths, or whatever, to pay homage.

So, wanting to make a cenotaph and realizing that it had to go into space, the idea was then very simple: One of Einstein's great contributions had to do with the speed of light. He didn't measure it and he wasn't the one who discovered it—even Newton was talking about the speed of light, and there was a pretty firm idea of what the speed of light might be—but there was also this idea that outer space was filled with something called, right up until Einstein's theories, the *ether*. The ether was a substance that would transmit particles—like light particles—through space, because people couldn't imagine that things would just travel through an empty void without there being a medium. Einstein's first theory of relativity didn't challenge the idea of the ether—he just didn't mention it, and he didn't need it. It all came down to the idea of *electromagnetism*.

So I thought: What if the cenotaph is somehow launched into space on a beam of light? The beam of light is fired into space, and the cenotaph is designed to ride that beam of light. Now, of course, that's a contradiction, because no material object is capable of going at the speed of light—its mass would be infinite. There's also the fact that space is curved, so if we did fire a beam of light into space, we could hypothesize that, eventually, it would return to Earth. Space is not flat and infinite—it returns on itself. This is one of the consequences of Einstein's thought. So I designed the cenotaph to follow a beam of light, and eventually it would return to Earth, in eons of time—at least in theory.

We would have the Einstein tomb—it would exist for us—but we couldn't see it or visit it, except in the design drawings. I felt that I'd addressed the paradox of Einstein's theories as well as his wishes not to be commemorated with a monument.

BLDGBLOG: So it was kind of an architectural boomerang?

Woods: In that it returns—exactly. Of course, in many religions—particularly Hinduism—there is an idea that things will return, that there is a cycle of time. It's not just an infinite progression of time. It's also the idea of the expansion of the universe—that there was a big bang, and the universe is expanding, and it's going to go and go and go—but at some point, it's going to collapse back in on itself because of gravity. Then it will all go into an infinitesimally small ball and explode again—and there'll be a new cycle. Physicists are discussing this today in a serious way—it's a theory—but the idea is that there is a finite cycle of time and space inside of which the universe repeats. Of course, the philosopher Nietzsche wrote in his books about the idea of the eternal return—that there would be this big cycle—and of course he's borrowing that from mythology, not from science.

Eventually, I abandoned that direction in my work, sometime in the mid-'80s, I'd say. I just went as far as I could go with it, and I couldn't do much more with it. In earlier years I had a philosophical concern, and actually was not at all concerned with specifics. I'd say that the philosophical element still runs throughout my work, but I've tried, now, to relate it much more to the world around me—to the world around all of us, really. I find the architecture of space programs and even much sci-fi architecture much too technological. The *Einstein Tomb* certainly doesn't look technological.

But I just remembered Arthur Clarke's book, *Rendezvous with Rama*, while we were talking. In *Rendezvous with Rama*, this object is detected coming into the outer solar system. People are worried about what it is—they can't figure it out—and so they send a spaceship to intercept it. It turns out to be a cylinder: it doesn't have any sexy shape, or any aerodynamic this or that, or any technological protrusions. It's just a cylinder flying through space. The crew boards it, and they go inside, and it turns out that the cylinder is rotating along its long axis, creating an artificial field of gravity, at least on the inner surfaces. Then there's a neutral axis, the axis of rotation, where

there's no gravity. That strikes me as being very interesting space architecture, because it wasn't based on a high-techy-looking thing like the Mars Lander or the Hubble telescope. It was just a cylinder. Anyway, they go in and explore it, but they never really figure out what it is before they have to leave—at which point it falls into the sun. So they don't know why it was there or what it was doing. There was obviously no one inhabiting it, but it was something like 16 miles long. Of course, Clarke was the guy who came up with the monolith in *2001*, so you can see the relationship there.

BLDGBLOG: What about the *Lower Manhattan* image? How did that project come about?

Woods: This was one of those occasions when I got a request from a magazine—which is very rare. In 1999, *Abitare* was making a special issue on New York City, and they invited a number of architects—like Steven Holl, Rafael Viñoly, and...oh god, I don't recall. Todd Williams and Billie Tsien. Michael Sorkin. Myself. They invited us to make some sort of comment about New York. So I wrote a piece—probably 1,000 words, 800 words—and I made the drawing.

The main thought I had, in speculating on the future of New York, was that, in the past, a lot of discussions had been about New York being the biggest, the greatest, the best—but that all had to do with the *size* of the city. I commented in the article about Le Corbusier's infamous remark that "Your skyscrapers are too small." Of course, New York dwellers thought he meant they're not *tall* enough—but what he was referring to was that they were too small in their ground plan. His idea of the Radiant City and the Ideal City—this was in the early '30s—was based on very large footprints of buildings, separated by great distances, and, in between the buildings in his vision, were forests, parks, and so forth. But in New York everything was cramped together because the buildings occupied such a limited ground area. So Le Corbusier was totally misunderstood by New Yorkers, who thought, *Oh, our buildings aren't tall enough—we've got to go higher!* Of course, he wasn't interested at all in their height—more in their plan relationship.

Remember, he's the guy who said, "The plan is the generator."

So I was speculating on the future of the city, and I said, "Well, obviously, compared to present and future cities, New York is not going to be able to compete in terms of size anymore. It used to be a large city, but now it's a small city compared with São Paulo, Mexico City, Kuala Lumpur, or almost any Asian city of any size." So I said, "Maybe New York can establish a new kind of scale"—and the scale I was interested in was the scale of the city to the Earth, to the planet. I made the drawing as a demonstration of the fact that Manhattan exists, with its towers and skyscrapers, because it sits on a rock—on a granite base. You can put all this weight in a very small area because Manhattan sits on the Earth. Let's not forget that buildings sit *on the Earth*.

I wanted to suggest that maybe lower Manhattan—not lower downtown, but *lower* in the sense of *below the city*—could form a new relationship with the planet. So, in the drawing, you see that the East River and the Hudson are both dammed. They're purposefully drained, as it were. The underground—or *lower Manhattan*—is revealed, and, in the drawing, there are suggestions of inhabitation in that region. So it was a romantic idea—and the drawing is very conceptual in that sense. It's peeling back the surface to see what the planetary reality is. It's not geologically correct, I'm sure, but the idea is there.

BLDGBLOG: One of the things I like so much about your work is that you re-imagine cities and buildings and whole landscapes as if they've undergone some potentially catastrophic transformation—be it a war or an earthquake—but you don't respond to those transformations by designing, say, new prefab refugee shelters or more durable tents. You respond with what I'll call *science fiction*: a completely new order of things—a new way of organizing and thinking about space. You posit something radically different than what was there before. It's exciting.

Woods: Well, I think that, for instance, in Sarajevo, I was trying to speculate on how the war could be turned around, into something

that people could build the new Sarajevo on. It wasn't about cleaning up the mess or fixing up the damage; it was more about a transformation in the society and the politics and the economics *through architecture*. I mean, it was a scenario—and, I suppose, that was the kind of movie aspect to it. It was a "what if?"

I think there's not enough of that thinking today in relation to cities that have been faced with sudden and dramatic—even violent—transformations, either because of natural or human causes. But we need to be able to speculate, to create these scenarios, and to be useful in a discussion about the next move. No one expects these ideas to be easily implemented. It's not like a practical plan that you should run out and do. But, certainly, the new scenario gives you a chance to investigate *a direction*. Of course, being an architect, I'm very interested in the specifics of that direction—you know, not just a verbal description but: This is what it might look like.

That was the approach in Sarajevo—as well as in this drawing of *Lower Manhattan*, as I called it.

BLDGBLOG: Part of that comes from recognizing architecture as a genre. In other words, architecture has the ability, rivaling literature, to imagine and propose new, alternative routes out of the present moment. So architecture isn't just *buildings*, it's a system of entirely re-imagining the world through new plans and scenarios.

Woods: Well, let me just back up and say that architecture is a multidisciplinary field, by definition. But, as a multidisciplinary field, our ideas have to be comprehensive; we can't just say: "I've got a new type of column that I think will be *great* for the future of architecture."

BLDGBLOG: [*laughs*]

Woods: Maybe it will be great—but it's not enough. I think architects—at least those inclined to understand the multidisciplinarity and the comprehensive nature of their field—have to visualize something that embraces all these political, economic, and social changes. As well as the technological. As well as the spatial.

But we're living in a very odd time for the field. There's a lack of discourse about these larger issues. People are hunkered down, looking for jobs, trying to get a building. It's a low point. I don't think it will stay that way. I don't think that architects themselves will allow that. After all, it's architects who create the field of architecture; it's not society, it's not clients, it's not governments. I mean, we architects are the ones who define what the field is about, right? So if there's a dearth of that kind of thinking at the moment, it's because architects have retreated—and I'm sure a coming generation is going to say: *Hey, this retreat is not good.* We've got to imagine more broadly. We have to have a more comprehensive vision of what the future is.

BLDGBLOG: In your own work—and I'm thinking here of the Korean DMZ project or the Israeli wall-game—this "more comprehensive vision" of the future also involves rethinking political structures: engaging in society not just spatially, but politically. Many of the buildings that you've proposed are more than just buildings, in other words; they represent new forms of political organization.

All images by Lebbeus Woods: *Lower Manhattan* (1999) and *Einstein Tomb* (1981). I was interested to read, meanwhile, in September 2008, that an "unusual object" had been discovered by the Hubble space telescope. In a paper published by the *Astrophysical Journal*, credited to Barbary et al., we read that a routine supernova survey carried out in 2005-2006 detected an "unusual optical transient" that simply disappeared from view 100 days later. What if we do someday detect structures of intelligent life—but they just whiz past, a million light-years away, lost forever again to space?

lebbeuswoods.net

Woods: The making of buildings is a huge investment of resources. The financial, as well as material, intellectual, and emotional, resources of a whole group of people get involved in a particular building project. And any time you get a group, you're talking about politics. To me politics means one thing: How do you change your situation? What is the mechanism by which you change your life? That's politics. That's the political question. It's about negotiation, or it's about revolution, or it's about terrorism, or it's about careful step-by-step planning—all of this is political in nature. It's about how people, when they get together, agree to change their situation.

As I wrote some years back, architecture is a political act, by nature. It has to do with the relationships between people and how they decide to change their conditions of living. And architecture is a prime instrument of making that change—because it has to do with building the environment they live in, and the relationships that exist in that environment.

BLDGBLOG: There's also the possibility that a building project, once complete, will actually change the society that built it. It's the idea that a building—a work of architecture—could directly catalyze a transformation, so that the society that finishes building something is not the same society that set out to build it in the first place. The building changes them.

Woods: I love that. I love the way you put it, and I totally agree with it. I think, you know, architecture should not just be something that follows up on events, but should be a *leader* of events. That's what you're saying: that, by implementing an architectural action, you actually are making a transformation in the social fabric and in the political fabric. Architecture becomes an instigator; it becomes an initiator.

That, of course, is what I've always promoted—but it's the most difficult thing for people to do. Architects say: *Well, it's my client, they won't let me do this.* Or: *I have to do what my client wants.* That's why I don't have any clients! [*laughter*] It's true. But at least I can put the ideas out there and somehow it might seep through, or filter through, to another level.

Gold Star Hurricane

1) Weather has been observed on the surface
of a star for the first time. Astronomers have
now seen clouds of mercury moving through
the turbulent skies of the star Alpha Androme-
dae, *New Scientist* reported back in June 2007.
Because the star does not have a magnetic field,
however, scientists have been left scratching
their heads over what caused the mercury
clouds to form. For the time being, no one
really knows where these things come from,
and they don't yet know if there might ever be
precipitation: frozen mercury snowing down
toward the star's core on slow currents of
helium gas.

I'm curious, as well, if there might be
any religious systems that use "hurricanes of
mercury" as a kind of divine threat. *You will
be struck down by a hurricane of mercury.* After
all, aren't Mormon fundamentalists worried
about being consumed by "hurricanes of fire"?
In which case a hurricane of, say, argon—or a
tornado of germanium—isn't all that much of
a stretch. Or perhaps a hurricane of transition
metals could come blowing in over the islands
of Stockholm, coating that city in a smooth new
shell of mineralogical forms.

2) Some stars are plated in gold. "Scattered
through space," we read in an October 1996
issue of *New Scientist*, "are some peculiar stars
that seem to contain more gold, mercury and
platinum than ordinary stars such as our Sun."
These stars are referred to as being "chemically
peculiar." One star, in particular, which astronomers have named chi Lupi, has 100,000 times
as much mercury as the Sun, and 10,000 times
as much gold, platinum, and thallium. What's
particularly interesting about this, though, is
that chi Lupi can apparently be thought of as
a series of concentric shells, where each shell
consists primarily of one element; the locations
of these shells are determined by the atomic
weights of the elements they contain. In other
words, "the heavy metals in the star were
pushed outwards by the radiation pressure of
the star's ultraviolet light, but were kept from
escaping by gravity." On chi Lupi, for instance,
there is a shell of mercury in the "stellar pho-
tosphere." Thin outer layers of gold can thus be
found on this and other "chemically peculiar"
stars throughout the universe.

Their skies are rare geology.

3) Finally, continuing with *New Scientist*, on
June 27, 2007, we read that "one of the largest

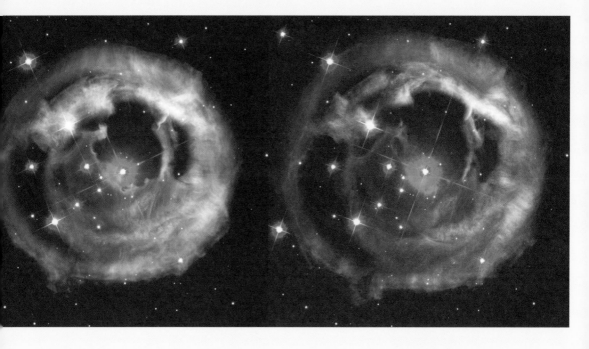

and most luminous stars in our galaxy" is also "a surprisingly prolific building site for complex molecules important to life on Earth." The discovery furthers an ongoing shift in astronomers' perceptions of where such molecules can form, and where the chain of events begins that leads from raw atoms to true biology.

The fact that "true biology" can be traced back to the stars is nothing new; but the discovery that a red hypergiant star called VY Canis Majoris is burning with prebiotic compounds, "including hydrogen cyanide (HCN), silicon monoxide (SiO), sodium chloride (NaCl) and a molecule, PN, in which a phosphorus atom and a nitrogen atom are bound together," as *New Scientist* went on to explain, is still an extraordinary discovery. Astrobiologists had previously thought that molecules like PN (which contains the phosphorous metabolically necessary for both RNA and DNA) would have been "destroyed by the intense ultraviolet radiation emitted by the star." An expanding star, it was thought, thus sterilized its progeny, like something out of the Greek myths. It now seems that this "ejected material" that later seeds fledgling solar systems with prebiotic compounds also "contains clumps of dust particles that apparently shield the molecules and can shepherd

them safely into interstellar space." I'm reminded of Peter Ackroyd's 1996 biography of poet William Blake, where Ackroyd writes that "human bodies are woven upon shining looms" in Blake's mythology—but perhaps those *shining looms* were biologically active stars.

First, let me quickly say that I am genuinely awestruck by the idea that biologists are beginning to study stars in their quest to understand the chemical origins of molecular biology; and, second, I'm curious about what might happen if we combined these three articles—asking: Could storms of living matter form on the outer surface of a star, reaching hurricane strength as they blow in whorls and vortical currents across gold-plated skies?

This sequence of images captures an expanding "light echo" around the star V838 Monocerotis which exploded in January 2002, temporarily becoming 600,000 times brighter than the Sun. The visual effect here is compared by NASA to "a spelunker taking a flash picture of the walls of an undiscovered cavern"—where the "cavern" in question is an exploding sphere of light. Photos courtesy of NASA, ESA and H.E. Bond (STScI).

Image courtesy of NASA, ESA,
and J. M. Apellániz (IAA, Spain).

→ next page
A "stellar spire" in the Eagle Fair
Nebula, described as a "tower"
9½ light-years high. Image Courtesy
of NASA, ESA, and The Hubble
Heritage Team (STScI/AURA).

hubble.nasa.gov

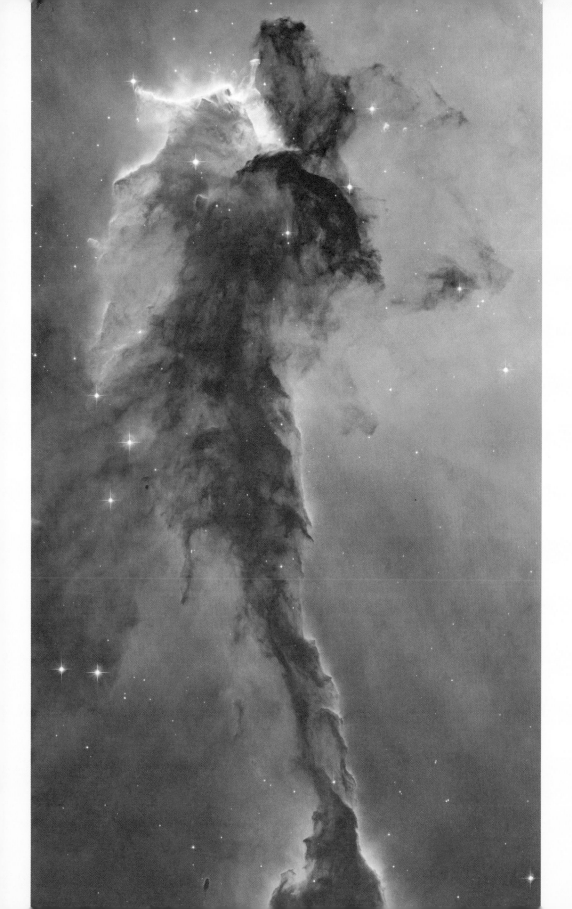

Unrecognized for What They Are

Physicist Paul Davies suggests that alien life might already exist on Earth—but it would be unrecognizable to microbiologists, and thus ignored or wrongly identified.

The early Earth, in its so-called *Hadean* phase, was a constantly exploding storm of rocks and asteroid impacts. Lava flows wider than the Mediterranean, and deeper, snaked across igneous landscapes, forming barren deltas of volcanic glass—that were then shattered by iron-rich debris falling from space. This went on for millions of years. No rocks survive from this period; it was a landscape that literally destroyed itself.

"How did life emerge amidst this mayhem?" Davies asked in a *New York Times* editorial from April 10, 2005. "Quite probably it was a stop-and-go affair, with life first forming during a lull in the bombardment, only to be annihilated by the next big impact. Then the process was repeated, over and over." What's interesting here is that one colony of microbes finally survived long enough to get its foot, if you'll excuse the anatomical metaphor, onto the evolutionary escalator, and eventually became life as we know it—what we call terrestrial life.

But, Davies asks, what if another microbe colony, locked in its place of safety—burrowed into bedrock, or buried under rising seas and 6 million years of near-constant rainfall as the surface of the planet cooled—*what if it, too, survived?* "It's possible that pockets of microbes could have survived in obscure niches," Davies writes, "opening up the tantalizing prospect of two or more different forms of life co-existing on the same planet. Although they would compete for resources, one type of life is not necessarily bound to eliminate the rest." He thus concludes that "microbes from another genesis—alien bugs, if you will—could conceivably have survived on Earth until today." He calls this "a form of biology that is unrelated to familiar life."

Are you *sure* that's your little brother...?

In a review of the book *Life as We Do Not Know It* by Peter Ward, meanwhile, Davies mentions some even more extraordinary things. The planets in our solar system, for instance, "are not completely quarantined from each other. Debris splattered into space by comet and asteroid impacts gets distributed around the solar system. Mars and Earth in particular have been trading rocks throughout their history, and it is clear that microbes could hitch a ride and be transported in relative safety from one planet to the other." Davies expands on the idea "that alien organisms may lurk all around us, unrecognized for what they are because they fail to respond to standard biochemical analysis." There is even a chance, he hints, "that some viruses could be relics of ancient alternative forms of life." In other words, your next cut could get infected with a 4-billion-year-old, parallel form of life. A celestial infection—like living fossils—your wounds would cultivate patches of alien worlds.

Perhaps one could even imagine a series of classified landscapes grown by infrared in an artificial cave beneath Los Alamos National Laboratory. Incomprehensible genetic lines, discovered during a deep-sea oil-drilling expedition, are pruned and crossbred into a kind of post-terrestrial Versailles. Weird topiary mazes of symmetrical creeper vines expand behind sealed government airlocks. Fountains of amino acids wash slowly over alien flowers.

But we needn't go beneath the Earth's surface, in a quest for Hadean refugees, to find unexpected future directions for terrestrial biology; we can just send our earthbound seeds into space. For several years, the Chinese government has been doing just that, pursuing what they call "space breeding." Seeds for important food crops like wheat and barley have been launched into low-earth orbit, on state-sponsored satellites and even sometimes on weather balloons, in order to expose them to solar radiation. If beneficial mutations arise, then these seeds might provide something like a new agrarian revolution, creatively tapping the power of the sun as an innovative and business-friendly source for botanical mutation.

When those satellites come back down, then, crashing to Earth in places like western Australia, the seeds are recovered, tested, and planted anew. Cultivating purposefully divergent species through genetic interaction

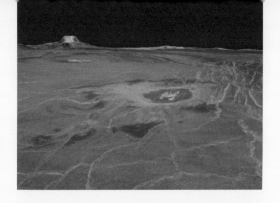

with the unfiltered radiation of the universe could surely herald the birth of a new era in landscape design—and possibly a temporary stopgap for the ongoing world food crisis. According to a May 2000 article in *Space Daily*, China might already have "nearly 405,000 hectares of rice fields planted with space seeds and 8,100 hectares of space vegetable growing. An estimate of 243,000 hectares of space rice fields will be added this year."

If Hadean biology is ever discovered, though, this particular type of space-based biofuturism might, ironically, have something it can learn from. Ancient and decidedly *not* man-made organisms have been around us all along, it seems, hiding out in rocky niches deep below ground—perhaps with surprising lessons in biological novelty for us latecomers to the planet.

Simulated images of Venus, courtesy of NASA and the National Space Science Data Center (NSSDC).

nssdc.gsfc.nasa.gov

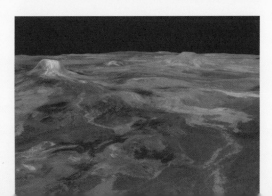

Liquid Films and Water-Signs

Over the past few years, a number of water-nozzle printers have been developed. What's a water-nozzle printer? Bitfall, for instance, by designer Julius Popp, prints images in space using carefully timed drops of water. Falling from a strip of 128 tiny nozzles, the drops become something like short-lived pixels in an image that must be produced again—and again—by more falling water drops. What appears simply to be a decorative waterfall, in other words, installed in your office lobby, turns out to contain images: it's a kind of liquid cinema.

While this is already interesting in and of itself, such a machine also brings with it some fairly unbelievable landscape design implications. You're in Rome, say, and you decide to visit the Trevi Fountain—but you're confused. Is that an *image* you see in the cascading water...? You look closer and recognize a telenovela in the water itself. The whole city, in fact, is full of fountains, and they're all playing films, news shows, and stationary reproductions of Italian Renaissance masterworks. It begins raining later that evening, and you swear you see *cartoons* in the falling water... Then Bitfall-like fountains are installed in red-light districts around the world, screening porn. The next summer, huge gates are attached to the top of Niagara Falls, and every August a film festival begins: You sit down on the Canadian side of the border and watch Hitchcock and Truffaut—an almost subliminal cinema roaring downward into the mist with the water.

A computer-controlled showerhead is installed in your home bathroom, and you watch the news or weather report before getting dressed for the day. Headlines fall on your shoulders from above. Hotel lobbies with fake waterfalls are transformed into stock tickers, with market prices and mineral futures trickling down the corporate surface of the falls. From different angles you receive different information; from further away you see different films.

Soon trees are genetically altered to form images in their bark: tree-screens. After a car accident in rural Bavaria, you accidentally stumble into a test forest. All of the trees around you seem to be covered in pictures, which, viewed from certain angles, add up into an IMAX featurette about volcanoes. Film stills from award-winning directors of the past are put into genetically modified flowers; you look closely and it's *Hollywood Ninja*, growing frame by frame in your best friend's garden. When a breeze comes, short scenes are animated, looped. Then flowers replace DVDs, and we go from visiting libraries to planting special trees. Landscapes everywhere bear encoded information.

Over time, a huge, Buckminster Fuller–like dome is built over New York City. As rain falls, the water is filtered bit by bit through the dome to form texts: images, signs, and financial information. You pay to have your logo displayed, coming down in liquid curtains on the city. The weather-advertising complex. The rain industry. Endless information, printed three-dimensionally in space.

"10 Mile Spiral" by Benjamin Aranda and Chris Lasch, from their book *Tooling*. terraswarm.com

10 Mile Spiral

In their 2006 book *Tooling*, architects Benjamin Aranda and Chris Lasch propose, among other things, a "10 mile spiral" that would "serve two civic purposes for Las Vegas":

> First, it acts as a massive traffic decongestion device...by adding significant mileage to the highway in the form of a spiral. The second purpose is less infrastructural and more cultural: along the spiral you can play slots, roulette, get married, see a show, have your car washed, and ride through a tunnel of love, all without ever leaving your car. It is a compact Vegas, enjoyed at 55 miles per hour and topped off by a towering observation ramp offering views of the entire valley floor below.

Drivers will enter this vertical labyrinth of concrete, approaching its whirligig-like compression of the desert horizon, and gradually lift off into the sky. Wound up like a snake on the periphery of the city, it's a herniation of space through which you could theoretically drive forever—a world with no outside, lit from within by cars.

I'm reminded of J. G. Ballard's voiceover for the 1971 film *Crash!*, directed by Harley Cokliss: "Take a structure like a multi-story car park, one of the most mysterious buildings ever built. Is it a model for some strange psychological state, some kind of vision glimpsed within its bizarre geometry? What effect does using these buildings have on us? Are the real myths of this century being written in terms of these huge unnoticed structures?"

Ballard's questions could as easily be asked of the 10 Mile Spiral.

Kitka River from the *Museum of Nature* by Ilkka Halso.

ilkka.halso.net

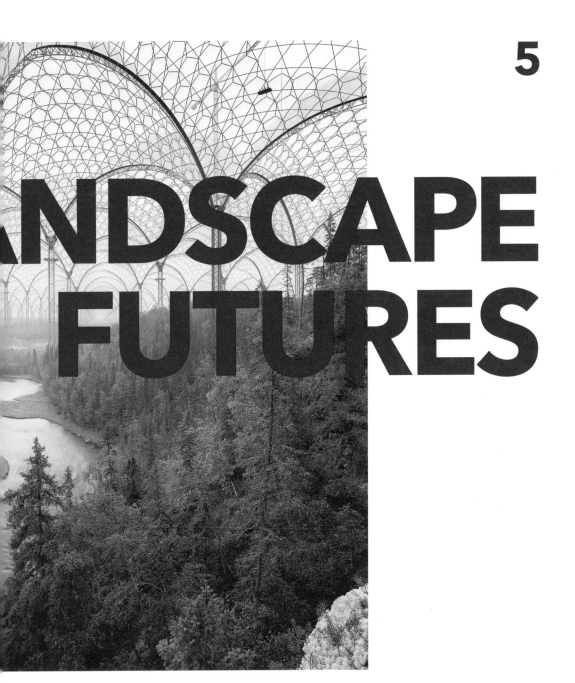

5

ANDSCAPE FUTURES

PORK FUTURES, GOLD FUTURES, OIL FUTURES—but what about *landscape* futures?

What values can be assigned to certain landscapes because of their beauty, or their history, or their sheer functional worth? A certain spatial arrangement for new subdivisions proves so popular with residents that the developers file a patent on it; the landscape thus becomes subject to the laws of intellectual property. It can be franchised. Should anyone format a similar landscape without explicit permission, he can be sued for landscape piracy. A new corporate plaza in Manhattan proves to be so comfortable, and so beneficial for casual business conversation, that it is reproduced elsewhere and given a value. It is *worth more* than other such landscapes—and that value can be traded on the market of landscape futures.

Of course, *landscape futures* has another meaning, referring simply to the future of certain landscapes. Thinking about landscape futures in this sense means asking: What will happen to these spaces over great spans of time? What long-term processes of tectonic change or artificial rearrangement are still in store for different parts of the world—for the whole planet, for other planets, for the electromagnetic breadth of space itself—and how can landscape architects prepare for, even help guide, such things?

What is the role of the world to come—of *landscape futures*—in understanding the world we know today?

Roller Coaster and *Museum I* from the
Museum of Nature by Ilkka Halso.

ilkka.halso.net

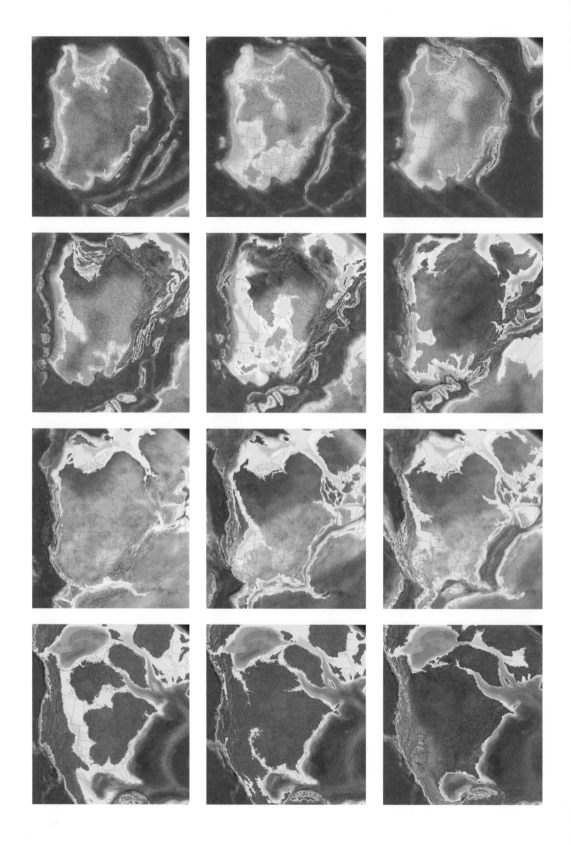

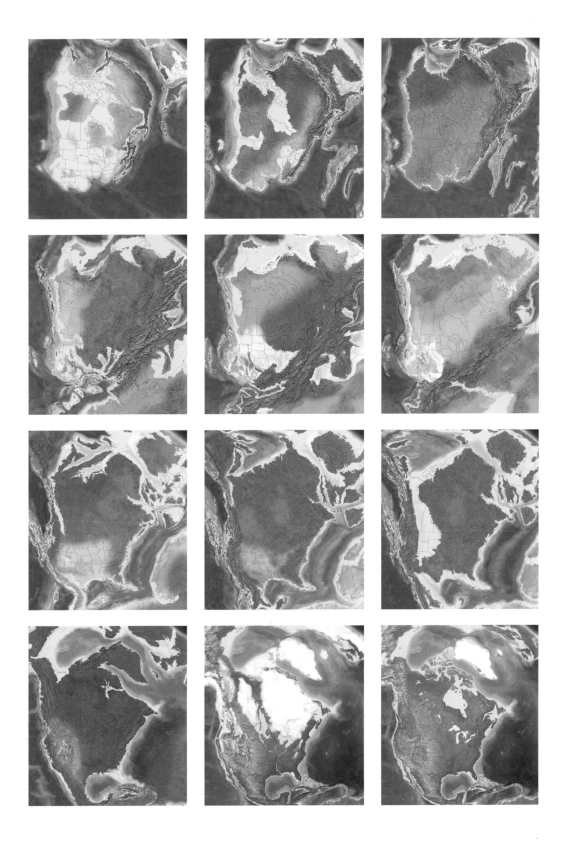

ABSTRACT GEOLOGY

For more than a decade, beginning in 1947, something called the Delicate Arch Stabilization Project was under serious consideration by the staff of Arches National Park in Moab, Utah.

The problem was that Delicate Arch, a fifty-two-foot-tall sandstone arch and one of the Park's most famous natural wonders, faces eventual collapse, as it is regularly threatened by rain, ice, and seismic activity. The solution, outlined in a series of documents that were photocopied for me in spring 2008 by a curator at Arches National Park, was clear: the arch should be stabilized. This "minor stabilization," we read in an internal memo dated February 6, 1953, "could be done in such an unobtrusive manner as to be hardly distinguishable and would not in any manner detract from the natural appearance of the Arch." It would not be *structural*, in other words, using cross-braces or encaging the arch in Gothic cathedral–like buttresses. Instead, the geological formation would be sprayed with a transparent aerosol adhesive. This fine mist of glue would then seep down into the rock's porous sandstone surface and harden there, locking the arch in place. The arch would be preserved—or geologically shellacked, if you will.

According to a March 9, 1954, report (helpfully marked with the phrase "Not to be taken from this room"), the spray, as the original list states:

1. Would penetrate the sandstone to a depth of approximately ½" or more
2. Would bring together the sandstone particles to resist wind erosion
3. Would itself offer resistance to wind erosion
4. Would resist the penetration of moisture
5. Is clear, colorless, and dries to a surface not glossy
6. Would remain plastic enough to allow expansion and contraction by freezing, thawing, and sunlight
7. Would retain spalling pieces of sandstone in place
8. Does not require special conditions of application unattainable at the site of the arch

These papers are nothing if not specific: "To avoid building a scaffold, the spray might be applied with an adaptation of long-nozzled orchard spray equipment." On April 19, 1954, the General Superintendent of Arches National Park notes that they have "received samples of two Geon lattices and of the products known as Daracone, Daraseal and Darastix. I suggest that all of these be field tested at Arches," he adds, along with "a silicon compound known as ethyl silicate."

↑ previous spread
Northern Arizona University professor of geology Ron Blakey has created some of the most stunning maps I've ever seen—including these looks at the paleo-tectonic evolution of North America. On Blakey's website—which is absolutely jammed full with other fascinating examples of geologic cartography—we read:

> The images presented here show the paleogeography of North America over the last 550 million years of geologic history...in time slices mostly 5-10 million years apart. By using such tightly spaced time slices, individual paleogeographic and tectonic elements can be followed and intuitively related from time slice to adjacent time slice. (...) The maps were prepared with the core of North America (Laurentia) fixed. All other tectonic elements are shown moving against or splitting away from Laurentia, thus showing clearly accretionary and rifting events in North America's geologic history.

What must it have been like, I wonder, to take a sailboat through those tropical seas, weaving around semicircular island chains, finding reefs and bays, lagoons and inlets, anchoring offshore and camping on beaches lit from above by stars—even the constellations different, forming alien patterns in the sky. Look closely at Blakey's maps, meanwhile, and you'll see that California is hardly a solid landmass at all, but a temporarily welded mass of remnant archipelagos. Down there in the coastal gravel are the buried edges of old island chains—and the whole state is still shivering with collision, making adjustments, jostling loose and sticking, always on the move...before stopping again. What future shapes might North America take?

jan.ucc.nau.edu/~rcb7

At this point the correspondence grows increasingly surreal. It begins referring to the flammable nature of these compounds; it points out (May 3, 1954) that certain of these materials risk "turning to an insoluable [*sic*] silica gel"; and it reveals (May 13, 1954) that "something similar to the usual tree sprayer leaving the spray pump and motor on the ground" had become one of the preferred methods of application. B. F. Goodrich, the maker of car tires, eventually gets involved, as they manufacture the chemical "lattices" proposed for future use; and (November 4, 1954) the Park Service's supply of something called "the Geon material," a vinyl chloride copolymer known for its stiffening properties, might actually be past its expiry date—so it should only be used with caution.

As if anticipating the whole conversation—or perhaps aware of its being conducted—a letter with almost religious overtones (March 5, 1956) is then sent by Douglass E. Cutler, a resident of Salt Lake City, to the Director of the National Park Service in Washington, D.C. Cutler writes:

Dear Sir:

As a lover of the great outdoors I am concerned with preserving our natural wonders for millions yet unborn. It is my view that each generation is a trustee, as it were, and is responsible for seeing that all earthly treasures, both animate and inanimate, are kept intact or, better still, improved upon if possible. This is certainly possible in regards to improving human life and the conditions of life.

At this time I am concerned with preserving the unique Delicate Arch, which I call truly one of the wonders of the world. I believe that the life of this marvel can be greatly extended beyond its natural life expectancy, an achievement greatly to be wished for. That is, barring a jolting earthquake, for which we have no defense.

I believe that a clear, erosion-resistant material could be sprayed upon the apparently weakest portion of this arch and thus prevent this section from becoming worn through. This spray may have a dull finish and be almost invisible. The treatment may have to be repeated once or twice a year, of course.

I would be pleased to know the reaction this suggestion produces.

On April 9, 1956, a Regional Director for the Park Service replies to Cutler, writing: "Natural arches are, geologically speaking, temporary structures which are doomed to fall eventually. However, we agree that any practical steps which might be taken to preserve the length of such inspiring features should be carefully investigated." A second letter is then sent (April 27, 1956) in which it's made clear not only that "a study was initiated to attempt to find preservative agents which would be of value," but that, somewhat incredibly, "several such agents were applied." Those agents proved "unsatisfactory," however, "because exposure to weather had caused them to turn white, or scale off, or both."

The very premise here is absurd, of course, but it's worth imagining for a moment what might happen if such a technique 1) actually worked, and 2) could be applied over a very broad area. Why stop at Delicate Arch, for instance? Why not spray the entirety of Arches National Park? Why not spray *all of Utah*? Indeed, we read (May 19, 1958) that a copy of the initial findings report had been mailed to park offices throughout Utah, including Bryce Canyon, Zion, and Cedar Breaks. A "pilot project" is mentioned in the same memo (May 19), and a meeting with the Utah Geological Society is proposed.

At that point, the chain of correspondence breaks off.

But if a literally impenetrable, perhaps even unremovable—perhaps even bombproof—spray adhesive could be developed, could you use it on, say, the buildings of Manhattan, or Stonehenge, or Angkor Wat? We need never worry about damage again; all of architecture could be sealed for eternity beneath

CARBON TOMBS

The underground storage—or "geological disposal"—of carbon dioxide that has been harvested from the atmosphere requires a whole new class of landscape architecture: the carbon tomb. Carbon tombs, according to a June 2006 report from the Associated Press, are "underground storage reservoirs" in which industrially produced CO_2 can be more or less safely sequestered.

After "capturing carbon dioxide from factory emissions and pressurizing it into liquid form," we read, "scientists can inject it into underground aquifers, gas fields or gaps between rock strata, safely keeping it out of the air." While today's carbon tombs are simply depleted oil fields, drained aquifers, and natural rock pores, it is not out of the question to assume that *artificial* carbon tombs may yet be produced. Massive digging projects, perhaps coupled with impermeable, lead-reinforced concrete walls, could very well result in gigantic bunkers for "underground carbon dioxide storage operations."

However, carbon tombs, like some future pharaonic depository in which we will bury pieces of the sky, might always be in danger of rupturing, releasing all of that trapped, highly pressurized CO_2 back into the atmosphere. The tombs will thus be monitored constantly by seismic engineers armed with ground-penetrating echo-location devices, using sound waves to make sure all the CO_2 has stayed in place. Horizontal migrations of the gas will be carefully tracked: a cold tide moving in darkness through unmapped caves below ground.

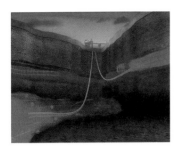

An underground carbon-storage facility in Sleipner, Norway. Image courtesy of Alligator Film/ BUG/StatoilHydro.

statoilhydro.com

a transparent coating of "the Geon material." Perhaps it would even be graffiti-proof.

If geology is, in fact, subject to chemical preservation, by what criteria would we decide to preserve it? The state of California, for instance, is famous for its natural landscapes—it contains one of the continent's highest mountain ranges, as well as its lowest point, Death Valley—but the state is also increasingly at risk from overdevelopment, sprawl, drought, and pollution. Perhaps we need to be more aggressive in our preservation efforts—more aggressive in our deployment of experimental preservation techniques. Why not cover the whole state in an artificial glacier of translucent plastic, thus saving its various landscapes for all time?

We could pour several million gallons of liquid polymer into Death Valley, for instance, creating an inland sea of sealant that would harden in California's dry heat. Soon we'd be slipping down semitransparent slopes of white plastic that extend to the desert horizon. These new plastic hills would be easy to clean— and you could charge admission to anyone who wishes to see them. Full-page advertisements featuring the white hills of California would immediately appear in European travel magazines: *America—A Land of Plastic*. A plasticized landscape— glowing and geometric in direct sunlight—could even serve a practical purpose: not only preserving but *visually enhancing* natural rock formations, ensuring their stable existence for generations to come.

However, if your ultimate goal is to laminate whole stretches of the American West, even beyond the National Parks of California, why not take a slightly different approach and *alter rock itself*? Transform ancient stone into plastic. A new geology arrives upon the surface of the earth: man-made, semitransparent, abstract. The Alps, sealed before your amazed eyes beneath a hard shield of pure white. You could roller-skate down Mont Blanc. The winter Olympics is forced to adapt immediately. New lines of sporting equipment are released.

This idea is not without its industrial uses. Whole continents of plastic could be mined for building materials, sculpted into small, white briquettes; these are then shipped halfway around the world to form new buildings by Richard Meier. Churches do away with stained-glass windows altogether, bathing altarpieces in virginal white.

Incredibly, the realization of such a scenario might not be far off. It was announced nearly a decade ago that *light-transmitting concrete* had been invented by a Hungarian architect named Áron Losonczi. Called Litracon, the new material is equal in strength to regular concrete, but small glass fibers embedded in the mix allow light to pass through. "In theory," the architect explains on the production company's website, "a wall

structure built from light-transmitting concrete can be several meters thick, because the fibers work without almost any
loss of light up until 20 meters." Litracon could easily be used
in the construction of future tower blocks, stadiums, and even
urban infrastructure—translucent streets, sewers, bridges, and
international motorways—all of which would suddenly cast no
shadows. You would look up to see the hazy silhouettes of cars
passing by in a fog of concrete like a cloud that spans the road
above you.

But because we can't turn rock into plastic—yet—it's worth
asking how we might turn *plastic* into *rock*. A few clues come to
us from the June 27, 1998, issue of *New Scientist*. There, we learn
that, hundreds of millions of years from now, many of our cities
will fossilize. These *fossil cities* will be "a lot more robust than
[fossils] of the dinosaurs," geologists Jan Zalasiewicz and Kim
Freedman write. They'll consist of "the abandoned foundations,
subways, roads, and pipelines of our ever more extensive urban
stratum," becoming the "future trace fossils" of a lost form of
life. Of course, this all depends on the tectonic fate that awaits
certain regions. Los Angeles, for instance, "is on an upward
trajectory, pushed by pressure from the adjacent San Andreas
Fault system, and is doomed to be eroded away entirely." For
those cities that will be flooded, buried in sand, or otherwise
absorbed downward, however, "the stage is set to produce ideal
pickling jars for cities. The urban strata of Amsterdam, New
Orleans, Cairo and Venice could be buried wholesale—providing, that is, they can get over one more hurdle: the destructive
power of the sea." This is also the fate that awaits London; faced
with rising sea levels and the slow sinking of southeast England, London, too, will be underwater perhaps even within two
centuries.

Elsewhere, the already buried, subterranean undersides of
our modern cities, from transport tunnels to secret government
bunkers, "will be hard to obliterate," Zalasiewicz and Freedman continue.

> They will be altered, to be sure, and it is fascinating to spec-
> ulate about what will happen to our very own addition to
> nature's store of rocks and minerals, given a hundred million
> years, a little heat, some pressure (the weight of a kilometer
> or two of overlying sediment) and the catalytic, corrosive
> effect of the underground fluids in which all of these struc-
> tures will be bathed.

Plastics, for instance, "might behave like some of the long-chain
organic molecules in fossil plant twigs and branches, or the col-
lagen in the fossilized skeletons of some marine invertebrates."
A hundred thousand Evian bottles, then, might someday be

URBAN FOSSIL VALUE

Nazi architect Albert Speer
infamously proposed that all
cities should be built so that they
will look good as future ruins.
He called this *Ruinenwert*—ruin
value. But ruins are so obvious,
so romantically 18th century; why
not strive for *fossil value* instead,
tens of millions of years in the
future when all of this urban infrastructure has turned to sludge
and radiative terrestrial heat has
cooked old bricks into something
resembling trace fossils? This way
our cities will still be beautiful.
The future footprints of fossilized
cities—entire autobahns and
highway systems—forming skel-
etal impressions in rock. Can
we design for this fate? Can we
plan urban fossils ahead of time?
Can we give our constructions
urban *fossil value*?

A strato volcano in Ngauruhoe, New Zealand, erupting in January 1974. Courtesy of the University of Colorado and the NOAA/NGDC Natural Hazards Photo Archive.

ngdc.noaa.gov

transformed by compression into a new type of quartz: vast and subterranean veins of mineralized plastic.

In other words, plastics likely *will* form a new geological layer upon the earth; plastics will become our future geology. It may take a hundred million years, but it will happen. Future desert adventurers will stumble upon belts of plastic, compressed into ribbons between layers of bedrock. Volcanoes of the future will erupt, belching transparent magma—liquid plastic—rolling out in great sheets, boiling everything in its path. Unlucky animals will be entombed as it cools, trapped in that plastic amber, fossilizing slowly over another million years, till the hardened remains of extinct species will seem to hover inside translucent hillsides, like specimens in a resinous vitrine, an open-air museum. Future Darwins will open their sketchbooks, stunned.

After thousands of years, perhaps a forest moves in, learning to metabolize this strange rock into transparent soil. Roots grow steadily downward through what appears to be air—the ground like transparent plastic or glass—and people come out just to sit there in the sun, watching those slow and ancient roots push deeper and deeper into the earth. Worms wriggle as if through space, leaving tunnels—underground landscapes of air. After the sun goes down, you walk out into the middle of the woods and shine a flashlight down through the surface of the earth, illuminating tangles of roots and buried streams.

Given time and the right chemical composition, these underground stratigraphies of white plastic could begin to dissolve, forming caves. Blurred and colorless stalactites will hang over subterranean lakes where blind fish swim, sensing rather than seeing the milky walls and abstract rock formations hovering all around them. A distant descendant of Steven Spielberg will direct his own version of *Journey to the Center of the Earth*, setting the film inside enormous tunnels of white plastic that extend tens of thousands of feet into the planet. One by one, actors lose consciousness and fall to the ground, passing out in contemplation of the apparently infinite abyss that extends for miles beneath their feet . . . hypnotized by the hazy white glow that comes from the very core of the planet.

As Jules Verne once wrote: "Look down well! You must take a lesson in abysses."

In this case, those abysses may well reflect us.

Of course, you could justifiably argue that all that plastic will simply compress into a geological layer no more than a centimeter wide—at most—or that it will melt away, burning off into hydrocarbon gas over time spans reaching 100 million years. Indeed, the same fate could await any other future translucent material: the deep actions of rocks and magmatic heat will undo these artificial geologies. On the other hand, some translucent rocks can *only* exist under such extreme conditions. For

THE GEOLOGIC TIME SPIRAL

Joseph Graham, William Newman, and John Stacy have created a "geologic time spiral" as an educational aid for the U. S. Geological Survey. Their poster-sized image shows the ongoing adventure of terrestrial evolution: the geological eras, waves of speciation, and tectonic rearrangements through which the Earth continues to flow. The image helps give visual form to the stratigraphic nature of planetary history, from the Cambrian to the Jurassic to the present day.

The spiral begins in a helical cloud 4.5 billion years ago, when the Earth was still forming, ribboning up and outward to show representative landscapes, organisms, and whole ecological systems from our planet's inhuman past. The first scattered invertebrates of the Precambrian give way to the well-forested eras of the Mississippian and Pennsylvanian (the buried remains of which form today's industrial coal supplies), passing forward into the heavily volcanic epoch of dinosaurs and towering gymnosperms—uncoiling still further to the metropolitan age of architecturally-inclined human beings—the Earth's history takes on the feel of an endless diorama. This effect is heightened by the illustration's style: stippled and sepia-toned landscapes, dotted with lone examples of often extinct species, sit either side of a central waterway that rushes upward, making literal the idea that time is a river.

These landscapes record what Charles Lyell called, in his seminal 1830 book The Principles of Geology, "monuments of ancient mutations in the earth's crust." Indeed, the planet is in a state of continual self-updating, Lyell writes:

The renovating as well as the destroying causes are unceasingly at work, the repair of land being as constant as its decay, and the deepening of seas keeping pace with formation of shoals.

Everything is dynamic and temporary, processes flowing one into the other.

In his 1998 book Annals of the Former World, John McPhee continues this line of thought, visualizing the planet as a surging liquid of proto-continental forms:

Human time, regarded in the perspective of geologic time, is much too thin to be discerned—the mark invisible at the end of a ruler. If geologic time could somehow be seen in the perspective of human time, on the other hand, sea level would be rising and falling hundreds of feet, ice would come pouring over continents and as quickly go away. Yucatáns and Floridas would be under the sun one moment and underwater the next, oceans would swing open like doors, mountains would grow like clouds and come down like melting sherbet, continents would crawl like amoebae, rivers would arrive and disappear like rainstreaks down an umbrella, lakes would go away like puddles after rain, and volcanoes would light the earth as if it were a garden of fireflies.

As William S. Burroughs would have it in his 1962 novel The Ticket That Exploded, there is, beneath the surface of the Earth, "a vast mineral consciousness near absolute zero thinking in slow formations of crystal." Burroughs's geomythological vision—a kind of artificially intelligent planetary hard drive—illustrates the difficulty of describing and giving literary shape to processes that are, for the most part, too slow to see and too alien to imagine.

The geologic time spiral itself is no exception to the challenge of representing terrestrial experience. For instance, the spiral has not been drawn to scale; it exaggerates the length of the Holocene—the era of human beings—while downplaying the Devonian—the age of warm, waist-high seas that once covered the globe—not to mention the 1.5-billion-year era before the appearance of recognizable microorganisms. Nonetheless, what the illustration does convey very clearly is the open-ended nature of the Earth's existence in time. The inevitability of further coils—layers hovering upon layers of future history—is made obvious by the propulsive energy of the spiral form itself. Deep time is one thing; deep future is another. The image is almost literally a cliffhanger, forcing viewers to imagine what might come next. It is sobering to remember that the Earth has existed for 4.5 billion years—with only 3 billion years of biology—but it has another 7.5 billion years during which to unfold before it's annihilated by an expanding sun.

What unimaginable terrestrial reformations—landscape futures—will unfold between now and that stellar rendezvous? What will this spiral look like when humans are as far in the past as dinosaurs are to us today?

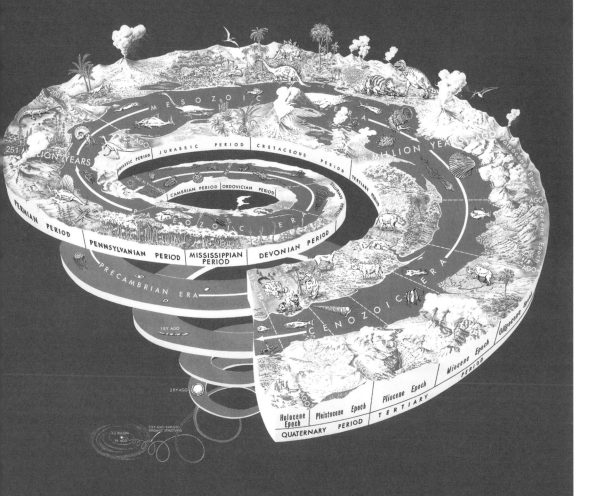

The Geologic Time Spiral by Joseph Graham, William Newman, and John Stacy, a "graphical representation of geologic time." From the U.S. Geological Survey's *General Interest Publication 58.*

usgs.gov

example, something called *amorphous carbonia* has been developed in an Italian lab. A solid form of carbon dioxide—a kind of carbon dioxide glass—the material only exists (for now) under extraordinary pressures; i.e., only inside the laboratory.

Unless, of course, amorphous carbonia exists on other planets: if carbon dioxide can be trapped within a planetary surface, and thus placed under geological pressures at the right temperature, then we could very well discover that certain unearthly worlds actually possess transparent bedrock made of glassine CO_2. Not unlike the aforementioned vision of California's plastic geology, you'd have miles and miles of translucent carbon dioxide glass spiraling downward beneath your feet, forming fissures and caves. Glass continents. Small earthquakes that sound like buried wind chimes.

More practically speaking, amorphous carbonia could perhaps—if it can ever be reproduced outside the lab—offer a new strategy for sequestering excess carbon dioxide from the atmosphere. Instead of letting all the CO_2 released by coal-burning power plants, cars, and heavy industry, among other sources, just float up into the atmosphere, where it will trap solar heat and accelerates climate change, we could simply compress the gas into huge transparent cubes of carbon dioxide. The more cars and factories pump out CO_2, the larger these perfectly Euclidean cubes will get, growing, reflective, looming on the edges of cities. They could even be put to use as a new building material, forming peripheral, abstract geometries of the purest avant-garde; amorphously carbonic buildings could be airlifted into the desert and stacked there.

THE CRYSTAL WORLD

In his 1966 novel *The Crystal World*, J. G. Ballard describes the uncontrolled crystallization of an African rain forest. A doctor named Edward Sanders has been sent into the forest to visit a leper colony, only to find himself surrounded by the hypnotic and jeweled landscape, its faceted surfaces seeming to emit light from within. The crystallization, however, is spreading, and it consumes anything exposed to it; the characters are soon brushing crystals off their trousers, and even out of their eyes. "Jeweled crocodiles glittered like heraldic salamanders on the banks of the crystalline river," Ballard writes.

In a kind of bio-mineralogical *Heart of Darkness*, the characters pass farther into the forest:

> The process of crystallization was more advanced. The fences along the road were so heavily encrusted that they formed a continuous palisade, a white frost at least six inches thick on either side of the palings. The few houses between the trees glistened like wedding cakes, their white roofs

and chimneys transformed into exotic minarets and baroque domes. On a lawn of green glass spurs a child's tricycle glittered like a Fabergé gem, the wheels starred into brilliant jasper crowns.

Dr. Sanders "stumbled on along the road, following the intricate patterns that revolved and expanded over his head like jeweled mandalas." The landscape there, "like some half-abandoned purgatory," later claims a crashed military helicopter:

The four twisted blades, veined and frosted like the wings of a giant dragonfly, had already been overgrown by the trellises of crystals hanging downwards from the nearby trees. The fuselage of the craft, partly buried in the ground, had blossomed into an enormous translucent jewel, in whose solid depths, like emblematic knights mounted in the base of a medieval ring stone, the two pilots sat frozen at their controls.

Perhaps, then, this is what a runaway chain reaction of amorphous carbonia would look like, with carbon dioxide crystals slowly forming a frost over the surface of the earth—a true crystal world, draining CO_2 from the sky.

Future canyons of glass will form, eroding from the surface down, abraded by sand-heavy winds. Decades later, you'll take walking tours of the Glass Caverns of Utah, staying in towns with names like New Carbonia, or Carbonia-on-Thames, where everything is made from uniform glass blocks and windows look out upon a faceted abyss of cubed mazes. Inside a crystalline world of self-generating reflections, future backpackers will perfect a new form of narcissistic existentialism, writing abstract poetry in their notebooks before being driven mad. A confrontation with your double that never ends.

Meanwhile, the skies will be cleared of all excess carbon dioxide, climate change will be reversed, and, like some sci-fi monster, these transparent ziggurats around the world will continue to grow.

INJECTED LANDFORMS

When a mud volcano began erupting in Java in the spring of 2006, spewing nearly 50,000 cubic meters of hot mud to the surface every day, burying whole villages, fields, and even an estimated 25 factories, no one quite knew what to do. "Every few seconds the earth jolts and another dollop of hot sediment belches out," a reporter for the *Guardian* wrote at the time, as if describing some rogue landscape giving birth to itself, creating literal *terra nova*.

The long-term effects of this event are extraordinary; after all, it wasn't only a surface landform that was created. That explosive tide of mud had to come from somewhere, and it's believed that a massive underground cavity is being created as the mud flows out onto the surface. In fact, it is entirely likely that the mud-flooded surface will simply collapse into the depressurized emptiness below. I was intrigued to see, however, that one of the earliest emergency response plans was to start three simultaneous drilling operations, poking into the subterranean pocket from different angles. The underground void would then be injected with concrete. The mud flow would thus be capped—and a new, artificial geological formation would be produced: a hard, uneven bulge of injected concrete in the exact size and shape of the mud reservoir it had filled.

I immediately thought of Emilio Grifalconi, a character in George Perec's 1978 novel *Life: A User's Manual*. At one point Grifalconi comes across an old table. "Its oval top, wonderfully inlaid with mother-of-pearl, was exceptionally well preserved," we read, "but its base, a massive, spindle-shaped column of grained wood, turned out to be completely worm-eaten. The worms had done their work in covert, subterranean fashion, creating innumerable ducts and microscopic channels now filled with pulverized wood. No sign of this insidious labor showed on the surface."

Grifalconi comes to the conclusion that "the only way of preserving the original base—hollowed out as it was, it could no longer support the weight of the top—was to reinforce it from within; so once he had completely emptied the canals of their wood dust by suction, he set about injecting them with an almost liquid mixture of lead, alum and asbestos fiber. The operation was successful; but it quickly became apparent that, even thus strengthened, the base was too weak"—and so the table would have to be discarded. As he prepares to throw out this useless piece of furniture, however, Grifalconi stumbles upon a new idea, that of "dissolving what was left of the original wood" in the table's base. This dissolution would reveal what Perec calls "the fabulous arborescence within, this exact record of the worms' life inside the wooden mass: a static, mineral accumulation of all the movements that had constituted their blind existence."

So if we could fill the Indonesian mud reservoir using ultra-durable, long-lasting concrete, might geotechnical engineers in 100 years' time come through with high-powered hoses to wash away the mud, rock, and topsoil, uncovering that almost literal earthwork, an unintended sculpture in the ground? And could they haul it up to the surface, as if fishing abstract forms from the earth itself? Perhaps we could try something like this with subsurface voids all over the planet: injecting concrete into porous bodies of rock, only to uncover those hardened subterranean forms years later.

British sculptor Rachel Whiteread, for instance, has become quite famous—and won a Turner Prize—for making plaster casts of architectural space: the space around a bathtub, the space of a stairwell, the spaces between the walls of a London row house. But what if she were to turn her attention to landscapes and infrastructure, filling caves with plaster—then removing those abstract sculptures piece by piece and reassembling them in the open air? Carlsbad Caverns, on display now in Berlin—or the sewers of San Francisco, cast in plaster and displayed in their entirety, sprawling across the hills of Dia:Beacon, upriver from New York City.

NEST-CASTING

Florida State University biologist Walter Tschinkel has been studying "the nest architecture of the Florida harvester ant" by filling the underground nests with dental plaster and/or liquid metal, and then removing the filled material after it hardens. In a paper called "Subterranean ant nests: trace fossils past and future?," published in 2003 in the journal *Palaeogeography, Palaeoclimatology, Palaeoecology*, Tschinkel describes these subterranean spaces as "shaped voids in a soil matrix." For the most part, these three-dimensional networks "are composed of two basic units: descending shafts and horizontal chambers," as Tschinkel wrote in a 2004 paper for the *Journal of Insect Science*. There are shafts and helices, he continues, lobes and indentations, all of which share a "looping, connected morphology." Tschinkel goes on to refer to "movement zones," in which "partially overlapping sequences from the center of the nest to the periphery" are traced and retraced by individual ants; these movements gradually erode the walls, expanding surfaces into rooms. The "spaces," then, that define these underground ant architectures are really the physical results of social activity, in which a surface becomes a route becomes a chamber—and further branchings spread outward (or downward) from there.

CITY OF THE PHARAOH

Wormholes, voids, and subsurface absences form a parallel landscape, yet to be revealed—and the exposure of this hidden world of shapes and spaces is often a matter of chance.

Skara Brae is a 4,000-year-old Stone Age village located in the Orkney Islands of Scotland. Had it not been for a freak windstorm in the winter of 1850, however, Skara Brae might

SLOW SCULPTURE

In his novel *Iron Council*, sci-fi novelist China Miéville proposes something called *slow sculpture*. Miéville describes an artist who creates geological works of art on a timescale that exceeds the individual human life:

Huge sedimentary stones... each carefully prepared: shafts drilled precisely, caustic agents dripped in, for a slight and so-slow dissolution of rock in exact planes, so that over years of weathering, slabs would fall in layers, coming off with the rain, and at very last disclosing their long-planned shapes. Slow-sculptors never disclosed what they had prepared, and their art revealed itself only long after their deaths.

STORMFRONT

When I first heard about Skara Brae, in the 7th grade, I actually hand-wrote an entire 198-page novel, regrettably titled *Stormfront*, which I still have saved away somewhere. The book is set in a small town in rural Wisconsin, and it was inspired by equal parts Skara Brae, Stephen King, and the Cahokia Mounds, a 1,000-year-old Native American city of abandoned earthworks that I must have seen at some point in a television documentary. The basic plot is that a massive, multiday storm has begun to wash away all the hills outside town...uncovering, beneath all that mud and gravel, the outlines of old walls, ceilings, doors, and something a lot like the gates of hell. The book, my first response to the story of Skara Brae, is absurdly—unreadably—bad.

never have been discovered. Blowing away loose coastal grasses and the sand dunes upon which those grasses grew, the storm uncovered the well-preserved walls, roofs, and roadways of this previously unknown village. It was archaeology by accident—and it opens an entire universe of implications about what else might be waiting to be uncovered elsewhere, by a similar unseasonal storm.

I'm reminded in many ways of the December 2004 Asian tsunami. Beyond the obvious devastation of the tidal wave and the massive offshore earthquake that accompanied it (an earthquake so large that it actually affected the rotation of the earth), an unexpected archaeological act was performed: The wave not only washed ancient artifacts up onto the beach in Tamil Nadu, in southeast India, but it also partially uncovered a buried temple. Believed possibly to be part of the legendary flooded city of Mahabalipuram, the temple's remains, and the sculpture of a large lion found with it, were washed clean of sand by the tidal wave's violent retreat. What's more, the tsunami helped excavate other sites further inland, including a 2,000-year-old brick temple that bears evidence of having been destroyed by a tsunami in its own historical era.

In other words, natural disasters often play an important role in archaeology—and even paleontology. I'm further reminded here of the story of Mary Anning, an amateur "fossilist" in 19th-century England. In his 2001 book *The Dragon Seekers*, Christopher McGowan describes how Anning would often find new fossils of dinosaurs—including the plesiosaur, a dragonlike, undersea species of which Anning is the credited discoverer—after massive coastal landslides, known as "slumps." But even the most basic processes of erosion and daily weathering could do the job:

Although [Anning] had an eye for fossils, she could not find them until they had been exposed by weathering—an achingly slow process. But when wind and rain and frost and sun had done their work, she would find them, peeking through the surface. Others were buried so deeply in the cliffs that it would be aeons before they were ever discovered.

Indeed, what else could still be locked in the hills of England, awaiting deep enough coastal erosion to be found?

Skara Brae was also the first thing that came to mind when I heard the following story about film director Cecil B. DeMille. When DeMille made his legendarily lavish 1923 film *The Ten Commandments*, he had what was then the largest film set in the world dismantled and buried in the sands of the California desert. And the set—an instant city—was extraordinary. According to the website *DeMille's Lost City*: "Sixteen hundred laborers built hieroglyph-covered walls 110 feet tall, flanked by four statues of Ramses II and 21 sphinxes, 5 tons each. DeMille populated his city with 2,500 actors and extras, housing them in tents on an adjacent dune." Not one to leave his creation around, however, lest someone else use the set for their own future film, the whole thing was buried—becoming known as the "lost city of Cecil B. DeMille."

It wasn't until 1983—sixty years later—that two friends and classic film fans, Peter Brosnan and John Parker, read DeMille's autobiography and noticed what sounded like a clue to the set's location. To make quite a long story short, Brosnan and Parker got hold of some ground-penetrating radar equipment, drove out into the California desert, near the town of Guadalupe—and, incredibly, found the set, digging up plaster statues and fragments of lost props. Of course, the Egyptian theme of DeMille's film lent a strange air of hyper-realism to the proceedings; after all, if the site had been excavated, say, five hundred or six hundred years later, what might future archaeologists have assumed?

Combine Skara Brae with DeMille's lost city, and perhaps these future archaeologists might well conclude that what we know to be a "real" city—Chicago, say, or neotropical Miami—was not an actual dwelling place at all, but a *monumental film set.* Excavations continue—leading to the controversial conclusion that human civilization in North America had really been a kind of massive performance art piece, from sea to shining sea—a cinematic installation upon the plains—and so whatever film had been made there must surely still exist…. Thus begins a whole new, Paul Auster–like chapter of future archaeology, in which our descendants hunt for the lost and secret films of a buried North America.

WRECK-DIVING LONDON

More than film sets will be lost to history, of course. As mentioned earlier, London itself, one of the oldest, continuously inhabited cities on the planet, will also someday disappear—and its future undersea fate is extraordinary.

Little Venice is a small riverine village east of Notting Hill on the man-made canals of Victorian London. The waterways on which it sits were designed in the early 1800s by Isambard Kingdom Brunel, the same engineer behind the machinery that excavated London's first Tube tunnels.

Now, however, the Romantic canals and artificial rivers of Little Venice might offer something of an unintended glimpse of the London yet to come. Brunel's work, here, becomes a model for how architects might design in accidental anticipation of a landscape's future.

LONDON CANYONLANDS

There are Grand Canyons everywhere, just waiting to form: "If we could wave a tectonic magic wand," British natural historian Richard Fortey writes in his excellent book *Earth: An Intimate History*, "and gently elevate southern England, the River Thames would excavate a canyon of its own, another magnificent thing—and, deep enough, there would be the equivalent of the [Grand Canyon's] Vishnu schist. If we do the same in northern France, the Seine would carve through a sequence of hard and soft layers back to a deep and ancient metamorphic foundation. The same goes for Texas, or the Pirana Basin, or the Arabian Peninsula, or western Africa, or much of Siberia." The question, for me, would be: what can we do to accelerate this process? Fortey himself compares the Grand Canyon to a massive act of carpentry: "The strata appear unwaveringly horizontal, like an infinity of stacked plywood worked with a giant fretsaw." So what are our geotechnical options? Could we carve a new Grand Canyon into the rocks of Afghanistan, franchising that landscape elsewhere—and would we be accused of geological imperialism? Dedicate it entirely to scientific research and perhaps Harvard will buy it. A geological research land, carved to order.

TATIVILLE

Lost films sets are nothing new. Film sets are dismantled and even sold part by part on eBay. It's not uncommon to visit someone's house in Los Angeles, for instance, and find yourself staring somewhat uncomfortably at a table in the corner of the room— because you know you've seen it somewhere before…only to learn, later, that it had been used in *Minority Report*. These sets—architectural constructions all—are atomized, broken into pieces, and distributed throughout the social world, where confused people bump into them, convinced they must be experiencing *déjà vu*.

In any case, there's an equally interesting story to be found in Tativille, the instant city and film set built for Jacques Tati's 1967 film *Playtime*. "Tativille came into existence," we read in a PDF hosted by the website *Potential Films*, "on the 'Ile de France' on a huge stretch of waste ground" in Paris:

> Conceived by Jacques Tati and designed by Eugene Roman, it was strictly a cinema town, born of the needs of the film: big blocks of dwellings, buildings of steel and glass, offices, tarmacked roads, carpark, airport and escalators. About 100 workers labored ceaselessly for 5 months to construct this revolutionary studio with transparent partitions, which extended over 15,000 square meters. Each building was centrally heated by oil. Two electricity generators guaranteed the maintenance of artificial light on a permanent basis.

During preproduction, we read, "Tati visited many factories and airports throughout Europe before his cinematographer Jean Badal came to the conclusion that he needed to build his own skyscraper. Which is exactly what he did." In fact, he built an entire city inhabited by no one but actors—who left at the end of each day of filming. One estimate puts the total mass of built space and material at "11,7000 square feet of glass, 38,700 square feet of plastic, 31,500 square feet of timber, and 486,000 square feet of concrete. Tativille had its own power plant and approach road, and building number one had its own working escalator." As Tati himself later explained, "there were no stars in the film, or rather, the set was the star, at least at the beginning of the film. So I opted for the buildings, facades that were modern but of high quality because it's not my business to criticize modern architecture"—it was only his job to film it.

However, those hoping to visit the set's cinematically Romantic remains are out of luck: "I would like to have seen it retained—for the sake of young filmmakers," Tati claimed, "but it was razed to the ground. Not a brick remains."

Or so he said. Perhaps Tati was just pulling a DeMille. Perhaps Tativille is still out there. Perhaps, in the summer of 2016, a Ph.D. candidate from New York University, studying architectural history and writing her thesis on the lost sets of mid-20th-century French cinema, will fly to Paris for three months. There, she'll rent a flat near the Seine, sketch buildings wistfully in blue ink on café napkins, and set up a series of informational interviews with the people who worked on Tati's set: carpenters, gaffers, manual laborers. Soon enough, she begins to suspect that Tativille wasn't destroyed at all. She special orders DVDs of later French films, pausing them at exact and very brief moments where you can actually see fragments of Tati's old set, reused as secondary props in the background. She takes notes, making a map of Tativille's distributed appearance across the history of modern French cinema.

Then, after one of these interviews, our overcommitted student discovers that a small note has been slipped inside her jacket pocket. The note is actually a map, however, with directions addressed solely to her. Outside the city, she sees, in an arson-plagued *banlieue*, an old cluster of import warehouses silently waits.

She takes the train—and a small pocketknife. Then, standing alone in the rain outside one of those warehouses, flashlight in hand, she slides open a heavy wooden door to find—

"Tide levels are steadily increasing owing to a combination of factors," the UK's Environment Agency warns. "These [factors] include higher mean sea levels, greater storminess, increasing tide amplitude, the tilting of the British Isles (with the south-eastern corner tipping downwards) and the settlement of London on its bed of clay." *Post-glacial rebound* is the technical term for this "tilting of the British Isles." That tilt comes as northern Scotland's deglaciated mountain valleys rise steadily upward, decompressing from the weight of lost ice caps. Like a slow-motion, geological amusement park ride, the British Isles are thus "tilting," with Scotland's rebound pushing London into the sea.

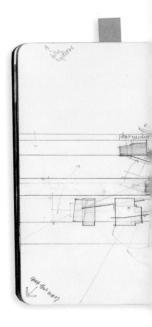

Using satellite measurement, tide gauges, GPS, and devices called "absolute gravimeters," a 2007 study performed for the Environment Agency showed that London is moving downward into the Earth's surface in "a general pattern of subsidence of 1–2 mm a year," as the BBC described it. "With waters rising in the region by about 1 mm a year, the combined effect is a 2–3 mm a year rise in sea level with respect to the land." Do some basic math, and London, incredibly, will have passed through the other side of the planet in less than—

Wait—

To help protect against these encroaching waters, the city contains or is surrounded by a rarely noticed hydrological labyrinth—"300 km of tidal defenses including embankments, walls, gates and barriers," the BBC writes. However, "at some stage, [these will] have to be adapted or moved"—at least until "new types of defenses [are] created that make better use of the natural floodplain." I'm increasingly convinced that if architectural magazines really want to discuss what the London of tomorrow will look like, then they would have stopped talking to architects a long time ago—and would now have flood consultants on the phone. The future of London will not be determined by architects, but by hydrological engineers.

Short of capping the Highlands in new glaciers of lead, then, or tethering gigantic hot air balloons to the spires of churches to pull the city skyward, London will eventually flood: its undersea fate is geologically inevitable. Climate change only adds to the city's worries. Whether this occurs in a hundred years or a hundred centuries, London will become a city of canals—before it is lost to the sea entirely. It is a new Atlantis, sinking deeper each day into a hydrological embrace.

But perhaps such an outcome isn't tragic at all. Perhaps, if we view this future with a certain *architectural curiosity*, then we can respond with something that even resembles enthusiasm. In which case, what future city might we see upon the Thames?

In a June 2007 report called *Living with Water: Visions of a Flooded Future*, prepared for the Royal Institute of British

Architects, authors Paul Ruff and Glen Moorley attempted to answer that question. In a scenario plan they call "Go with the Flow," Ruff and Moorley describe a number of infrastructural shifts for the eastern extremes of Greater London, including school boats—"so that the children of each town would not have their education affected by any prolonged periods of flooding"—and what they describe as "vast retention lakes" in which flood waters could be stored. These artificial lakes would not only be reservoirs, they would also encourage windsurfing "and other water-sports." Ruff and Moorley go on to describe a rather Archigram-like turn toward prefabricated "bolt-on" architecture, including "bolt-on bay windows, plug-in balconies and instant attic conversions," as people living in flood zones will seek "to increase space within houses above ground level." This architectural flexibility would be in the face of "hard flood defenses," as the authors describe them.

A more ambitious, if openly unbuildable plan, comes from the London-based firm Smout Allen. In response to coastal flooding and the erosion of the British shoreline—with whole villages, formerly miles from the sea, now tumbling off cliffs into the tides below—architects Mark Smout and Laura Allen have proposed a "retreating village" on rails. "The village is mounted on steel and concrete skids that allow each house to be dragged across the landscape," the architects wrote in their 2007 book *Augmented Landscapes.* Operating the village "mimic[s] techniques for hauling boats from the waves." In other words, the houses are more like machines, attached to complicated devices of retreat that have been anchored into the earth much farther inland. "The village is slipped, dragged, and rotated by a mechanism of anchors, ground beams, and concreted arcs," with each house "manipulated by no fewer than three pulleys that are anchored in the landscape and attached to the frame mounted above the skids and below the floor of the house." This also has the effect of making the village look, from above, like a gigantic stringed instrument—these are what the architects call "rope gardens," part of the "paraphernalia of haulage" necessary for the town's "inevitable withdrawal from the edge."

However unrealistic this plan may be, it would be stunning, I think, to discover someday, while you're out exploring the railyards west of Paddington Station or northwest from King's Cross, a whole subsidiary landscape of train tracks, all of which seem to disappear beneath the nearby buildings. You don't know what they are, who put them there, or what they do; so you do some research. It turns out that they are railed evacuation routes for the hauling of London—all of London—further back and faster inland, should the Thames ever catastrophically overflow. The city itself retreats on rails into the British Midlands…and then goes back, when the waters recede.

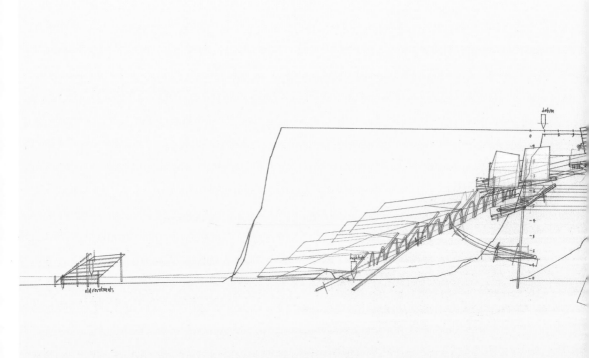

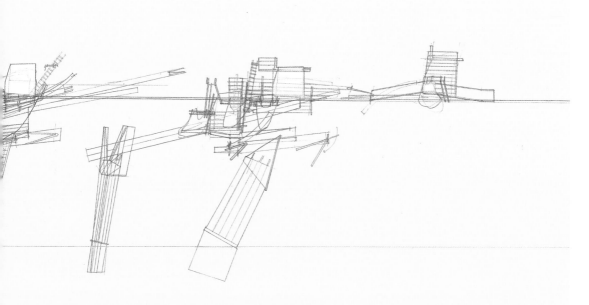

A section through the Retreating
Village, complete with mobile
coastline, by Mark Smout
and Laura Allen, from their book
Pamphlet Architecture 28:
Augmented Landscapes.

Of course, one could also build a *floating city*—and here science fiction becomes a viable planning resource for tomorrow's city administrators. In his 2002 novel *The Scar*, British author China Miéville proposes a kind of counter-Atlantis—a city that cannot sink—called Armada, "the ship-city." Armada is lashed together from the hulls of captured ships into one floating metropolitan unit. It is a "flotilla of dwellings," he writes. "A city built on old boat bones."

> What had once been berths and bulkheads had become houses; there were workshops in old gundecks. But the city had not been bounded by the ships' existing skins. It reshaped them. They were built up, topped with structure, styles and materials shoved together from a hundred histories and aesthetics into a compound architecture. Centuries-old pagodas tottered on the decks of ancient oarships, and cement monoliths rose like extra smokestacks on paddlers stolen from southern seas. The streets between the buildings were tight. They passed over the converted vessels on bridges, between mazes and plazas, and what might have been mansions. Parklands crawled across clippers, above armories in deeply hidden decks. Decktop houses were cracked and strained from the boats' constant motion.

Miéville's ship-city is not locked into its topography. It is dynamic, responsive, and buoyant: "Armada moved constantly, its bridges swinging side to side, its towers heeling. The city shifted on the water." Could this, then, be a prophetic vision of the London to come? In 600 years, will we see London, a great nomadic amalgamation of ships, set loose upon the waters of the north Atlantic?

Miéville's city is easily dismissed as mere science fiction, but it resembles, at least in spirit, a project already built—and currently under expansion—in the Netherlands. In 2005, the *New Yorker* ran a series of articles by Elizabeth Kolbert called "The Climate of Man," an investigative look at climate change. The third article in Kolbert's series ended with a description of how "one of the Netherlands' largest construction firms, Dura Vermeer, received permission to turn a former R.V. park into a development of 'amphibious homes'." They had built a floating city, in other words: a Dutch Armada.

"The amphibious homes all look alike," Kolbert explained. Floating there on the River Meuse in Maasbommel, Holland, "they resemble a row of toasters. Each one is moored to a metal pole and sits on a set of hollow concrete pontoons. Assuming that all goes according to plan, when the Meuse floods the homes will bob up and then, when the water recedes, they will gently be deposited back on land."

CLOUD CITY

For a 2007 competition called *What If New York City...*, architects were asked what New York should do, in planning its future infrastructure, to help alleviate the aftermath of a direct hit by a Category 3 hurricane. Local designers Studio Lindfors offered a weirdly hilarious response to the call for projects in the form of habitable blimps. They called it *Cloud City*.

"Though perhaps an unusual proposal," the architects write in a description of the project on their website, "*Cloud City* is literally an uplifting experience that will allow communities to remain intact as they pull themselves out of the rubble."

It's an instant city in the sky— a refugee camp amongst the clouds:

> The homes can be rapidly deployed with minimal site preparation. They are intended to "plug in" to existing utility services, and can be deployed by a team of four workers in roughly an hour. Once airborne, the floating homes allow construction crews below to work unimpeded, speeding up the recovery effort. This in turn reduces cost overruns and unnecessary delays.

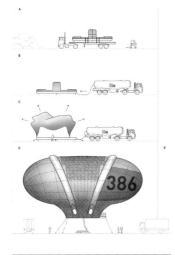

The hovering metropolis is an emergency city, held in reserve, waiting for a flood to strike. Might cities other than New York, but also at high risk from flooding, like London, Amsterdam, or Venice, someday have permanent hot-air balloon districts, hovering over the tides...? Of course, there's no reason to wait till disaster strikes; we could simply *migrate into the sky*. Renewing ourselves–becoming literally airborne–in a vertical migration that evacuates the earth.

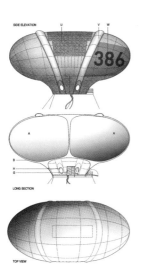

As Dura Vermeer's environmental director pithily remarks to Kolbert: "There is a flood market emerging"—and the Dutch are the pioneers in this particular kind of landscape futurism. For instance, there's Frits Schoute, a former professor at Delft University. According to Kristina Kessler, writing in the May 2006 issue of *Urban Land* magazine, Schoute is "developing a stabilizing platform that allows communities to live in the middle of the oceans, unaffected by waves. He expects people to start living and working on these platforms by 2020, and envisions floating cities by 2050." The *Guardian* describes this rather optimistically as "colonizing the sea." This radical take on the concept of maritime urbanism could just as well scrap solid ground altogether. Indeed, in a further, philosophically vertiginous, step away from terrestrial stability, we learn that Dura Vermeer has actually built what sounds, to Oliver Burkeman of the *Guardian*, writing on June 30, 2005, "like a bizarre folly: an experimental floating greenhouse."

Made out of polystyrene slabs clicked together like Lego pieces, then overlain with concrete, it was built on the water, rather than being constructed on dry land. As a result, there is no obvious limit to the size of the platforms that could be built this way—and Dura Vermeer, certainly, envisages cities of floating homes, floating offices and floating restaurants.

Almost incredibly, Burkeman adds, "a further development could allow the greenhouse to move with the sun, so that the plants will grow faster"—implying that this groundless state of dynamic heliotropism carries advantages and opportunities that land-based inflexibility simply could never offer. It was everywhere remarked that 2008 saw the majority of the earth's human population living in cities for the first time in the history of the species; will there someday be an equally historical turning point, after the polar ice caps have melted, *when humans no longer live on land*?

There is an alternative to architectural flexibility, however, and that is *fortification*. What version of London might we see then? In the estuarial distance, perhaps a thousand new artificially intelligent Thames Barriers will lift and fold their bulwarked walls against the onslaught of the sea—a kind of hydrological Maginot Line made of levees and powered by tides, encircling the British archipelago. We'll drive across inland lagoons on floating motorways. Houseboats and cargo ships will anchor 10 meters above the pavements of Trafalgar Square, unloading cargo, Admiral Nelson wreathed in robes of seaweed. Adventure tourism firms will lead scuba diving expeditions through the reefs of Westminster; wealthy clients will spearfish eels in the back rooms of flooded estate agents. But

London's underwater fate presents us with at least two intriguing
lines of speculation. On the one hand you've got possible next
steps for Greater London's imperial flood control regime, as the
city hardens its position, building higher and higher walls
against the coming flood. On the other, you've got a vision of
managed retreat: the city gradually evacuated, left half-collapsed
and abandoned after the city's oceanic war has been lost.

Either way, the future of London lies with the sea. It's easy
to imagine, in fact, that the entire English coastline might soon
be buttressed behind 40-meter-high locks and channels—and
it would be a beautiful sight to see, as if King Arthur's castle
had been rebuilt as a hydrological fortress along the Thames.
Thames Water, already struggling to keep the Tube dry from
river overflow, would perhaps need its own nuclear power
plants, droning into the 27th century, just to fuel its complex networks of pumps and aquatic regulators. New canals, distributing North Sea storm surges up toward marshland desalination
plants, could store that water in huge inland seas, reservoirs well-
protected for drinking. A new Lake District, militarized, utopian,
and entirely man-made, walled behind concrete, might be visited
by future Wordsworths, with Coleridge and his Ancient Mariner
setting sail up the Thames, now freshly dredged as far as Leeds.

But once those defenses fail, and London slips further
beneath the waves? The London Underground will be lost first,

transformed into both sewer and urban aquarium. Cellars and the steps that lead to them will make London a city of valves, pulsing from below with subsurface waters that burst upward and outward from the windows of buildings, all of London a new Versailles—an unintended architecture of choreographed fountains—showing off in arcs sprayed upon the facades of abandoned shopping centers. Perhaps no one will even be around to witness all this: Cold water will lap across the bleached dome of St. Paul's, unseen for centuries…till, someday, a distant heir of J. M. W. Turner returns sunburnt from the tropics to find London an archipelago of failed sea walls and waterlogged high-rises, the suburbs an intricate filigree of uninhabited canals, bonded warehousing forming atolls amidst sandbanks and deltas. Atop new islands of former rooftops, this man will rename future constellations to fit British geography as it used to be: Piccadilly Circus, King's Cross, Tottenham Court Road, all burning above a city that rots, stagnant, in a soup of black waters. Perhaps there will even be a cluster of stars named after Little Venice, as its namesake rebounds further and further beneath the sea.

Such visions have a long history, of course. In his 1885 novel, *After London; Or Wild England*, author Richard Jefferies envisioned London as it would be after the city has been abandoned by its human population. Jefferies wrote that parts of London have become a gigantic lake, and "vast marshes" have taken over

the city. The Thames is "partially choked," and water becomes London's true downfall:

> Now it is believed that when this had gone on for a time, the waters of the river, unable to find a channel, began to overflow up into the deserted streets, and especially to fill the underground passages and drains, of which the number and extent was beyond all the power of words to describe. These, by the force of the water, were burst up, and the houses fell in.

> For this marvelous city, of which such legends are related, was after all only of brick, and when the ivy grew over and trees and shrubs sprang up, and, lastly, the waters underneath burst in, this huge metropolis was soon overthrown. At this day all those parts which were built upon low ground are marshes and swamps.

More famously, J. G. Ballard's 1962 novel *The Drowned World* also brought with it scenes of a flooded London. The city has become sweltering and neotropical in the planet's increasing heat, Ballard writes; it is full of silt and entangled with Jurassic plant life, "a nightmare world of competing organic forms returning rapidly to their Paleozoic past." Huge iguanas laze around in the heat. Buildings regularly collapse, their lower six floors immersed in polluted seawater, "miasmic vegetation... crowding from rooftop to rooftop."

Ballard's story goes that a research biologist is traveling north with a small group of soldiers, boating from hotel to hotel across inland seas, recording the types of plants that are infesting the city. Meanwhile, monsoons are coming up from the south, everyone is dying of skin cancer, and no one can sleep. The intensity of the sun's radiation is making everything mutate. In between some eyebrow-raising moments of pop-Nietzschean pseudo-philosophy, there are some amazing descriptions of London's new urban tropics:

> Giant groves of gymnosperms stretched in dense clumps along the rooftops of the submerged buildings, smothering the white rectangular outlines. (...) Narrow creeks, the canopies overhead turning them into green-lit tunnels, wound away from the larger lagoons, eventually joining the six hundred-yard-wide channels which broadened outwards toward the former suburbs of the city. Everywhere the silt encroached, shoring itself in huge banks against a railway viaduct or crescent of offices, oozing through a submerged arcade. (...) Many of the smaller lakes were now filled in by the silt, yellow discs of fungus-covered sludge from which

THE SUPER-VERSAILLES

Humans channel, contain, and redirect water through the use of levees, irrigation ditches, ornamental fountains, sewage systems and filtration ponds, freshwater reservoirs, dredged wetlands, hydroelectric dams, underground pipelines, and even Evian bottles. The sum historical total of these projects, worldwide, from prehistory to ten thousand years from now, constitutes a unified endeavor—a kind of running subtheme for the anthropological experience. This is what landscape blogger Alexander Trevi calls the *Super-Versailles*.

When asked about the idea, Trevi replied that the Super-Versailles is "the agglomeration of past, present, and future hydro-engineering, from the Garden of Eden to Martian terraforming." The Super-Versailles, then, is coextensive with civilization—each generation engineering ever more forms in which to reorganize, however temporarily, Earth's finite supply of water molecules. The aquatic foundations of Venice, Three Gorges Dam, Dutch polders reclaimed from the bottom of the sea, the Los Angeles Aqueduct, deltaic shrimp-fishing villages in the Sundarbans of Bangladesh and India, Malaysian kelongs, the Great Man-Made River of Libya—all redirective interactions with water can be considered distant, abstract branches of Alexander Trevi's Super-Versailles.

pruned.blogspot.com

GLASS SUBMARINES
Subsidence of the Mediterranean
seabed north of Alexandria, Egypt,
means that archaeological ruins
have collapsed beneath the waters
of the harbor. Stone columns now
stand amidst sewage and fish.
While a Seuthopolis-style circular
walled city might certainly be one
means of rescuing this architectural heritage from the deep, a
2006 article in Egypt's *Al-Ahram
Weekly*—asking "Will Egypt build
the first offshore underwater
museum?"—suggests something
far more imaginative: a "glass submarine" that could be used to
explore the flooded ruins. Perhaps,
then, glass submarines—not walled
cities—are just what we need for any
future exploration of Doggerland:
No coastal city will be complete
without an undersea archipelago
of glass submarines, offshore
buildings roaming the seafloor.

UNDERSEA PALEOLANDSCAPES
The North Sea Paleolandscapes
Project, run by the Institute of
Archaeology and Antiquity at
England's University of Birmingham, has been using "3D seismic
reflection data" to investigate
"one of the largest and best
preserved prehistoric landscapes
in Europe"—Doggerland, at the
bottom of the North Sea.
   Seawater, which "rapidly inun-
dated" several sites of human
habitation and caused a "massive
loss of European land," here acts
as an unexpected preservative:
Those early floods from melting
glaciers set the stage for an
undersea museum of submerged
landscapes, a "lost world" of
human prehistory that we're only
now beginning to map.

iaa.bham.ac.uk

a profuse tangle of competing plant forms emerged, walled gardens in an insane Eden.

In Ballard's new alluvial world of fresh earth, architecture is reduced to deltas of sand. Old eroded reefs of brickwork fester in lagoons of pollution.

DOGGERLAND

Losing human settlements to rising sea levels is not something new in anthropological history—and I'm not referring to the occasional urban flood. At the end of the last ice age, during what's referred to as the Last Glacial Maximum, there was so much water stored in the polar ice sheets and in high mountain glaciers that sea level around the world was more than three hundred feet lower than it is today. Accordingly, huge tracts of dry land were exposed: Florida, for instance, was almost twice as wide as it is today; the Red Sea was an inhabitable valley; Sri Lanka was a peninsula, not an island, jutting southeast from India; and you could all but walk to Australia from mainland Asia, across an Indonesia that was mostly one continuous land mass.

One of these expanses of exposed dry land was something called Doggerland. Doggerland was a massive extension of the European continent northward into what is now the North Sea. From Denmark to England, stretching northward from Germany and France, a series of hills and river estuaries—the Rhine, the Seine, the Thames—stood, dry, for thousands of years. And it was inhabited by humans. How do we know this? As Steven Mithen, an archaeologist at the University of Reading, writes in his 2003 book *After the Ice*: "The first awareness of this lost Mesolithic world came in 1931. The *Colinda*, a trawler, was fishing at night about twenty-five miles east of the Norfolk coast near the Ower bank. Its skipper, Pilgrim E. Lockwood, hauled up a lump of peat and broke it open with a spade. He struck something hard—not a piece of rusty metal but an elegant barbed antler point." What we now call the Dogger Bank, a rich fishing ground east of England in the North Sea, used to be the Dogger Hills. Fishing for archaeology.

It's only obvious to point out, then, that as the glaciers began to melt, sea levels rose—and humans were around to see it happen. Mithen memorably describes this transformative process:

The Mesolithic coastal dwellers of Doggerland began to see their landscape change—sometimes within a single day, sometimes within their lifetime, sometimes only when they recalled what parents and grandparents had told them about lagoons and marshes now permanently drowned by the sea. An early sign of change was when the ground became boggy, when pools of water and then lakes appeared in hollows as the water table rose. Trees began to drown while the sea remained quite distant. Oak and lime were often the first to go, alder normally the last, surviving until sea water was splashing upon its roots and spraying upon its leaves.

High tides became higher and then refused to retreat. Sandy beaches were washed away. Coastal grasslands and woodland became salt marsh—land washed daily by the sea which saturated the soil with salt. (...) Marine waters worked their way into the valleys and around the hills; new peninsulas appeared, became offshore islands and then disappeared for ever.

But if this lost land of the earliest Europeans is still down there, being periodically dredged up by commercial fishing fleets, might there be another, more organized way, to rescue this particular chapter in human history?

I'm reminded of a startling proposal by Bulgarian architect Jeko Tilev. Tilev hopes to build a circular dam wall around the submerged Thracian archaeological site of Seuthopolis, in what is now Bulgaria. Those ruins, flooded by a dam project within just a few years of their discovery in the 1940s, would thus be returned to dry land; you could stand amidst the moss-covered walls of a Thracian metropolis, surrounded by a fortified ring holding back the reservoir waters. The protective dam walls would even be complete with an embedded tourist interpretation center, a concert hall, and a café.

Could a dozen Seuthopoli be built in the North Sea, in a multinational act of architectural dredging—massive ring cities in the form of hydrological projects, encircling the flooded landscapes of Doggerland? Build some boutique hotels out there—and you've got yourself a tourist gold mine.

Unfortunately, the answer to these questions might come the other way round: It is infinitely more likely that cities such as London will become preemptive Seuthopoli, surrounding themselves with walls in advance of the encroaching waters—till someday they, too, are archaeological sites from a lost phase of European civilization.

AN EARTH WITHOUT HUMANS

In 2006, *New Scientist* took a long look at what the Earth would look like following the complete disappearance of humans. Cites would revert to vast meadows and wild forests would

FISHING BENEATH MANHATTAN

In the summer of 2007, a short-lived architecture blog called *Urbablurb* reported on a little-known phenomenon: people fishing in the basements of Manhattan. *Urbablurb* quotes from a letter sent to the *New York Times* back in 1971. The letter's author, Jack Gasnick, claims that he used to fish in the basement of his Manhattan hardware store:

> We had a lantern to pierce the cellar darkness and fifteen feet below I clearly saw the stream bubbling and pushing about, five feet wide and upon its either side, dark green mossed rocks. This lively riverlet was revealed to us exactly as it must have appeared to a Manhattan Indian many years ago.

> With plum-bob and line, I cast in and found the stream to be over six feet deep. The spray splashed upwards from time to time and standing on the basement floor, I felt its tingling coolness.

> One day I was curious enough to try my hand at fishing. I had an old-fashioned dropline and baited a hook with a piece of sperm-candle. I jiggled the hook for about five minutes and then felt a teasing nibble. Deep in the basement of an ancient tenement on Second Avenue in the heart of midtown New York City, I was fishing.

The lost rivers of Manhattan are real; hundreds of streams and whole wetlands were paved over and filled so that the roots of buildings could safely grow. But whether or not you could ever fish in them—and this whole thing sounds like Dr. Seuss to me—was the subject of a May 2007 post on the also now defunct blog *Empire Zone*, to which *Urbablurb* brought our attention. On *Empire Zone*, a commenter informs us that fishing for eyeless carp in the underground cisterns of Istanbul is something of a national pastime—but we're also told, alas, as to the question of "whether any carp could be found swimming under Manhattan today," the answer, sadly, is no.

Still, how much would I love to find myself in New York City for a weekend, perhaps sent there to cover a story for work—when the phone rings in my hotel room. It's 11 p.m. I'm tired, but I answer. An old man is on the other end, and he clears his throat and says: "I think this is something you'd like to see." I doubt, I delay, I debate with myself—but I soon take a cab, and, as the clock strikes 12 a.m., I'm led down into the basement of a red brick tenement building on East 13th Street.

I step into a large room that smells vaguely of water—and six men are sitting around an opening in the floor, holding fishing poles above a river in the darkness.

conquer the streets. "If tomorrow dawns without humans," we read, "even from orbit the change will be evident almost immediately, as the blaze of artificial light that brightens the night begins to wink out. (. . .) The loss of electricity will also quickly silence water pumps, sewage treatment plants and all the other machinery of modern society."

The same lack of maintenance will spell an early demise for buildings, roads, bridges and other structures. Though modern buildings are typically engineered to last 60 years, bridges 120 years and dams 250, these lifespans assume someone will keep them clean, fix minor leaks and correct problems with foundations. Without people to do these seemingly minor chores, things go downhill quickly.

For instance, in his book *The World Without Us*, discussed earlier, Alan Weisman writes that "the only thing that has kept New York from flooding already is the incessant vigilance of its subway crews and 753 pumps." These pumps, of course, require a constant supply of electricity, so when there is even a routine interruption of electrical service, the hydrological consequences can be disastrous. Just a few days without active pumping could result in Manhattan's subways flooding—let alone a few months, a few decades, or a thousand years. An engineer actually suggests to Weisman that 36 hours without pumps during heavy rain might be enough to flood the New York subway system entirely. And if there's no one around to fix and clean them up?

At that point, water would start sluicing away under the pavement. Before long, streets start to crater. With no one unclogging sewers, some new watercourses form on the surface. Others appear suddenly as waterlogged subway ceilings collapse. Within 20 years, the water-soaked steel columns that support the street above the East Side's 4, 5, and 6 trains corrode and buckle. As Lexington Avenue caves in, it becomes a river.

And so on. The city folds into itself. Soon, "a layer of soil will start forming atop New York's sterile hard shell, and seedlings will sprout," Weisman writes.

Way back in 1996, *New Scientist* offered a very similar look at what would happen if London was abandoned to the marshes and earthworms. It would only be one year, for instance, before weeds as mundane as dandelions would begin to colonize the street's gutters and sidewalks. Unmaintained roads and building fronts would begin to crack with winter ice, and species like buddleia would escape from gardens and spread, kick-starting

the dismantling of the city. "Buddleia grows fast, and its light seeds are easily dispersed by the wind," the magazine informs us. "Brought to Britain from the Himalayas to adorn Victorian gardens, buddleia is already everywhere in London, poised to rid the city of its concrete and brick."

Then, "[w]ithin five years, roads, pavements, parking places and the great squares of the city are carpeted with weeds and a rich turf of clover." At that point, an "understory of grasses and shrubs gradually spreads over the city. As the soil layer builds up, deeper-rooting plants take hold. Trees start to grow and their roots smash through what's left of the pavement and tarmac." The city will become a perfect nesting place for birds:

> The concrete-and-steel office blocks in the City financial district and out east to Canary Wharf are immensely strong. Although the streets have turned green, the concrete buildings merely look neglected. Windows are broken, or have fallen from their frames, and the concrete is stained by the smoke of fires. But their structures are in as good shape as ever…

> The condition of the buildings is good news for cliff-nesting birds. At the end of the first decade, the complex of pipes and stairwells that adorn the Lloyd's building supports a huge population of kestrels, sparrowhawks and even a few rough-legged buzzards from Scandinavia.

The article's parting shot: "In a floodplain like London's, inundation of foundations and natural soil movements would leave very few buildings standing after 1,000 years. By that time, both the oak and the floodplain forests would be mature and the rubble of Canary Wharf would have sunk into the marsh." And so the whole of London looks more like Angkor Wat than Notting Hill.

I'm reminded of Percy Bysshe Shelley, who wrote of a time "when St. Paul's and Westminster Abbey shall stand, shapeless and nameless ruins, in the midst of an unpeopled marsh."

Of course, the world doesn't have to be "unpeopled" for this sort of decay to set in. At one point in his book *The Rings of Saturn*, author W. G. Sebald describes the slow collapse of large manor houses as they fail to survive years of inadequate maintenance:

> Keeping up the houses even in the most rudimentary way had long been impossible. The paintwork was flaking off the window encasements and the doors; the curtains became threadbare; the wallpaper peeled off the walls; the upholstery was worn out; it was raining in everywhere, and people put out tin tubs, bowls and pots to catch the water. Soon they were

As photographer Jacob Carter explains on his website, "the constant urge to improve upon or change the surrounding environment has given rise to vivid cityscapes. Empty wharfs, unused power stations, and other now derelict buildings of industry stand as the ruins and remains of once cutting-edge technologies." Throughout his work, Carter explores an interest "in the aesthetics of early photographic methods, in particular color postcards from the 19th-century." He does this using "specifically chosen expired film stock (expiry date 1970) and then perfecting the images digitally." The photographs here are from his *River Thames Series* (2006).

jacobcarter.co.uk

obliged to abandon the rooms on the upper stories, or even whole wings, and retreat to more or less usable quarters on the ground floor. The window panes in the locked-up rooms misted over with cobwebs, dry rot advanced, vermin bore the spores of mould to every nook and cranny, and monstrous brownish-purple and black fungal growths appeared on the walls and ceilings, often the size of an ox-head. The floor-boards began to give, the beams of the ceilings sagged, and the paneling and staircases, long since rotten within, crumbled to sulphurous yellow dust, at times overnight. Every so often, usually after a long period of rain or extended droughts or indeed after any change in the weather, a sudden, disastrous collapse would occur in the midst of the encroaching decay that went almost unnoticed, and had assumed the character of normality. Just as people supposed they could hold a par-ticular line, some dramatic and unanticipated deterioration would compel them to evacuate further areas, till they really had no way out and found themselves forced to the last post, prisoners in their own homes.

The owners might still live inside the building; certain rooms might still even be taken care of; but the inexorable process of rot continues apace. The buildings literally collapse around their residents. It's an architectural form of managed retreat.

THE RUINS PARK

In the late 1990s, photographer and urban sociologist Camilo José Vergara began to discuss a different form of managed retreat—on the scale of whole cities—when he controversially proposed that a "skyscraper ruins park" be built in downtown Detroit. In his book *American Ruins*, Vergara wrote that, "as a tonic for our imagination, as a call for renewal, as a place within our national memory, a dozen city blocks of pre-Depression skyscrapers be stabilized and left standing as ruins: an Ameri-can Acropolis." Continuing this line of thought in a later article for *Metropolis* magazine, Vergara suggests:

> We could transform the nearly 100 troubled buildings into a grand national historic park of play and wonder, an urban Monument Valley.... Midwestern prairie would be allowed to invade from the north. Trees, vines, and wildflowers would grow on roofs and out of windows; goats and wild animals—squirrels, possum, bats, owls, ravens, snakes and insects—would live in the empty behemoths, adding their calls, hoots and screeches to the smell of rotten leaves and animal droppings.

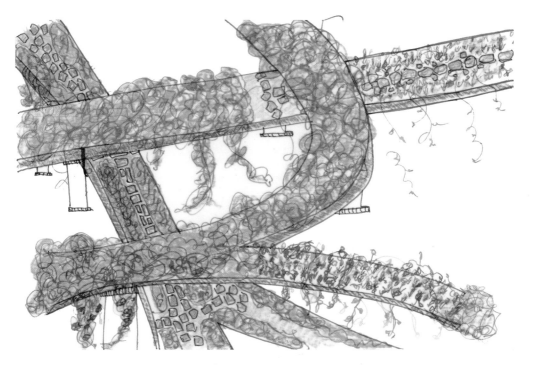

Perhaps you could pitch a new breed of entertainment complex to an oil-rich emir: Build a ruined city on the shores of an artificial island somewhere southwest of Dubai. Invite tourists to explore those haunted canyons of steel and broken glass; they can bring their families. For the low, low, discount price of only $75,000 a day, you can rent the entire park for yourself—and pose as Will Smith in *I Am Legend*, wandering through ruined department stores and sunbathing in weed-filled plazas. The ruined city could even be co-sponsored by Warner Bros.

At the very least, imagine the political implications of such a park: touring the ruins of the West by visiting the Middle East—where the shattered remnants of Euro-America are nothing but a theme park for future Chinese tourists. With recognizable buildings from London, New York, Chicago, Paris, Rome, and so on, it'd be a bit like the 2007 film *Resident Evil: Extinction*, wherein we see the lost lights of Las Vegas buried in desert sand. Only here it's a simulacrum of the entire Western world, laid out as waste at the feet of Dubai's glass towers and air-conditioned boulevards. It's an end-of-civilization theme park, complete with half-ruined hotels and flooded lobbies.

EARTH, A.D. 7,500,000,000

Of course, well beyond the era of human habitability, the earth will continue to change. Don't forget "the distant future," a December 2003 article in *New Scientist* warned—referring to an era 7.5 billion years from now when "the sun will loom 250 times larger in the sky than it is today, and it will scorch the Earth beyond recognition." The earth's surface will be entirely reconfigured into something called *Pangaea Ultima*:

> Existing [subduction] zones on the western edge of the Atlantic ocean should seed a giant north-south rift that swallows heavy, old oceanic crust. The Atlantic will start to shrink, sending the Americas crashing back into the merged Euro-African continent. So roughly 250 million years from now, most of the world's land mass will once again be joined together in a new supercontinent that [Christopher] Scotese and his colleagues [at U-Texas, Arlington] have dubbed Pangaea Ultima.

It would be interesting here to project, however unrealistically, where urban infrastructure will end up in this new tectonic configuration—for instance, if New York will collide with the docklands of London, and what that new city would then be called, and if you could set a novel in a situation like that. Your characters could take rowboats out to visit the half-collapsed towers of Manhattan, that ghost city adrift on mantled currents of earthquake-prone rock. Or perhaps it'd be possible for an architect—or two architects, on opposite sides of the ocean—to design, today, different buildings meant to merge in millions of years, to collide with each other and link into one building through plate tectonics, a delayed urban self-completion via continental drift.

After Pangaea Ultima, we read, runaway greenhouse warming and a literally expanding sun will mean that everything "gets worse. In 1.2 billion years, the sun will be about 15 percent brighter than it is today. The surface temperature on Earth will reach between 60 and 70°C and the . . . oceans will all but disappear, leaving vast dry salt flats, and the cogs and gears of Earth's shifting continents will grind to a halt. Complex animal life will almost certainly have died out."

Jeffrey Kargel, from the U. S. Geological Survey's office in Flagstaff, Arizona, offers his own vision of planetwide erosion: "Imagine a steaming Mississippi river delta with 90 percent of the water gone," he told the magazine. "There'll be lots of sluggish streams and the whole Earth will be flattening out. All the mountains will be eroded down to their roots. Huge swathes of the Earth might resemble today's deserts in Nevada and southern Arizona, with low, rugged mountains almost buried in their own rubble."

Kargel believes that the Earth might even become "'tidally locked' to the sun. In other words, one side of the planet will be in permanent daylight while the other side will always be

Architectural Ruins—a Vision (Bank of England in Ruins) (1798-1832) by Joseph Gandy, courtesy of the Trustees of Sir John Soane's Museum. This painting of what was, at the time, a brand-new building by Gandy's friend John Soane reveals the strange imaginative game those two would play: Gandy would frequently depict Soane's structures in the distant future, long after they had become ruins, covered with vines, half-collapsed upon themselves in feral darkness.

soane.org

↓ next spread
A Bird's-Eye View of the Bank of England (1830) by Joseph Gandy, courtesy of the Trustees of Sir John Soane's Museum.

soane.org

dark." The side of the planet always in the glare of triumphant Apollo will eventually consist of huge, roiling seas of red hot, liquid rock—perhaps ready for the return of Coleridge's Ancient Mariner, sailing on magmatic tides. "7.57 billion years from now, the magma ocean directly in the glare of the sun will reach almost 2200°C. 'At that kind of temperature, the magma will start to evaporate,' says Kargel." We've already discussed airborne geology—but does this mean we can assume the future existence of aerial rock weather and mineral hurricanes, on the planet we now know as Earth? From *New Scientist*: "Kargel thinks the night side of the Earth could be…about -240°C. And this bizarre hot-and-cold Earth will set up some exotic weather patterns."

> On the hot side, metals like silicon, magnesium and iron, and their oxides, will evaporate out of the magma sea. In the warm twilight zones, they'll condense back down. "You'll see iron rain, maybe silicon monoxide snow," says Kargel. Meanwhile potassium and sodium snow will fall from colder dusky skies.

So it would seem possible from this to figure out the melting point of Manhattan—i.e., the point at which rivers of liquid architecture will start flowing down from the terraces of uninhabited high-rise flats, and when the top of the Chrysler Building, all but invisible behind superheated orange clouds of toxic greenhouse gases, will form a glistening silver stream of pure metal, boiling down into what used to be the Atlantic Ocean. If cities are viewed, in this instance, as geological deposits, then there must be a way to account for them in the equations of future geophysicists: all of London reduced to a pool of molten steel, swept by currents of gelatinous glass, as sedimentary rocks made of abraded marble, granite, and limestone form from compression in the lower depths. A new Thames of liquid windows and parti-walls flows out into an evaporating sea.

GROUND CONDITIONS

It is a little-known fact that parts of Manhattan island are actually constructed from British war ruins. In his excellent 2005 book *Rubble: Unearthing the History of Demolition*, author Jeff Byles describes how Nazi bombers destroyed more than 4.5 million housing units, displacing at least 16 million people. "With London and Coventry knee-deep in rubble by the fall of 1940," he writes, "a phalanx of 13,500 troops from the Royal Engineers got busy ripping down war-ravaged structures." But what to do with all that rubble?

↑ previous spread
For the past ten years, students enrolled in Nic Clear's Unit 15 at London's Bartlett School of Architecture have used the tools of cinema and film production to turn out short classics of architectural science fiction. Employing narrative, animation, real-time actors, and Hollywood-quality special effects, often all at the same time, Clear's studios are one part Archigram, one part Steven Spielberg—with a dash of Fritz Lang's *Metropolis* thrown in for good measure. But it's not a film studio, Clear was quick to point out in an e-mail exchange with BLDGBLOG: "We are an architecture unit that uses film." Here we see images from *After the Rain* by Ben Olszyna-Marzys, set in a London both Edenic and postapocalyptic: We see a new London full of rock arches and jungle canopies, consumed with heavy vegetation and drowning in lagoons of pollution. The Millennium Dome and Tower Bridge compete with herds of giraffes and elephants for the viewer's attention.

bartlett.ucl.ac.uk

Around that same time, New York's FDR Drive was being constructed, which ran along the east side of Manhattan. "Much of the landfill on which it is constructed consists of the rubble of buildings destroyed during the Second World War by the Luftwaffe's blitz on London and Bristol," the historian Kenneth T. Jackson wrote. "Convoys of ships returning from Great Britain carried the broken masonry in their holds as ballast."

The obvious implication here is that when you're driving on the FDR—or, for that matter, when you're simply looking out over the east side of Manhattan—you and your gaze are passing over fragments of British cathedrals and London slums, the shattered doorframes and lintels, eaves, vaults, and bedroom floors of whole towns—pieces of Slough and Swindon perhaps—embedded now in asphalt.

Down in the foundations of cities are other cities.

And there are also ships. In preparation for a move to San Francisco in the summer of 2007, I found myself flipping through *The Lonely Planet Guide to San Francisco*—where I read that parts of San Francisco are actually built on the remains of old ships. Lonely Planet writes that many of the streets near the Embarcadero are actually built over reclaimed land, "some of it layered over the scores of sailing ships scuttled in the bay to provide landfill." In fact, the basements of some San Francisco homes weren't basements at all—*they were the hulls of old ships*. Well into the 19th century, apparently, some houses—built directly on land that had been filled in around abandoned boats—simply used those ships as basements (perhaps for storage, perhaps for entertaining; who knows). In other words, when you walked downstairs in certain buildings to grab a jar of preserved fruit, you stepped into the remains of an old ship. It's like a deleted scene from *The Goonies*.

Some of the underground boats' locations are well-known; right around the corner from my office, for instance, is a bar called the Old Ship Saloon. The original bar had been built out of the remains of a boat called *The Arkansas*; when you went in to order a drink at the turn of the 20th century, you actually stepped into the hull of a grounded seagoing vessel.

But still more ships are down there, unremembered and being discovered even today. A website called *Interesting Thing of the Day* had this to offer on the subject:

In the late 1960s, as San Francisco was building its BART subway system, discoveries of ships and ship fragments occurred regularly. Over the following decades, ships and pieces of ships appeared during several major construction projects along the shore. As recently as 1994, construction

workers digging a tunnel found a 200-foot-long (61-meter) ship 35 feet (11 meters) underground. Rather than attempt to remove the ship—which would have been both costly and dangerous—they simply tunneled right through it. When buried ships are found, they're sometimes looted for bottles, coins, and other valuable antiques frequently found inside. Among the prizes found in the ships have been intact, sealed bottles of champagne and whiskey, nautical equipment, and a variety of personal effects from the passengers and crews.

An entire armada of lost fishing ships, now rotting in the mud, nameless and undiscovered, shivering with every earthquake.

If there can be something as surreal as British war ruins in the island foundations of New York City, and 19th-century ships beneath the hotels and bars of San Francisco, then how else might we create new land—stretching the habitable surface of the earth beyond its natural shores?

FUTURE NATURE

Japan recently embarked upon a project to grow artificially enhanced coral reefs in a bid to extend its territorial sovereignty further south into the Philippine Sea.

Successfully transplanting and cultivating these reefs would, in theory, allow Japan "to protect an exclusive economic zone off its coast," the BBC reported in the summer of 2007—expanding Japanese maritime power more than 1,000 miles farther from Tokyo.

> According to the Law of the Sea, Japan can lay exclusive claim to the natural resources 370 km (230 miles) from its shores. So, if these outcrops are Japanese islands, the exclusive economic zone stretches far further from the coast of the main islands of Japan then it would do otherwise. To bolster Tokyo's claim, officials have posted a large metal address plaque on one of them making clear they are Japanese. They have also built a lighthouse nearby.

However, the major geopolitical question remains: Are these reefs truly islands?

At the moment, the Okinotori Islands (as they're called) are merely "rocky outcrops"; but, by enhancing their landmass through reefs—using reef "seeds" and "eggs"—Japan can create *sovereign territory*. This, in turn, means that it will win economic control over all the minerals, oil, fish, natural gas, etc., located in the area—providing friendly sea routes for American military ships in the process. The United States, of course, thinks that

Japan's sovereign reefs are a great idea; China, unsurprisingly, thinks the opposite. In fact, we read in the February 20, 2005, edition of the *Wall Street Journal*:

> Chinese interest in Okinotori lies in its location: along the route U.S. warships would likely take from bases in Guam in the event of a confrontation over Taiwan. China's efforts to map the sea bottom, apparently so its submarines could intercept U.S. aircraft carriers in a crisis, have drawn sharp protests from Japan that China is violating its EEZ.

Which means that these artificial encrustations of living matter, planted for political reasons at the beginning of the 21st century, could very well influence the future outcome of marine combat between the United States and China.

The rest of this story could go in any number of directions:

1) If this establishes a legal precedent for other such experimental terrains, might it lead to a new and exciting summer course at SCI-Arc, guest-taught by BLDGBLOG: *From Gothic Cathedrals to Sovereign Reefs: The Science Fiction of Architectural Structures…*? Or perhaps it could mean that the United States will turn away from Treasury-depleting global military adventures abroad to spend money on more interesting projects within its own borders—funding a whole new series of Hawaiian islands, designed by Thom Mayne, that would extend United States territory archipelagically toward Asia. It would be the outright geo-architectural construction of whole new landmasses, islands, and offshore microcontinents—terrains governed by Colonel Kurtz–like technocrats with iron fists, whose unchecked cruelty will inspire the literary classics of the 22nd century. Greece will be motivated to expand the Cyclades with a cluster of designer islands, slowly growing to dominate the Mediterranean once again— a kind of inverse-*Odyssey* in which the islands themselves do the traveling. Or maybe there will be a whole new terrestrial future in store for Scotland's Outer Hebrides, or for the Isle of Man, or for Friesland—or perhaps even a whole new Nova Scotia, extending hundreds of nautical miles into the waters of the north Atlantic, a distant, fog-shrouded world of melancholic introspection, visited only by poets.

2) It's worth remembering that the possession of land and territory was not always a recognized marker of political sovereignty—and so the Earth, in the sense of *geophysical terrain*, is here being swept up into a model of human governance that has only existed for a few hundred years, and which may only exist for a few decades more. So, under a

Spanish architect Vicente Guallart's
projects include tips on "how to make a
mountain": "put forward a mineralogical
system that will guide its functioning,"
he advises. Guallart's work is often more
geological than architectural, involving
the literal design of new territory. The
recent book *Geologics* documents his
studio's work.

guallart.com

Photograph by Eran Brokovich, courtesy of the photographer.

BRANDED LANDFORMS

A team of Israeli and Jordanian scientists, led by professor Nadav Shashar from the Hebrew University of Jerusalem, has been designing an artificial reef in the Red Sea.

The reef could be described as prefab: It is made from modular concrete sections that link together beneath the waves. However, the project is also a bio-architectural study in interspecies communica-tion: The reef must be inviting enough that fish and other aquatic wildlife move in to colonize the structure, but it must also be so alluring that human divers will want to explore it and not the natural reef nearby—which this concrete reef is being built to protect.

The fact that the new reef has the logo of its maker, the Israeli firm Ocean Brick System (OBS), visible on the upper flank of the module pictured here, brings with it an incredible implication: That is, hundreds or even thousands of years from now, divers unaware of the reef's history might snap off some coral...and find a logo underneath. Imagine if Sir Edmund Hillary had reached the summit of Everest—only to discover an insignia for the firm that con-structed it.

different political system, these artificial reefs would be quite literally meaningless: just a weird experiment in the middle of the sea.

3) Nonetheless, the generation of new territory for the purpose of extending—or consolidating—political power is nothing new. As but one example, in *The Conquest of Nature: Water, Landscape, and the Making of Modern Germany*, David Blackbourn describes "how Germans transformed their landscape over the last 250 years by reclaiming marsh and fen, draining moors, straightening rivers, and building dams in the high valleys." The relevance of this here, in the context of artificial Japanese reefs in the South Pacific, is that Frederick the Great used hydrological reclamation projects—i.e., marsh draining and river redirection—literally to create new territory; this expanded the political reach of Prussia by generating more earth upon which German-speaking settlers could then build farms and villages. All in all, this was a process of both "agricultural improvement and internal colonization," and it "increasingly assumed the character of a military operation." As Blackbourn further notes: "External conquests created additional territory on which to make internal conquests, spaces on the map out of which new land could be made." Indeed: "For Prussia, a state that was expanding through military conquest across the swampy North European plain, borders and reclamation went together."

This future nature of artificial reefs, drained wetlands, and engineered tropical island chains comes with its own architectural implications. At the very least, not only will architects need to brush up on their marine geotechnical skills—hiring underwater construction crews as often as they bring on summer interns—but they'll need to be increasingly well read in the legal issues of political sovereignty.

Of course, these examples also point to the shifting relationship between humans and the planet, and to the disputed jurisdictions that accompany all embryonic geographies—as the Earth becomes unearthly, indeed. ⊗

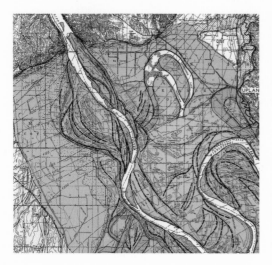

Fossil Rivers

The geological history of the Mississippi River has been extensively documented by the U. S. Army Corps of Engineers for more than a century. The Corps has produced maps, charts, graphs, and illustrated reports. Taken together, these offer a snapshot of the Mississippi, from source to sea, including the river's "subsurface conditions," its ancient geological forms, and its present-day urban surroundings. We see the grids of existing cities—New Orleans, Baton Rouge, St. Louis—built upon the shores of the world's fourth-largest river; and we see remnant landscapes of eroded bedrock from a time before humans set foot in North America. This is the "ancestral" Mississippi, a lost waterscape of "meander belts" and "alluvial aprons," now visible only to the eyes of trained geologists.

The Corps' maps are visually spectacular—beautiful to the point of disbelief. Colors coil around other colors; abstract shapes knot, circle, and extend like Christmas gift ribbons. This is geology as a subset of Abstract Expressionism: rocky loops of the Earth's surface in the hands of Jackson Pollock.

In the maps, different colors represent routes of the Mississippi as recorded by the Corps at "approximate half-century intervals"—indeed, the river can shift that much, tracing whole new geometries in less than a century. We glimpse the Mississippi in its true historic

dimensions, where it becomes a labyrinth of conflicting riverbeds, each one disappearing slowly, inevitably, over thousands of years, only to be replaced, abruptly, by new directions and forms—that will themselves disappear later. These maps document *time*, in other words, as much as they document *geography*.

The sheer fact that cities have been built in the midst of this mobile terrain is vaguely hilarious. The "land" all these cities are constructed on is actually hundreds of thousands of acres of displaced mud, thick sheets of soil washed down from the north and compacted over time into something approximating solid ground. Yet there is no solid ground here: It is an unstructured mush of erased landscapes, a syrupy blur. The river meanders, creating surface here, surface there—solidity nowhere. The waters curve eastward, then westward, then back again, redesigning the central landscape of the United States even as they drain North America.

Indeed, what the Army Corps of Engineers discovered while producing these maps is that the Mississippi River has *changed channel completely*—and it has done this hundreds, even thousands, of times. In fact, the river's endless self-alteration still occurs, even as you read this: The Mississippi, like all rivers, is migratory, destined to wander across the landscape for as long as it continues to flow. It drifts back and forth—sometimes a few feet, sometimes a mile—walled in by its own silt and debris, until

The Mississippi River's ancestral channels, unearthed through cartography by the U. S. Army Corps of Engineers. These maps, part of the Lower and Middle Mississippi Valley Engineering Geology Mapping Program, were produced in collaboration with geologists from the Engineering Geology and Geophysics Branch. Courtesy of the U. S. Army Corps of Engineers.

lmvmapping.erdc.usace.army.mil

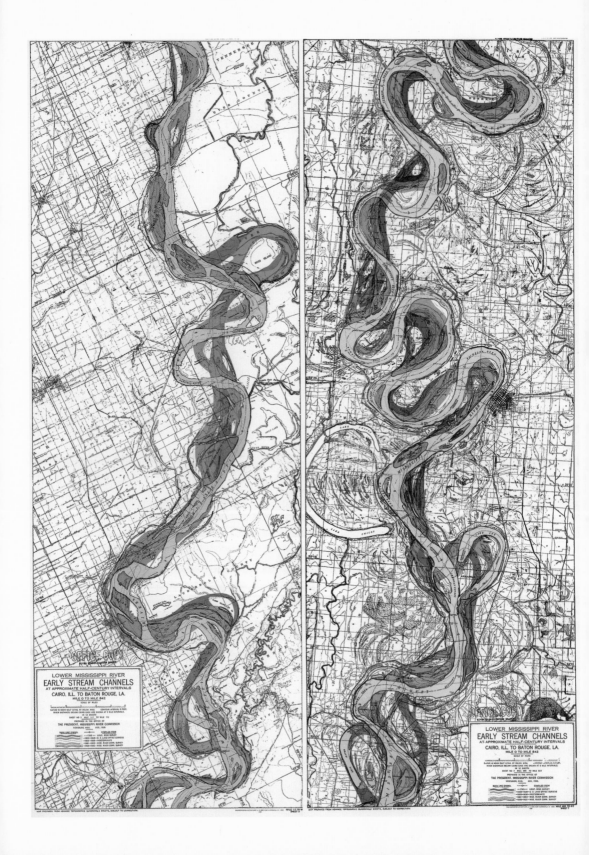

there is change: A natural levee fails, or a storm surge bursts into another watercourse nearby, and the river finds itself on a quick new route to the sea.

These old routes, of course, leave traces: Eroded deep into rock and soil, or piled high in distant mounds, running across the backyards of farms, forming ponds, they are the fossils of ancient landscapes—lost rivers locked in the ground around us.

If you are the Army Corps of Engineers, however—a branch of the U.S. military—then your mandate is to secure the nation's waterways. The Mississippi's relentless change in shape and direction is thus not a topic for poetry but a matter of national security. Through their infinite encyclopedia of the river—constantly updated, never complete—the Corps hopes to control these riverine transformations. Their goal is made almost comically obvious when you note that these maps are printed by the "War Department." This is a battle strategy: It is *geomorphic warfare*.

Simultaneous with the realization that the Mississippi is a landscape on the move, the Army Corps of Engineers launched a much-larger project: to fix the path of the Mississippi in place—forever. It sought to do this *through architecture*, installing monumental locks and dams up and down the river's route, controlling rates of flow, sediment, ship traffic, flash floods, and so on. For thousands of miles, the Mississippi would be a landscape held literally under martial law.

This can be seen as sheer folly for anyone who looks at the Corps' own maps. Meadows and hillsides once located hundreds of miles away have been reduced to nothing but mud braided on the bottom of the Mississippi River, clumped high in deltas, spread wide over lobes upon which whole towns have now been built. And someday even the Corps' pharaonic locks and dams will be mere sand on the shores of a future Mississippi. All these misguided control structures—and the cities they protect—will disappear, glittering in the currents like Rheingold…before they, too, are lost to the river forever.

Maps courtesy of the U. S. Army Corps of Engineers.

lmvmapping.erdc.usace.army.mil

Tectonic Warfare

Enlisting geology for violent ends—or putting the Earth itself into military service—is something of which we'll see much more in the coming decades. Defense budgets are growing, geotechnical know-how has bloomed, and global military ambitions continue to push further and further into what would once have been science fiction. There are several imaginative precedents for what might be called *terrestrial weaponization*—but one that has always stuck with me as a prime example of tectonic warfare is the 1985 James Bond film *A View to a Kill.*

Christopher Walken plays the bad guy, Max Zorin. Zorin is blond, he was born as part of a Nazi experiment, and he goes speed-boating with Grace Jones. He likes to race horses and he grins a lot. His plan? To blow up the San Andreas fault outside San Francisco, which will cause a massive earthquake and thus flood Silicon Valley. This will allow Zorin to corner the world microchip market.

Wonderfully, Zorin's plan is worked out using a model of San Francisco Bay, while he and a group of potential investors fly above the region in a blimp. In other words, he first hovers antigravitationally above the planet, simulating a plan to weaponize the earth; later, he travels beneath the earth's surface wearing a hard hat, where he gets into a discussion with engineers about the geotechnical nature of the San Andreas Fault—including how to blow the thing sky high. Max Zorin, in other words, has declared tectonic war on American private industry. Bond, of course, played by Roger Moore, teams up with a female geologist to thwart this evil plan; needless to say, Bond succeeds.

But man-made earthquakes don't only exist in James Bond films. In late 2006, Swiss engineers found to their surprise that they had set off a series of small tremors in the city of Basel when they began injecting water into a freshly drilled geothermal well on the outskirts of town. Some dams in the Pacific Northwest have also been linked to increased regional seismic activity due to the weight of all that impounded water.

Most interesting of all, a December 2005 article in the *Guardian* suggested that Taipei 101, one of the tallest (and heaviest) buildings on earth, might actually have reopened a dormant fault beneath the island nation of Taiwan; the skyscraper was a kind of seismic acupuncture point. There are several interesting implications here—including what it might mean if the building had been planned by Chinese engineers. China-Taiwan relations not being the greatest these days, what if Taipei 101 had been a kind of seismological Trojan horse, deliberately constructed by a Chinese engineering firm to be so big, and so precisely located, that it would cause later earthquakes, thus demolishing what China considers to be a rogue province? What would the UN say or do? Could you declare tectonic warfare on another country simply by *building* there?

On the other hand, it might be possible to achieve the exact opposite: Through sheer mass and fortuitous location, a building could perfectly weight a fault line…preventing it from shifting again. A building—a whole city—that acts to prevent earthquakes. Think of it as a geological piano damper. Anti-earthquake city. When my wife and I moved out to Los Angeles, I found myself thinking about earthquakes quite frequently—but I also found myself wondering if the surprising lack of seismic activity in the greater Los Angeles area over the past century and a half has been precisely *because* of the amount of buildings there. Is it possible that Los Angeles itself—its massive urban obesity—is a kind of anti-Taipei 101? In other words, could Los Angeles be so big and so heavy that it has shut down the major tectonic faults running beneath the city? If one hydroelectric dam in the well-forested canyons of Washington state can cause minor earthquakes, then surely an entire metropolis could stop equally minor earthquakes—at the very least—from occurring?

I would love to discover that the Los Angeles freeway system performs a kind of constant seismic massage on local tectonic plates by spreading the tension outward. Specific bus lines, say—traveling north on Figueroa, or down La Brea, or west on Venice—would have the totally unexpected effect of *releasing local tension out of the earth.* Whole new classes of vehicles could come into existence: Like hyper-industrial street cleaners, these slow-rolling, anti-earthquake machines would drone

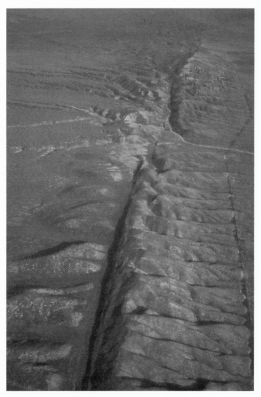

An aerial view of the San Andreas
Fault, courtesy of the NOAA/NGDC
Natural Hazards Photo Archive.

ngdc.noaa.gov

might hold the faults in place for a while—a
decade, a century—before the earth regains the
strength to break free.

In March 2008, *New Scientist* indirectly
answered this question. They wrote that
"earthquakes happen less often in areas covered by ice caps"—but that "quakes come back
with a vengeance when the ice melts." From
the article:

> Andrea Hampel at Ruhr University in
> Bochum, Germany, and colleagues (…)
> found that the vertical stress placed on the
> Earth's crust by a heavy ice sheet can sup-
> press many types of fault from slipping and
> causing a quake.
>
> Though the faults are pinned down for a
> time, stresses in the crust continue to build,
> so when the ice melts, earthquakes occur
> more strongly and more frequently.

Might it be possible that, as long as L. A.
continues to grow, it will function like an ice
sheet—an artificial glacier made of steel,
drywall, and excess pickup trucks—and thus
remain safe from major earthquakes? Only
when it begins to lose population will there be
earthquakes in L. A. again. I was interested to
see, then, that a commenter on BLDGBLOG
named Diego Makinara came back to the
original post in which I first proposed this
to comment:

through the twisting, fractal valleys of Hollywood, pressing strain out of the bedrock.

I'm reminded of David L. Ulin's book *The
Myth of Solid Ground*. Ulin introduces us to a
man named Donald Dowdy, who once found
himself under FBI investigation for taunting
the United States Geological Survey with "a
bizarre series of manifestos, postcards, rants,
and hand-drawn maps…forecasting full-bore
seismic apocalypse around an elusive, if biblical, theme." But Dowdy also claimed that, "in
the pattern of the L.A. freeway system, there is
an apparition of a dove whose presence serves
to restrain 'the forces of the San Andreas
fault'." This is absurd—yet I find myself wondering if more and more people were to move
to Los Angeles, and more and more buildings
were to be constructed there, then perhaps we

> I was reminded of this post during an earth
> science class this afternoon. My prof didn't
> think any city, even L. A., could hold the
> plates in place enough to prevent earth-
> quakes. But he was intrigued by the idea that
> constant construction might be continually
> breaking the brittle earth around the plate
> boundary, preventing the elastic stretch and
> subsequent snap that causes earthquakes.

Till proven otherwise, then, Los Angeles could
be the world's first tectonic utopia: As long as
everyone sticks together out there, they'll be
just fine.

Photos by Richard Mosse.

richardmosse.com

Air Disaster Simulations

In the winter of 2008, photographer Richard Mosse got in touch with BLDGBLOG to share his recent photographs of air disaster simulations: fire crews racing to put out temporary infernos amidst fake airplane bodies on the runways of airports all over Europe and the United States.

"I spotted my first air disaster simulator on the tarmac at JFK," Mosse wrote. "You can see it yourself next time you fly into that airport. It's an intimidating black oblong structure situated dangerously close to one of the runways. Ever since, I have hunted for air trainers while taxiing across each new airport that I've had the chance to fly into."

When I asked him about the act of setting himself up near burning, abstract airplanes in order to get the right shot, Mosse replied: "They are extremely difficult to photograph. First the water jets are turned on to douse the fuselage in water. This is in order to stop the

metal from warping under the intense heat of the flames. Then a pilot light comes on—and the spectacle begins."

This is all part of Mosse's larger attempt to show "the ways in which we perceive and consume catastrophe."

> The actual disaster is a moment of contingency and confusion. It's all over in milliseconds. It's hidden in a thick cloud of black smoke and you cannot even see it. Battles, ambushes, hijackings, air strikes, terrorism: It's the same with all of these, too. But the catastrophe lives on before the fact and after the fact, as this spectacle. That's why I wanted to photograph the air disaster simulators; they are the air disaster more than the thing itself.

"I think it's important," Mosse concludes, "that we understand where catastrophe exists in our cultural imagination—where it actually is in reality—which is why I do what I do."

Structures of Mass Wasting

In a giddily good essay called "Los Angeles Against the Mountains," originally published in the *New Yorker* in September 1988, John McPhee describes how buildings survive in the fallout paths of rock slides, debris slugs, and other flows of geologic mass wasting.

The scene? Southern California's San Gabriel Mountains—"divided by faults, defined by faults, and framed by them," McPhee writes—against which Los Angeles has grown, its outermost neighborhoods now encroaching upon what McPhee calls the "real-estate line of maximum advance."

"The San Gabriels are nearly twice as high as Mt. Katahdin or Mt. Washington, and are much closer to the sea. From base platform to summit, the San Gabriels are three thousand feet higher than the Rockies," McPhee informs us. Further, although the San Gabriels are "in their state of tectonic youth, they are rising as rapidly as any range on earth…. Shedding, spalling, self-destructing, they are disintegrating at a rate that is also among the fastest in the world." Rising up, rising down—the San Gabriels produce, in the process, some of the most extraordinary rock slides ever documented in North America: "On the average, about seven tons disappear from each acre each year—coming off the mountains and heading for town."

These slides are referred to as *debris slugs*, and they "amass in stream valleys and more or less resemble fresh concrete. They consist of water mixed with a good deal of solid material, most of which is above sand size. Some of it is Chevrolet size." Debris slugs have been known to contain "propane tanks, outbuildings, picnic tables, canyon live oaks, alders, sycamores, cottonwoods, a Lincoln Continental, an Oldsmobile, and countless boulders five feet thick." And all of it comes crashing down—frequently going right through people's houses.

If a house is to survive in the face of "this heaving violence of wet cement," then new architectural techniques are desperately needed. "At least one family," for instance, "has experienced so many debris flows coming through their back yard that they long ago installed overhead doors in the rear end of their built-in garage. To guide the flows, they put deflection walls in their back yard. Now when the boulders come they open both ends of their garage, and the debris goes through to the street." Deflection walls, overhead doors, feeder channels, concrete crib structures: The lived vocabulary of dwelling expands dramatically in the presence of geologic collapse.

Except, of course, that this shift is not limited to houses—the whole city's in on it. Los Angeles County "began digging pits to catch debris," McPhee writes, surrounding itself with voids to counteract the unleashed brawn of surprise geology. These debris pits are "quarries, in a sense, but exceedingly bizarre quarries, in that the rock [is] meant to come to them." They are, you could say, strange attractors: "Blocked at their downstream ends with earthfill or concrete constructions, they are also known as debris dams. With clean spillways and empty reservoirs, they stand ready to capture rivers of boulders—these deep dry craters, lying close to the properties they protect."

In all their megalithic abstraction—like great walls of pharaohs, embedded in the Los Angeles hills—these basins can be "ten times as large as the largest pyramid at Giza." Yet they are *empty*—vast concavities—ready to be filled with a single night's rush of silt. The attack of the debris slugs. These artificial mini-anti-quarries, so to speak, bearing nearly "four million tons of rock, gravel, and sand" in some of the deeper basins, eventually become something of a highway-builder's wet dream: A "private operator," for example, "has set up a sand-and-gravel quarry," using these reservoirs as rock mines. You can almost feel McPhee kicking himself for not thinking of it first.

But the rock slide–ready house, complete with internal avalanche channels and overhead doors, perhaps offers us a new domestic typology: a house that will also serve as a valve for natural processes.

Several variations ensue: For instance, you could build a house on a migration route for international waterfowl. It should be a very, very large house, and the international waterfowl should be very, very stubborn. They will not change course. They are committed, and your house is in the way. Every March, therefore, a ritual begins: You roll up your garage doors, you slide open the glass living room walls, you throw plastic tarps over all of your furniture—and then, all afternoon, massive flocks of waterfowl come arcing straight through, clouds of temporary house inhabitants. Soon you charge admission to total strangers and, at $5 a head, you're a millionaire: People come from all over the world to sit inside your house, in specially placed chairs, just to watch the migrating birds fly through.

So, as debris slugs continue to pour down out of the San Gabriel Mountains, reclaiming the terrain of peripheral Los Angeles, perhaps Californian houses can learn to *open up*: pop out a door here, a window there, perhaps attach some chutes and kiddie slides between them, till they're all ramps and moving surfaces, and you've got a valve house: flexibility in the face of what should have been destruction. Thus, the spectacle of mass wasting begins: sand, pebbles, rocks, boulders, canyon live oaks, Oldsmobiles, migratory birds, and even forest fires—everything nature's got, whirling through your house in a geotechnical storm. And there you are, at the center of it, sitting ready, open to the world, tectonic.

Milton, Atomicist

John Milton's *Paradise Lost* is perhaps the world's first—and only—epic poem about an insurrectionary terrorist invasion of Heaven. Writing in 1667, Milton describes "materials dark and crude," lying "deep under ground," that will open up to "shoot forth" light like "Heaven's ray":

> These in their dark nativity the Deep
> Shall yield us, pregnant with infernal flame,
> Which, into hollow engines long and round
> Thick-rammed, at the other bore with
>   touch of fire
> Dilated and infuriate, shall send forth
> From far with thundering noise among
>   our foes
> Such implements of mischief as shall dash
> To pieces, and overwhelm whatever stands
> Adverse, that they shall fear we have disarmed
> The Thunderer of his only dreaded bolt.

Thus armed, the demons prepare their deicidal uprising:

> …in a moment up they turned
> Wide the celestial soil, and saw beneath
> The originals of Nature in their crude
> Conception: sulfurous and nitrous foam
> They found, they mingled, and, with
>   subtle art,
> Concocted and adjusted, they reduced
> To blackest grain, and into store conveyed,
> Part hidden veins dug up (nor has this Earth
> Entrails unlike) of mineral and stone,
> Whereof to found their engines and
>   their balls
> Of missive ruin

While this could simply describe gunpowder, Milton's mineral activation of the Earth as a resource for high-tech weaponry sounds like the Manhattan Project three centuries ahead of itself. Atomic bombs, read through the lens of *Paradise Lost*, become a kind of *geological pursuit*.

Wounded Landscapes: An Interview with David Maisel

In his own words, photographer David Maisel has a "fascination with the undoing of the landscape." Perhaps his most widely known project—and my personal favorite—is a series of aerial photographs of Owens Lake, California; the surreally abstract images were taken from nosebleed-inducing heights of 13,000 feet. As cinephiles will no doubt know, Owens Lake was drained in the early 20th century to water the lawns of suburban Los Angeles, an act of hydrological theft that found its way into American cultural mythology through Roman Polanski's film *Chinatown*. Owens Lake is now a Dantean wasteland, one of the most toxic sites in North America.

As Maisel describes it on his website:

> The only moving things are the dust devils that coalesce and spin in the afternoon heat, swirling white towers of cadmium, arsenic, sulfur, chlorine, iron, calcium, nickel, potassium, aluminum, chlorine. The lakebed emits 300,000 tons of such matter every year; thirty tons of it arsenic, nine tons of it cadmium. We had dreamed of building cities, fields of glittering towers, urban fantasies meant to house our hopes of progress; now we seek out dismantled landscapes, abandoned, collapsing on themselves. Rather than creating the next utopia, we uncover the vestiges of failed attempts, the evidence of obliteration.

In March 2006, my wife and I visited Maisel in his Bay Area studio to talk to him about his work.

BLDGBLOG: Your work is obviously different from, say, the work of Ansel Adams, whose documentary-style "nature photography" serves as an inevitable point of reference for landscape photographers today. You're not attracted to the same landscapes, for instance, and your technique—often using airplanes—is completely different from his. To my knowledge, there's no David Maisel series of Zion National Park, or of the Grand Canyon. Does straightforward "nature photography" interest you? Does there have to be some kind of human stain or industrial intervention in the landscape before you take a picture?

David Maisel: In Ansel Adams's era, I imagine that making such pictures meant something different than it would today. By now, this kind of work has been done to death, so to speak; I'm not certain there's much significance in making those pictures today. At least for me. I'm certainly guilty of it myself at times—I've been working in Iceland for two years, on a series of geothermal landscape images—but I actually find it somewhat self-indulgent. When I'm being particularly self-critical, I'll convince myself that making pictures of "unspoiled" places doesn't teach me anything, or offer me anything, or challenge me. At best, it's a placebo. But I still have found Iceland, for example, to be an intensely captivating place to work…so it's a bit of a conundrum.

For the most part, I'm interested in landscape images not merely for what they look like, but for what they make us *feel*, and for what they might represent metaphorically. I also want my pictures to take the viewer to places and sites that they've never seen before, with a resulting sense of alienation or displacement. I'm less interested in being warm and fuzzy than in being harsh and cruel! [*laughs*] Those possibilities don't exist when you're looking at the familiar.

So I look at landscape from a conceptual point of view—and that's fueled my pervasive interest in the work of Robert Smithson and Gordon Matta-Clark, two artists who explored the undoing of things, the endgame, the absent, the void. I'm drawn to aspects of the sublime, and to a certain kind of visceral horror—and, in a sense, I am using my imagery in order to get to that feeling, as much or even more than I am documenting a specific open-pit mine or cyanide-leaching field or clear-cut forest. I'll readily admit that my work might not hold up very well from a documentary standpoint.

BLDGBLOG: It struck me while looking at your work that the very word *landscape* is a bit inaccurate, because the sites you choose are

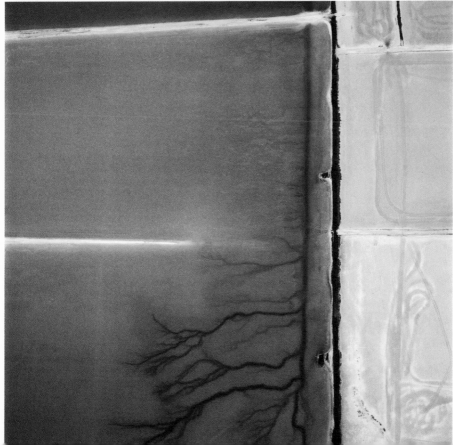

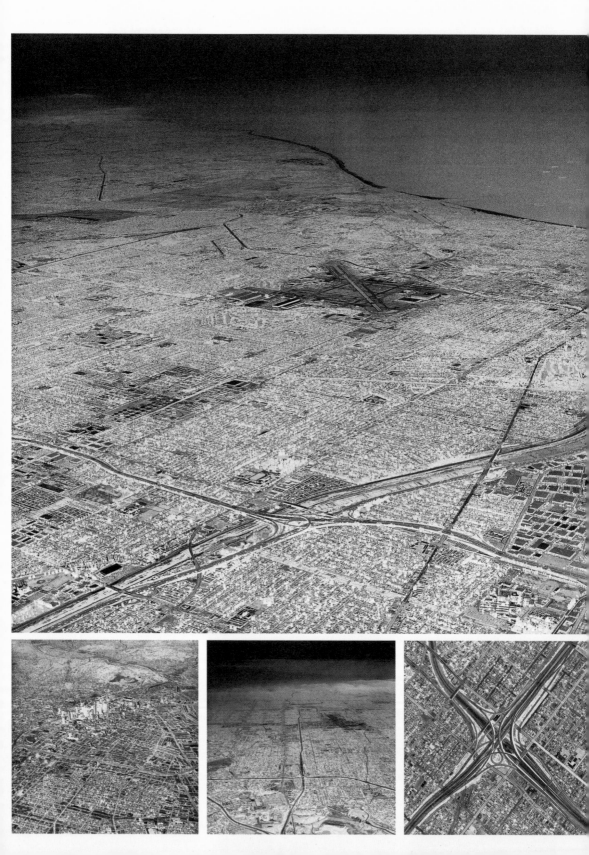

more like *events*. You photograph abraded lake beds, forests being clear-cut, copper mines, and so on. What do you think of that—that you're an *event* photographer? That a landscape itself can be an event, a process?

Maisel: Well, the word *landscape* is an interesting one—it implies a viewer who is making a judgment. A *landscape* is bounded by our own set of interests and values. The *land* exists without us; the *landscape* involves our own discernment. I suppose that you're actually very accurate. It's that sense of *turmoil*, or, really, it's the sublime, right? It's the dislocation of the viewer that interests me. It gets back to the same issue as Ansel Adams. I mean, his work at a particular moment in time probably had a different meaning than it does now—but I want to make work that has meaning *now*. And I think you really have decide what that is—*as an artist*. You have an obligation, in a way, to choose subject matter that has *meaning*.

BLDGBLOG: What do you think of the growing popularity of aerial images in this era of *Google Earth*?

Maisel: The aerial view has certainly become increasingly normative in our lifetimes. The impulse is to assume that we understand or know something concrete about a place because we've seen a photograph of it, whether aerial or otherwise. I don't necessarily subscribe to that view. Information can be just that: dumb and inert. It needs tools of interpretation, discernment, and judgment in order to have meaning. *Definitive meaning*, as such, is a slippery slope. In fact, the slope is steeper and more treacherous now as the sheer quantity of information (from *Google Earth*, etc.) grows. To see a photograph of a thing is to see an *interpretation* of it, whether by the photographer, the remote satellite camera, or the viewer. The same aerial photograph of a flooded New Orleans might be interpreted quite differently by a hydraulic engineer, a former resident of that city, a member of Congress, or a pastor. There are multiple truths in images—but, too frequently, singular truths are ascribed to them.

I should add that I don't think of my work as *aerial photography* or of as myself as an *aerial*

photographer, per se. It's simply a tool that I use in order to make the pictures that I want to make.

BLDGBLOG: This is a fairly abstract question, but those colors at Owens Lake are, fundamentally, the result of chemical processes—yet so is photography. Your prints, for instance, are literally their own landscapes, made from the same metals present at the sites you've been photographing. So I'm curious if you see any connection between the chemical act of photography itself and those processes of landscape discoloration. Owens Lake, in other words, is a kind of massive photographic plate, producing abstract hydrological imagery on its surface, twenty-four hours a day. Do you ever feel like you are taking photographs of photographs?

Maisel: Yes, conceptually it is part of the work—though I've never heard it so poetically described!

BLDGBLOG: I find, ironically, that your photographs make what happened at Owens Lake so beautiful that the images almost preclude an interest in intervening. Your photos aestheticize the abyss in such a way—

Maisel: [*laughs*] That's true.

BLDGBLOG: —that Owens Lake might almost become a place of artistic pilgrimage, with people coming out to see what you call its "beauty born of environmental degradation."

Maisel: Yeah, that impulse interests me, too. These places really are off the beaten path—or are less-known—whether that's Owens Lake or the mining sites. But I do think that the more people start to visit them, or start to bring them into their consciousness, the better off we'll be. We'll have a better understanding of what happened in these places.

BLDGBLOG: Of course, the draining of the lake could almost be seen as kind of avant-garde landscape architecture. I mean, you could easily imagine the lake having been drained for its *aesthetic impact*: a conscious attempt to reveal the geochemical iridescence

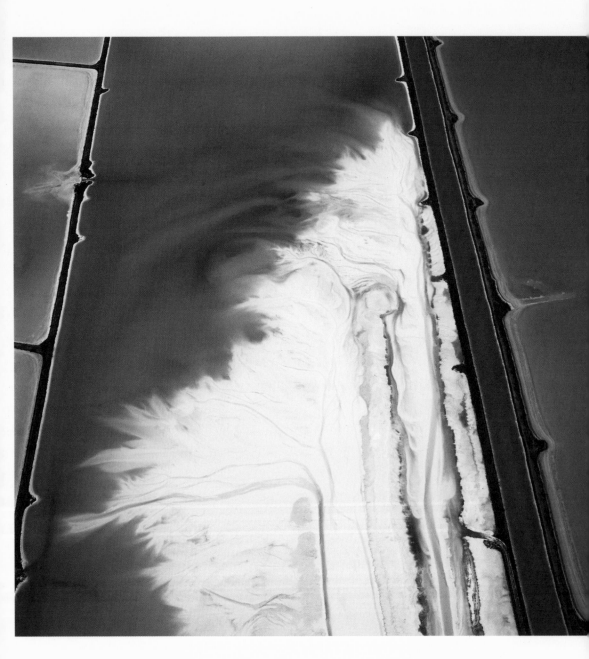

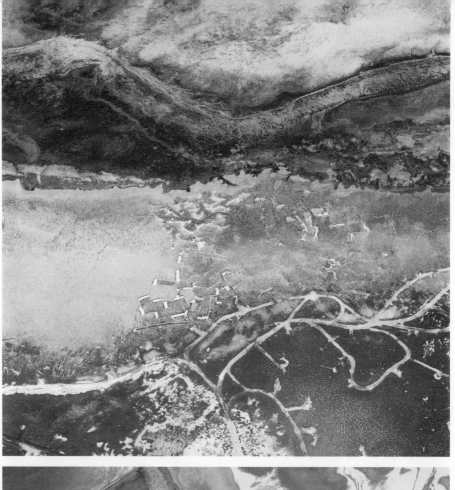

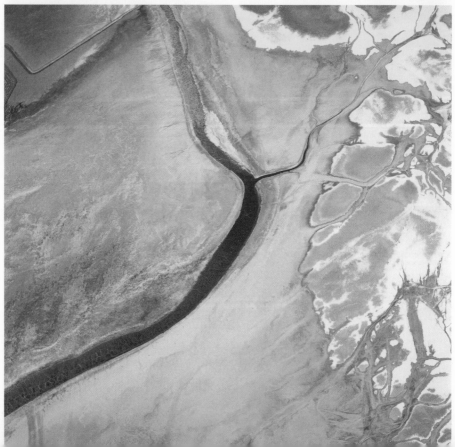

of the site. I'm curious if you're ever tempted to cheat—to make the site *more* polluted, *more* colorful, *more* inhuman—to make things temporarily worse before you take a photograph?

Maisel: Set fires in the desert so I can take a few pictures? [*laughs*] I've never had to—and I'm not capable of that kind of nihilism. At least not yet! I'm more interested in the cumulative nature of small decisions. You know, I'm sure no one ever said, "Let's drain this lake and cause huge, toxic dust storms." Yet that's exactly what happened. It was precisely *un*planned.

BLDGBLOG: So an intervention by you, the artist—

Maisel: It's not necessary. There are ways to achieve that sense of the base, the infected, the elemental without necessarily introducing poisons into the environment.

For example, in my next phase of work at Owens Lake I'd like to occupy a broader role as artist/sculptor/architect. My desire is to bring the viewer out of the gallery space and into the actual physical environment of the lake bed. My plans—quite preliminary and conceptual at this point—are to build two structures at the site: an observation tower and a footbridge. The observation tower, a spiraling, Tatlin-esque form, would rise on the edge of the Flood Zone. The Flood Zone is the most recent human intervention at the site, created to keep toxic windstorms from rising off the lake bed. It's like a replicant landscape: It *refers to* the Owens Lake that was drained. It's got a sterility, a coldness, a machine-made feel that I like.

So the footbridge would actually cross over the blood-red waters that remain in what was once the deepest part of the lake.

BLDGBLOG: Would that be for scientific purposes—to teach visitors about the history of Owens Lake—or more of a landscape installation, a kind of new *Spiral Jetty*?

Maisel: I think the net goal would be an aesthetic one. I don't see it necessarily as a place where knowledge would come prepackaged for you, the way many science museums do today. I think you could very easily introduce viewers to the history of Owens Lake, and let them draw their own conclusions and assess the state it's in now. That could be a very interesting idea. But I also wonder if there's not a way for the architecture itself to suggest those things, without needing to spell it out. Maybe the thing I'm more interested in is asking certain questions, rather than giving certain answers. I'm very wary of being didactic.

But, you know that footbridge: If there was a way to have an oculus in the bridge, so you're actually looking down, and straddling the gap—you're just suspended there above these blood-red waters—you would come away with a very different kind of knowledge. Maybe not a quantitative knowledge. Maybe more qualitative. But you would have a knowledge.

BLDGBLOG: You could do something with glass-bottomed boats. Take people out and punt around, like a Venice gondolier, with Muzak piped over hidden speakers.

Maisel: [*laughs*] I like that.

Mars Bungalow and the Prison of Simulation

"What would it be like to spend nearly two Earth years at the Martian north pole," *Building Design* asked back in February 2007, "a place where darkness falls for nine months of the year, carbon dioxide snow flutters down in winter and temperatures drop to a chilly minus 150 centigrade?" Well, I think it'd be wonderful.

As a means of actually answering that question, ANY Design Studios put together a speculative project meant to house "visitors" at the Martian pole. Their structure, complete with padded walls and well-made beds, is described as "a robot on legs built of Martian ice." What's particularly intriguing, however, is that, in the project renderings, the interior walls have been painted to look like the Pacific Northwest. Even on Mars, then, we will live within simulations. Indeed, the architects go on to explain that they have been "exploring the possibility of reproducing *programmable Earth environments* in a room we have called the 'Multi Environment Chamber.' Settlers on Mars may well be able to make themselves a cup of tea and settle into a chair with the sun gently warming their skin, cool breezes, and the sound of songbirds of an English orchard on a warm July afternoon"—assuming that such an experience wasn't precisely what you were trying to get away from in the first place.

These "programmable Earth environments," of course, bring up the question of what I like to call *surrogate Earths*: those portable versions of our planet's biosphere that pop up everywhere from hydroponic gardens, terrariums, and floating greenhouses to complex plans for manned missions to the moon. If only for the purpose of growing vegetables, how can we use technology—fertilizers, UV lights, and even TV screens—to reproduce terrestrial conditions elsewhere, in miniature? And what does it mean that the Earth itself can enter into a chain of substitutions—a whole economy of counterfeits and stand-ins, referring, through simulation, to a lost original—only to produce something so unearthly as a result?

These unearthly stand-ins for a kind of lost terrestriality should undoubtedly include a scenario in which a person can sit inside a room somewhere in southern California, but the room has been kitted out to look like a Martian base. And inside that Martian base a man sits, reminiscing about a room in southern California that he once decorated to look like a Martian bungalow…which could perhaps be referred to as the interplanetary architecture of *et cetera, et cetera, et cetera*. It comes with a free bottle of aspirin to keep the headaches at bay.

Phrased otherwise, of course, all of this would be an inversion of what author William L. Fox describes in his book *Driving to Mars*. There, Fox writes about "the idea of practicing Mars on Earth." He is referring to a small team of hopeful astronauts who, even as I write this, have been "practicing Mars" on a remote base in northern Canada. That is, they are acting as if they are already surrounded by Martian topography. It's a form of psychological training: act as if you have already arrived. If you turn this around, however, you find astronauts "practicing Earth on Mars." Act as if you never left.

But why not practice, say, Neptune, instead? Why not be even more ambitious and use each planet in the solar system as a base from which to simulate the rest? We'll build a Mercury Simulation Lab on Venus, and we'll simulate Uranus on Jupiter. Or we could just abandon simulation altogether, and experience Mars as Mars.

It's interesting in this context, then, to look at the nomenclature used by NASA to claim—or at least label—Martian territory. Landscapes on Earth toponymically reappear on the Martian plains. There is Bonneville Crater and Victoria Crater, for instance; there is Cape Verde and a cute little rock called "Puffin."

Mars is an alien landscape, then, in everything but name.

Even more fascinating is the small range of Martian hills now "dedicated to the final crew of Space Shuttle *Columbia*." Accordingly, these hills now appear on maps as the "Columbia Hills Complex." But an entire landscape named after dead American astronauts? Surely there's a J. G. Ballard story about something exactly like this.

COLUMBIA HILLS COMPLEX

Anderson Hill · Brown Hill · Chawla Hill · Clark Hill · Husband Hill · McCool Hill · Ramon Hill

All images courtesy of NASA and the California Institute of Technology Jet Propulsion Laboratory.

marsrovers.jpl.nasa.gov

Space Mountain

Norway's Kristian Birkeland was the first physicist to correctly speculate, in the early 1900s, that the titanic astral forces of the sun might somehow be interacting with the Earth's own magnetic field to produce the Northern Lights. As Birkeland's career developed, however, he became self-destructively obsessed with building a device that could reproduce those spectacular atmospheric light effects in miniature. He wanted his own auroras, in other words, and he would make them with a machine.

Unfortunately, Birkeland was propelled toward ruin by a strange double addiction: he drank near-psychotic amounts of caffeine in the Egyptian desert and he grew dependent on a new barbiturate called Veronal, which that well-known medical resource *Wikipedia* memorably describes as a "slow-acting hypnotic."

In her 2002 book *The Northern Lights*, a biography of Birkeland, British author Lucy Jago writes that, even as a young man, Birkeland wanted to build a "machine in which to recreate many phenomena of the solar system beyond the Earth." He called this machine a *terrella*—a kind of *little earth*. Birkeland's terrella was really just a vacuum chamber—but it was "unlike anything that had been made before." Indeed, Jago explains that the terrella would have acted as a "window into space." To construct it, Birkeland assembled a glass-walled chamber that was then "pumped out to create a vacuum" in which he could "produce charged particles" using a cathode ray—quite similar to the technology found in early television sets. As the cathode ray sent its charged particles passing through Birkeland's artificial void, it created stunning visual effects; these resembled "beautiful solar phenomena," Jago writes, such as "the sun's corona." Birkeland was even able "to simulate Saturn's rings, comet tails, and the Zodiacal Light."

Inspired by his success with the terrella, and by the stimulating powers of caffeine, Birkeland began to "take his Northern Lights theory one step further—into a complete cosmogony, a theory of the origins of the universe." He thus began to speculate about the "electromagnetic nature" of the material world. This intellectu-

ally supercharged period of his life is described by Jago as Birkeland's "immersion into the universe of his vacuum chamber."

In a letter written from a hotel in Aboukir, Egypt, where his interacting addictions to caffeine and Veronal had already begun to drive him insane, Birkeland wrote:

> And, finally, I am going to tell you about a great idea I have had; it's a bit premature but I think it will be realized. I am going to get some money from the state and from friends, to build a museum for the discovery of the *Earth's magnetism, magnetic storms, the nature of sunspots, of planets—their nature and creation*. On a little hill I will build a dome of granite, the walls will be a meter thick, the floor will be formed of the mountain itself and the top of the dome, fourteen meters in diameter, will be a gilded copper sphere. Can you guess what the dome will cover? When I'm boasting I say to my friends here, "next to God, I have the greatest vacuum chamber in the world." I will make a vacuum chamber of 1,000 cubic meters and, every Sunday, people will have the opportunity to see a ring of Saturn ten meters in diameter, sunspots like no one else can do better, Zodiacal Light as evocative as the natural one and, finally, auroras...four meters in diameter. The same sphere will serve as Saturn, the sun, and Earth, and will be driven round by a motor.

While this description of "the greatest vacuum chamber in the world," carved out of a granite mountaintop, complete with a gilded copper dome, conjures up imagery somewhere between *Frankenstein*, *Batman Begins*, Hindu theology, and perhaps a new film by Guillermo del Toro, it also suggests that it might be possible to model—even to *reproduce*—the universe using *architecture*. Birkeland's cosmogonic laboratory on a hill, inside of which "magnetic storms" would be re-created every Sunday for paying visitors, like some new church of the sky, would thus have been a true museum of space. It was an electromagnetic machine-altar—a kind of spherical television set inside of which we could have stood, to watch the uncoiling of the universe in miniature.

The San Francisco Bay Hydrological Model

Inside a warehouse in Sausalito, California, you will find the San Francisco Bay Hydrological Model. The Bay Model, as it's known, was built in 1957 by the Army Corps of Engineers; it is, the Corps explains on their website, "over 1.5 acres in size and represents an area from the Pacific Ocean to Sacramento and Stockton, including: the San Francisco, San Pablo and Suisun Bays and a portion of the Sacramento-San Joaquin Delta."

The Model served "as a scientific research tool from 1958–2000 to evaluate circulation and flow characteristics of the water within the estuary system." This allows Army Engineers "to simulate currents, tidal action, sediment movement and the mixing of fresh and salt water. Pollution, salt-water intrusion, barrier and fill studies were a few of the important research projects that have been undertaken at the Bay Model."

It's not in the greatest condition, unfortunately, and the faded primary color scheme leaves much to be desired, but the Model is no less fascinating for all that; any chance you get to walk along the shores of a microcosm is a good chance to do some thinking.

If I may briefly quote William Blake:

To see a world in a grain of sand
And a heaven in a wild flower
Hold infinity in the palm of your hand
And eternity in an hour.

I'll then also point out that the Bay Model exists within its own time zone: In the world of the Model, one day passes every 14.9 minutes. Thirty full days elapse every 7.2 hours. Complete tidal cycles run 3.8 minutes. You can practically feel yourself aging in the presence of this copyscape, its wetlands and alluvial braids of artificial rivers running through fields of pumps and power cords. Look closely and you'll see a "Tide Hut," where little gods of the Model enact catastrophe and unleash floods upon the surrogate world spread out before them. Look closer, and you'll see damage from a "hundred years of waves, subsidence, and boat wakes"—which, in Model time, is almost exactly one human year.

But I soon got to thinking about the politics of architectural models. Imagine what would happen, for instance, if some Navy SEALs raided a cave in Afghanistan and found the Bay Model sitting there: *What on Earth does al-Qaeda want with San Francisco's water supply?* Or a model of Greater London's Thames hydrology, complete with flood gates, barriers, and overflow sewers—which is one thing if it's in the possession of Tony Blair and quite another if found in the basement of, say, Abu Hamza or even Timothy McVeigh. *What were they trying to do with it?*

It's the politics of architectural models: An object of scientific curiosity in one person's hands is an issue of national security in another's. Landscape simulacra as a threat to homeland security.

A plot for a new film by Charlie Kauffman, or a Philip K. Dick novel, comes to mind: A man, perhaps a young Al Pacino, breaks into the Bay Model in the middle of the night. He barricades himself inside, turns on the power, and starts flooding the Model, demolishing bridges, rerouting estuarial confluences. He jumps up and down, causing modelquakes, before he accelerates the tides, obliterating Golden Gate Park under the force of a giant tsunami. He calls all the local newspapers and takes responsibility for the disasters now befalling San Francisco outside. But *what disasters?* they ask, and he thinks they're playing with him, conning him, denying his rage, because he's read St. Thomas Aquinas and he believes that everything he throws at that simulacrum there before him will have effects in the real world.

It's all building up to one moment, see, the big moment when he decides to flood the Bay Model's model of the Bay Model, opening up a rift in the universe and blasting him headfirst through the macrocosm.

Until the police break in, guns drawn....

The following list is not an exhaustive survey of all the books, films, websites, and so on that have inspired BLDGBLOG, nor is it a comprehensive bibliography of everything cited in the book. It is more of a rough guide to further research in some of the topics discussed both on BLDGBLOG and in the *BLDGBLOG Book*. The list is quite heavy with books, you will see, but trying to list every useful website I've ever discovered would risk an even more pronounced sense of incompletion and would be out of date within months. For an extensive list of other websites and blogs, please refer simply to the links available twenty-four hours a day on BLDGBLOG. Note, as well, that this list does not include publishers; as BLDGBLOG has quite a large readership in the UK and further afield, I thought I should simply include the original year of publication (or, in some cases, year of translation into English). Finally, this list also includes films, listed in alphabetical order by director.

Of course, BLDGBLOG's online archives, stretching back to July 2004, are always worth a long visit:

Ⓦ *BLDGBLOG* → bldgblog.blogspot.com

Ⓦ Website

Ⓕ Film

Ⓟ Periodical

Ⓜ Media

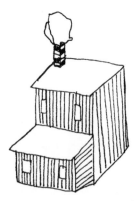

Bill Addis, *Building: 3,000 Years of Design, Engineering, and Construction* (2007)

Mark Anderson and Peter Anderson, *Prefab Prototypes: Site-Specific Design for Offsite Construction* (2007)

Benjamin Aranda and Chris Lasch, *Pamphlet Architecture 27: Tooling* (2006)

Ⓦ *Archinect* → archinect.com

Ⓦ *Architecture 2030* → architecture2030.org

Margaret Atwood, *The Handmaid's Tale* (1985)

Pier Vittorio Aureli et al., *Brussels, A Manifesto: Towards the Capital of Europe* (2007)

Paul Auster, *Moon Palace* (1989)

Mark Bain, "Sonic Architecture (Sonarchitecture)" (2002)

J. G. Ballard, *The Atrocity Exhibition* (1970), *Concrete Island* (1974), *Crash* (1973), The *Crystal World* (1966), *The Drowned World* (1962), *Empire of the Sun* (1984), *High-Rise* (1975), *Super-Cannes* (2000), *A User's Guide to the Millennium* (1996)

Clive Barker, "Down, Satan!" (1985)

Gabriele Basilico, *Beirut 1991 (2003)* (2008)

Stephen Battersby, "Designer Snowflakes" (2000)

Mary Beard, *The Roman Triumph* (2007), *The Wonders of the World Series* (ed.) (ongoing)

Ⓦ Jonathan Bell, *things magazine* → thingsmagazine.net

Janine Benyus, *Biomimicry: Innovation Inspired by Nature* (1997)

Robert Bevan, *The Destruction of Memory: Architecture at War* (2004)

Burkhard Bilger, "The Long Dig" (2008)

Tom Bissell, *Chasing the Sea: Lost Among the Ghosts of Empire in Central Asia* (2003)

David Blackbourn, *The Conquest of Nature: Water, Landscape, and the Making of Modern Germany* (2006)

William Blake, "Jerusalem: The Emanation of the Giant Albion" (1804–1820), "The Marriage of Heaven and Hell" (1790–1793), "Milton" (1804–1810), "Songs of Innocence and of Experience" (1794)

Ⓦ Ron Blakey, *Stratigraphy and Sedimentology on the Colorado Plateau* → jan.ucc.nau.edu/~rcb7

FURTHER READING

Philip Bobbitt, *The Shield of Achilles: War, Peace, and the Course of History* (2002)

Ⓦ Stefano Boeri → stefanoboeri.net

Giovanna Borasi and Mirko Zardini, *Sorry, Out of Gas* (2007)

Jorge Luis Borges, *Labyrinths* (1962)

Friedrich von Borries and Matthias Böttger, *Updating Germany: 100 Projects for a Better Future* (2008)

Paul Bowles, *The Sheltering Sky* (1949)

M. Christine Boyer, *The City of Collective Memory: Its Historical Imagery and Architectural Entertainments* (1994)

Ⓕ Danny Boyle, *28 Days Later* (2002)

Giordano Bruno, *The Expulsion of the Triumphant Beast* (1584)

William S. Burroughs, *Naked Lunch* (1959), *Nova Express* (1964), *The Soft Machine* (1961), *The Ticket That Exploded* (1962)

Edward Burtynsky, *Quarries* (2007)

Larry Busbea, *Topologies: The Urban Utopia in France, 1960–1970* (2007)

Jeff Byles, *Rubble: Unearthing the History of Demolition* (2005)

Ⓕ James Cameron, *Aliens* (1986)

Ⓕ John Carpenter, *The Thing* (1982)

Ⓦ Nick Catford et al., *Subterranea Britannica* → subbrit.org.uk

Ⓦ The Center for Land Use Interpretation → clui.org

Antony Clayton, *Subterranean City: Beneath the Streets of London* (2002)

Ⓦ Jace Clayton, *Mudd Up!* → negrophonic.com

Michael Conan, *The Crazannes Quarries by Bernard Lassus: An Essay Analyzing the Creation of a Landscape* (2004)

Joseph Conrad, *Heart of Darkness* (1902)

Ⓦ Michael Cook, *The Vanishing Point* → vanishingpoint.ca

Peter Cook et al., *Archigram* (1999)

Arthur Cotterell, *A Dictionary of World Mythology* (1979)

Devra Davis, *The Secret History of the War on Cancer* (2007)

Mike Davis, *City of Quartz* (1990), "Dead Cities: A Natural History" (2001), *Ecology of Fear* (1998), *Planet of Slums* (2006)

Roger Deakin, *Wildwood: A Journey Through Trees* (2007)

Ⓦ Régine Debatty, *we make money not art* → we-make-money-not-art.com

Guy Debord, tr. Donald Nicholson-Smith, *The Society of the Spectacle* (1994)

Manuel DeLanda, *War in the Age of Intelligent Machines* (1991)

Don DeLillo, *The Names* (1982), *White Noise* (1985)

Ⓕ Roger Donaldson, *The Bank Job* (2008)

Richard Doyle, *Flood* (2002)

Umberto Eco, *Foucault's Pendulum* (1989)

Shin Egashira and David Greene, *Alternative Guide to the Isle of Portland* (1997)

Mircea Eliade, *The Myth of the Eternal Return: Or, Cosmos and History* (1954)

Richard Ellis, *Aquagenesis: The Origin and Evolution of Life in the Sea* (2001)

Luigi Ficacci, *Piranesi: The Complete Etchings* (2000)

Ⓦ Bryan Finoki, *Subtopia*
→ subtopia.blogspot.com

James R. Fleming, "The Climate Engineers" (2007)

Richard Fortey, *Earth: An Intimate History* (2004)

Michel Foucault, *Discipline & Punish: The Birth of the Prison* (1975), *The Order of Things: An Archaeology of the Human Sciences* (1970)

William L. Fox, *Driving to Mars* (2006), *Terra Antarctica: Looking Into the Emptiest Continent* (2005), *The Void, The Grid & The Sign: Traversing The Great Basin* (2000)

Yona Friedman, *Pro Domo* (2006)

Cathy Gere, *The Tomb of Agamemnon* (2006)

Joe Ghiold, "The Sponges That Spanned Europe" (1991)

Allen Ginsberg, "Aether" (1960), *Indian Journals* (1978), *Journals: Early Fifties, Early Sixties* (1978), "Laughing Gas" (1958), "Paterson" (1949), "Siesta in Xbalba" (1954)

Ⓕ John Glen, *A View to a Kill* (1985)

Thomas Gold, *The Deep Hot Biosphere* (1998)

Steven Jay Gould, "A Humongous Fungus Among Us" (1992)

David Grann, *The Lost City of Z: A Tale of Deadly Obsession in the Amazon* (2009)

Stanley Greenberg, *Invisible New York: The Hidden Infrastructure of the City* (1998), *Waterworks: A Photographic Journey through New York's Hidden Water System* (2003)

Joseph Grima et al., *White House Redux* (2008)

Ⓕ John Guillermin, *King Kong* (1976)

Ⓕ John Guillermin and Irwin Allen, *The Towering Inferno* (1974)

Graham Hancock, *Underworld: The Mysterious Origins of Civilization* (2002)

Samantha Hardingham and David Greene, *L.A.W.U.N. Project #19* (2008)

David Harvey, *Spaces of Hope* (2000)

Kitty Hauser, *Bloody Old Britain: O. G. S. Crawford and the Archaeology of Modern Life* (2008)

Robert M. Hazen, "Life's Rocky Start" (2001)

Martin Heidegger, *Basic Writings* (1977), *The Question Concerning Technology* (1954)

Frank Herbert, *Dune* (1965)

Ⓕ Werner Herzog, *Grizzly Man* (2005)

Ⓦ Dan Hill, *City of Sound*
→ cityofsound.com

Ⓕ Alfred Hitchcock, *The Birds* (1963), *The Man Who Knew Too Much* (1956), *North By Northwest* (1959)

Richard Holmes, *Shelley: The Pursuit* (1974)

Homer, *The Odyssey*

Ⓕ Tobe Hooper, *Poltergeist* (1982)

Nannette Jackowski and Ricardo de Ostos, *Pamphlet Architecture 29: Ambiguous Spaces* (2008)

Ⓦ Sam Jacob, *Strangeharvest*
→ strangeharvest.com

Lucy Jago, *The Northern Lights: The True Story of the Man Who Unlocked the Secrets of the Aurora Borealis* (2002)

Richard Jefferies, *After London; or Wild England* (1885)

Ⓕ Jean-Pierre Jeunet and Marc Caro, *The City of Lost Children* (1995)

Franz Kafka, *The Castle* (1926), *Diaries: 1910–1923* (1948), *The Trial* (1925)

Ⓕ Cédric Kahn, *Roberto Succo* (2001)

Ⓕ Mathieu Kassovitz, *La Haine* (1995)

Richard Kenney, *The Invention of the Zero* (1993)

Stephen King, "Graveyard Shift" (1978)

Elizabeth Kolbert, *Field Notes from a Catastrophe: Man, Nature, and Climate Change* (2006)

Rem Koolhaas, *Delirious New York* (1978), "Junkspace" (2002)

Rem Koolhaas et al., *Mutations* (2001)

Jon Krakauer, *Into Thin Air: A Personal Account of the Mount Everest Disaster* (1997)

Ⓕ Peter Krieg, *Machine Dreams* (1988)

Ⓕ Stanley Kubrick, *2001: A Space Odyssey* (1968)

James Howard Kunstler, *The Long Emergency: Surviving the End of Oil, Climate Change, and Other Converging Catastrophes of the Twenty-First Century* (2005)

Ⓕ John Landis, *An American Werewolf in London* (1981)

Peter Lang and William Menking, *Superstudio: Life Without Objects* (2003)

Robert E. Lang and Jennifer Lefurgy, *Boomburbs: The Rise of America's Accidental Cities* (2007)

William Langewiesche, *The Outlaw Sea: A World of Freedom, Chaos, and Crime* (2004)

Ⓕ David Lean, *A Passage to India* (1984)

Alan Lee, *Castles* (1984)

Ⓕ Spike Lee, *Inside Man* (2006)

Ⓦ Sze Tsung Leong → szetsungleong.com

Sabrina van der Ley and Markus Richter, *Megastructure Reloaded: Visionary Architecture and Urban Design of the Sixties Reflected by Contemporary Artists* (2008)

Jeff Long, *The Descent* (1999)

Francisco López, "Environmental Sound Matter" (1998)

H. P. Lovecraft, *At the Mountains of Madness* (1931), "The Call of Cthulhu" (1928), "The Colour Out of Space" (1927), "From Beyond" (1934), "The Shadow Out of Time" (1936), "The Shadow Over Innsmouth" (1936)

David Macauley, *Underground* (1976)

Robert Macfarlane, *The Wild Places* (2007)

ⓦ David Maisel → davidmaisel.com

Geoff Manaugh, *Film Night* (unpublished novel, 2006)

Greil Marcus, *Lipstick Traces: A Secret History of the Twentieth Century* (1989)

Ⓕ Chris Marker, *La Jetée* (1962)

Cormac McCarthy, *Blood Meridian, or the Evening Redness in the West* (1985), *The Road* (2006), *Suttree* (1979)

Tom McCarthy, *Remainder* (2005)

Patrick McGrath, *Asylum* (1997), *The Grotesque* (1989)

Terence McKenna, *Food of the Gods: The Search for the Original Tree of Knowledge— A Radical History of Plants, Drugs, and Human Evolution* (1992)

John McPhee, *Annals of the Former World* (1998), "The Atlantic Generating Station" (1975), *The Control of Nature* (1989), "Minihydro" (1981)

Ⓕ John McTiernan, *Die Hard* (1988)

China Miéville, *Perdido Street Station* (2000), "Reports of Certain Events in London" (2004), *The Scar* (2002)

John Milton, *Paradise Lost* (1667)

Steven Mithen, *After the Ice: A Global Human History, 20,000–5,000 B.C.* (2003)

David R. Montgomery, *Dirt: The Erosion of Civilizations* (2007)

Ⓕ Errol Morris, *Fast, Cheap and Out of Control* (1997)

Oliver Morton, *Mapping Mars: Science, Imagination, and the Birth of a World* (2002)

ⓦ NASA, *Earth Observatory* → earthobservatory.nasa.gov

National Park Service, "A Report on the Stabilization of Delicate Arch," Arches National Park Museum Collection, Catalog Number ARCH 3334 (1954)

Reza Negarestani, *Cyclonopedia* (2008)

Victoria Nelson, *The Secret Life of Puppets* (2001)

Ⓟ *New Scientist* → newscientist.com

Ⓟ The *New Yorker* → newyorker.com

Ⓕ Christopher Nolan, *Following* (1998)

Simon Norfolk, *Afghanistan: Chronotopia: Landscapes of the Destruction of Afghanistan* (2003)

Ⓕ Claude Nuridsany and Marie Pérennou, *Microcosmos* (1996)

Michael Ondaatje, *The Conversations: Walter Murch and the Art of Editing Film* (2002)

Alice Oswald, *Dart* (2002)

George Packer, "The Megacity" (2006)

Ian Parker, "Traffic" (1999)

Ⓕ Chris Petit, *Surveillance* (1993)

Daniel Pinchbeck, *Breaking Open the Head: A Psychedelic Journey into the Heart of Contemporary Shamanism* (2002)

Edgar Allan Poe, "A Descent into the Maelström" (1841)

Robert Polidori, *Zones of Exclusion: Pripyat and Chernobyl* (2003)

Albert Pope, *Ladders* (1997)

Ⓜ Radiolab → wnyc.org/shows/radiolab

Mary-Ann Ray, *Seven Partly Underground Rooms and Buildings for Water, Ice, and Midgets* (1997)

Marc Reisner, *Cadillac Desert* (1986)

Ⓕ Ivan Reitman, *Ghostbusters* (1984)

Thomas Richards, *The Imperial Archive: Knowledge and the Fantasy of Empire* (1993)

Kim Stanley Robinson, *Mars Trilogy* (1992–1996)

Tim Robinson, *Stones of Aran: Pilgrimage* (1985)

Fernando Romero, *Hyperborder: The Contemporary U. S.–Mexico Border and its Future* (2007)

Justin Rosenberg, *The Follies of Globalization Theory: Polemical Essays* (2001)

Aldo Rossi, *The Architecture of the City* (1982)

Jim Rossignol, *This Gaming Life: Travels in Three Cities* (2008)

Ⓕ Franklin J. Schaffner, *Papillon* (1973)

Felicity D. Scott, *Ant Farm: Living Archive 7* (2008)

W. G. Sebald, "Ambros Adelwarth" (1993), *Austerlitz* (2001), *On the Natural History of Destruction* (2003), *The Rings of Saturn* (1999)

Iain Sinclair, *Lights Out for the Territory* (1996), *London Orbital* (2002)

P. W. Singer, *Corporate Warriors: The Rise of the Privatized Military Industry* (2003)

Ⓦ Siologen, *International Urban Glow* → siologen.net/pbase

Andrew Smith, *Moondust: In Search of the Men Who Fell to Earth* (2005)

Mark Smout and Laura Allen, *Pamphlet Architecture 28: Augmented Landscapes* (2007)

Gary Snyder, "Bomb Test" (1986), "The Call of the Wild" (1969), "It Pleases" (1973), "Logging" (1960)

Julia Solis, *New York Underground: The Anatomy of a City* (2004)

Michael Sorkin, *Local Code: The Constitution of a City at 42 Degrees North Latitude* (1996), *Some Assembly Required* (2001), *Wiggle* (1998)

Ⓕ Steven Spielberg, *Close Encounters of the Third Kind* (1977), *Indiana Jones and the Last Crusade* (1989), *Raiders of the Lost Ark* (1981)

Laura Spinney, "Return to Paradise: If the People Flee, What Will Happen to the Seemingly Indestructible" (1996)

Alexander Stille, *The Future of the Past* (2002)

Ⓦ *Strange Maps* → strangemaps.wordpress.com

Kim Stringfellow, *Greetings from the Salton Sea: Folly and Intervention in the Southern California Landscape, 1905–2005* (2005)

Manfredo Tafuri, *The Sphere and the Labyrinth: Avant-Gardes and Architecture from Piranesi to the 1970s* (1987)

Taipei Fine Arts Museum, *Archigram: Experimental Architecture, 1961–1974* (2003)

Michael Taussig, *My Cocaine Museum* (2004)

Rupert Thomson, *Divided Kingdom* (2005)

David Toop, *Ocean of Sound: Aether Talk, Ambient Sound, and Imaginary Worlds* (2000)

Ⓦ Alexander Trevi, *Pruned*
→ pruned.blogspot.com

David L. Ulin, *The Myth of Solid Ground: Earthquakes, Prediction, and the Fault Line Between Reason and Faith* (2004)

Ⓦ U. S. Army Corps of Engineers, *Lower and Middle Mississippi Valley Engineering Geology Mapping Program*
→ lmvmapping.erdc.usace.army.mil

Tom Vanderbilt, *Survival City: Adventures Among the Ruins of Atomic America* (2002)

Robert Venturi, Denise Scott-Brown, and Steven Izenour, *Learning from Las Vegas* (1972)

Jules Verne, *A Journey to the Center of the Earth* (1864)

Virgil, *The Aeneid*

Ⓕ Christian Volckman, *Renaissance* (2006)

Ian Warrell and Franklin Kelly, *J. M. W. Turner* (2007)

Alan Weisman, *The World Without Us* (2007)

Eyal Weizman, "Lethal Theory" (2006)

Lawrence Weschler, *Mr. Wilson's Cabinet of Wonder: Pronged Ants, Horned Humans, Mice on Toast, and Other Marvels of Jurassic Technology* (1995)

William Carlos Williams, *Paterson* (1963)

Ⓟ *The Wire*
→ thewire.co.uk

Ⓟ *Wired*
→ wired.com

Michael Wolf, *Hong Kong: Front Door/Back Door* (2005), *The Transparent City* (2008)

Lebbeus Woods, *Pamphlet Architecture 6: Einstein Tomb* (1980), *Pamphlet Architecture 15: War and Architecture* (1993)

John Wyndham, *The Day of the Triffids* (1951)

Frances A. Yates, *The Art of Memory* (1966)

Jan Zalasiewicz, *The Earth After Us: What Legacy Will Humans Leave in the Rocks?* (2008)

Jan Zalasiewicz and Kim Freedman, "Buried Treasure" (1998), "The Dawn of Slime" (2000)

Carl Zimmerman, *Landmarks of Industrial Britain* (2006)

Emile Zola, *The Kill* (1871)

It would be impossible to thank, or even list, everyone who's had a positive impact on the development of BLDGBLOG over the past five years—but it would be inexcusable not to tip my hat in at least a few directions.

Alan Rapp, my editor, kicked off the book by e-mailing me way back in January 2007, asking me to pitch him an idea. Alexander Trevi, Bryan Finoki, Joseph Grima, Sarah Rich, Dan Polsby, Dan Hill, Marcus Trimble, Jonathan Bell, Jim Webb, Brett MacFadden & Scott Thorpe (who designed this book), Brendan Callahan (who illustrated this book), everyone who has ever spoken at a BLDGBLOG event (including *Postopolis!*) or who has invited BLDGBLOG to speak, everyone I've ever interviewed (both for the website and for this book), everyone whose art or imagery appears in the book and on the blog, everyone who has ever asked me to write for their publication, Christopher Hawthorne, Lawrence Weschler, Robert Krulwich, William L. Fox, David Maisel, Tom Cohen, Matthew Coolidge, Steve Silberman, Walter Murch, Lebbeus Woods, Theo Paijmans, Simon Sellars, William Drenttel, the crew of *Archinect* (especially Javier Arbona), Alexis Madrigal, Christopher Stack, Jill Fehrenbacher, Alex Steffen, Alex Haw, Jeffrey Inaba, Mary-Ann Ray, Ed Keller, Gianluigi Ricuperati, Rob Jones, Nic Clear, Ruairi Glynn, Sonja Hall, Annalee Newitz, Josh Glenn and the Hermenautic Circle, David Haskell, Elias Redstone, Justin McGuirk, Leah Beeferman, Sam Jacob, Geoff Shearcroft, Mark Smout and Laura Allen, Jace Clayton, Jim Coudal, Erin Reinhardt, Mark Wigley, Detlef Mertins, the Los Angeles Forum for Architecture and Design, L. G., my family, Steve & Valerie Twilley, Molly McCall, Simon Norfolk, Stanley Greenberg, Michael Wolf, Frances Ander"ton, Phil Steinberg, Thomas Levin, Annette Fierro, Bruce Sterling, Douglas Coupland, Vicki Webster, and, of course, the site's multitude of commenters, who all continue to make BLDGBLOG worth writing. I also owe a very belated thank you to Allen Ginsberg for first taking me to Europe, and for giving me an unforgettable boost when I was just two decades old.

Finally, my wife, Nicola Twilley, one of the best editors I know, is a trusted and ongoing influence on the ideas, writing, and direction of both the book and the blog—and she is also my best friend. I owe her a huge thanks, for the patience, the feedback, and the fun.

THANK YOU

Paul Auster

J. G. Ballard

Mary Beard

David Byrne

Minsuk Cho

Jace Clayton

Peter Cook

Matthew Coolidge

Mike Davis

Don DeLillo

Umberto Eco

Richard Fortey

Joseph Grima

Zaha Hadid

Werner Herzog

Jeffrey Inaba

Bjarke Ingels

Sam Jacob

Rem Koolhaas

David Maisel

Thom Mayne

Cormac McCarthy

✕ _____

Patrick McGrath

✕ _____

John McPhee

✕ _____

China Miéville

✕ _____

The Mole Man of Hackney

✕ _____

Walter Murch

✕ _____

Christopher Nolan

✕ _____

Brad Pitt

✕ _____

Mary-Ann Ray

✕ _____

Siologen

✕ _____

Steven Spielberg

✕ _____

Alexander Trevi

✕ _____

Margaret & Christine Wertheim

✕ _____

Rachel Whiteread

✕ _____

Lebbeus Woods

AUTO GRAPHS

MORE
SOON